FOUNDATIONS OF SOFTWARE TESTING

ISTQB CERTIFICATION

THIRD EDITION

Rex Black

Erik van Veenendaal

Dorothy Graham

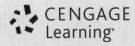

CENGAGE
Learning

Australia • Brazil • Japan • Korea • Mexico • Singapore • Spain • United Kingdom • United States

**Foundations of Software Testing: ISTQB
Certification, 3rd Edition**
Rex Black, Erik van Veenendaal,
and Dorothy Graham

Publishing Director: Linden Harris

Publisher: Brendan George

Development Editor: Annabel Ainscow

Content Project Editor: Kate Daniel

Production Controller: Eyvett Davis

Typesetter: Integra Software Services

Cover Design: Design Deluxe, Bath

For product information and technology assistance, contact
emea.info@cengage.com.
For permission to use material from this text or product,
and for permission queries, email
emea.permissions@cengage.com

This work is adapted from *Foundations of Software Testing* by Dorothy
Graham, Erik van Veenendaal, Isoleb Evans and Rex Black published by
South-Western, a division of Cengage Learning, Inc. © 2009.

British Library Cataloguing-in-Publication Data
A catalogue record for this book is available from the British Library.

ISBN: 978-1-4080-4405-6

Cengage Learning EMEA
Cheriton House, North Way, Andover, Hampshire, SP10 5BE
United Kingdom

Cengage Learning products are represented in Canada by Nelson
Education Ltd.

For your lifelong learning solutions, visit **www.cengage.co.uk**

Purchase your next print book, e-book or e-chapter at
www.cengagebrain.com

Printed in China by RR Donnelley
3 4 5 6 7 8 9 10 – 16 15 14

CONTENTS

FIGURES AND TABLES

ACKNOWLEDGEMENTS

The materials in this book are based on the ISTQB Foundation Syllabus 2011. The Foundation Syllabus is copyrighted to the ISTQB (International Software Testing Qualification Board) and was written by Thomas Müller (chair of the working party), Debra Friedenberg (vice chair of the working party), Rex Black (past vice chair of the working party), Armin Beer, Sigrid Eldh, Dorothy Graham, Martin Klonk, Klaus Olsen, Maaret Pyhäjärvi, Geoff Thompson, Erik van Veenendaal, and Rahul Verma. Permission has been granted by the ISTQB to the authors to use these materials as the basis of a book, provided that recognition of authorship and copyright of the Syllabus itself is given.

The ISTQB Glossary of Testing Terms, edited by Erik van Veenendaal (chair of the working party), and released as version 2.1 by the ISTQB in 2010, is used as the source of definitions in this book.

The other co-authors would like to thank Rex Black for his effort in updating this book to be fully aligned with the 2010 and 2011 versions of the ISTQB Foundation Syllabus and version 2.1 of the ISTQB Glossary.

Be aware that there are some defects in this book! The Syllabus, glossary and this book were written by people – and people make mistakes. Just as with testing, we have applied reviews and tried to identify as many defects as we could, but we also needed to release the manuscript to the publisher. Please let us know of defects that you find in our book so that we can correct them in future printings.

The authors wish to acknowledge the contribution of Isabel Evans to the previous editions of this book. Working with Isabel was a pleasure, and we wish her all the best as she embarks on a new direction for her career.

Rex Black, Texas, USA
Erik van Veenendaal, Kralendijk, Bonaire
Dorothy Graham, Macclesfield, UK
2011

PREFACE

The purpose of this book is to support the ISTQB Foundation Syllabus 2011, which is the basis for the international Foundation Certificate in Software Testing. The authors have been involved in helping to establish this qualification, donating their time and energy to the Syllabus, terminology glossary and the International Software Testing Qualifications Board (ISTQB).

The authors of this book are all passionate about software testing. All have been involved in this area for most or all of their working lives, and have contributed to the field through practical work, training courses and books. They have written this book to help to promote the discipline of software testing.

The initial idea for this collaboration came from Erik van Veenendaal, author of *The Testing Practitioner*, a book to support the ISEB Software Testing Practitioner Certificate. The other authors agreed to work together as equals on this book. Please note that the order of the author's names does not indicate any seniority of authorship, but simply which author was the last to update the book as the Foundation syllabus evolved.

We intend that this book will increase your chances of passing the Foundation Certificate exam. If you are taking a course (or class) to prepare for the exam, this book will give you detailed and additional background about the topics you have covered. If you are studying for the exam on your own, this book will help you be more prepared. This book will give you information about the topics covered in the Syllabus, as well as worked exercises and practice exam questions (including a full 40-question mock exam paper in Chapter 7).

This book is a useful reference book about software testing in general, even if you are not interested in the exam. The Foundation Certificate represents a distilling of the essential aspects of software testing at the time of writing (2011), and this book will give you a good grounding in software testing.

ISTQB AND CERTIFICATION

ISTQB stands for 'International Software Testing Qualifications Board' and is an organization consisting of software testing professionals from each of the countries who are members of the ISTQB. Each country representative is a member of a Software Testing Board in their own country. The purpose of the ISTQB is to provide internationally accepted and consistent qualifications in software testing. ISTQB sets the syllabus and gives guidelines for each member country to implement the qualification in their own country. The Foundation Certificate is the first internationally accepted qualification in software testing and its syllabus forms the basis of this book.

From the first qualification in 1998 until 2011, over 175,000 people took the Foundation Certificate exam administered by a National Board of the ISTQB, or by an Exam Board contracted to a National Board. All ISTQB National Boards and Exam Boards recognize each others' Foundation Certificates as valid.

The ISTQB qualification is independent of any individual training provider – any training organization can offer a course based on this publicly available syllabus. However, the National Boards associated with ISTQB give special approval to organizations that meet their requirements for the quality of the training – such organizations are 'accredited' and are allowed to have an invigilator or proctor from an authorized National Board or Exam Board to give the exam as part of the accredited course. The exam is also available independently from accrediting organizations or National Boards.

Why is certification of testers important? The objectives of the qualification are listed in the syllabus. They include:

- recognition for testing as an essential and professional software engineering specialization
- enabling professionally qualified testers to be recognized by employers, customers and peers
- raising the profile of testers
- promoting consistent and good testing practices within all software engineering disciplines internationally, for reasons of opportunity, communication and sharing of knowledge and resources internationally.

FINDING YOUR WAY AROUND THIS BOOK

This book is divided into seven chapters. The first six chapters of the book each cover one chapter of the syllabus, and each has some practice exam questions.

Chapter 1 is the start of understanding. We'll look at some fundamental questions: what is testing and why is it necessary? We'll examine why testing is not just running tests. We'll also look at why testing can damage relationships and how bridges between colleagues can be rebuilt.

In Chapter 2, we'll concentrate on testing in relation to the common software development models, including iterative and waterfall models. We'll see that different types of testing are used at different stages in the software development life cycle.

In Chapter 3, we'll concentrate on test techniques that can be used early in the software development life cycle. These include reviews and static analysis – tests done before compiling the code.

Chapter 4 covers test design techniques. We'll show you techniques including equivalence partitioning, boundary value analysis, decision tables, state transition testing, use case testing and statement and decision testing. This chapter is about how to become a better tester in terms of designing tests. There are exercises for the most significant techniques included in this chapter.

Chapter 5 is about the management and control of testing, including estimation, risk assessment, incident management and reporting. Writing a good incident report is a key skill for a good tester, so we have an exercise for that too.

In Chapter 6, we'll show you tools that support all the activities in the test process, and how to select and implement tools for the greatest benefit.

Chapter 7 contains general advice about taking the exam and has the full 40-question mock paper. This is a key learning aid to help you pass the real exam.

The appendices of the book include a full list of references and a copy of the ISTQB testing terminology glossary.

TO HELP YOU USE THE BOOK

1 Get a copy of the Syllabus: You should download the Syllabus from the ISTQB website so that you have the current version, and so that you can check off the Syllabus objectives as you learn.

2 Understand what is meant by learning objectives and knowledge levels: In the Syllabus, you'll see learning objectives and knowledge (or cognitive) levels at the start of each section of each chapter. These indicate what you need to know and the depth of knowledge required for the exam. We've used the timings in the Syllabus and knowledge levels to guide the space allocated in the book, both for the text and for the exercises. You'll see the learning objectives and knowledge levels at the start of each section within each chapter. The knowledge levels expected by the Syllabus are:

- K1: remember, recognize, recall; you will recognize, remember and recall a term or concept. For example, you could recognize one definition of 'failure' as 'non-delivery of service to an end user or any other stakeholder'.
- K2: understand, explain, give reasons, compare, classify, summarize; you can select the reasons or explanations for statements related to the topic, and can summarize, compare, classify and give examples for the testing concept. For example, you could explain that one reason why tests should be designed as early as possible is to find defects when they are cheaper to remove.
- K3: apply; you can select the correct application of a concept or technique and apply it to a given context. For example, you could identify boundary values for valid and invalid partitions, and you could select test cases from a given state transition diagram in order to cover all transitions.
- K4: analyze; you can separate information related to a procedure or technique into its constituent parts for better understanding, and can distinguish between facts and inferences. For example, you could analyze a document, software or project situation and propose appropriate test techniques to address features of the system.

Remember, as you go through the book, if a topic has a learning objective marked K1 you just need to recognize it. If it has a learning objective of K3 you'll be expected to apply your knowledge in the exam, for example.

3 Use the glossary of terms: Each chapter of the Syllabus has a number of terms listed in it. You are expected to remember these terms at least at K1 level, even if they are not explicitly mentioned in the learning objectives. You will see a number of **definitions** throughout this book, as in the sidebar.

Definition a description of the meaning of a word.

All definitions are taken from the *Standard Glossary of Terms Used in Software Testing* (version 2.1), edited by Erik van Veenendaal. A copy of this glossary is at the back of the book. All the terms that are specifically mentioned in the Syllabus, i.e. the ones you need to learn for the exam, are mentioned in each section of this book.

You will notice that some terms in the glossary are underlined. These are terms that are mentioned specifically in the Syllabus, or that are used in the Syllabus. These are the terms that you need to be familiar with for the exam.

4 Use the references sensibly: We have referenced all the books used by the Syllabus authors when they constructed the Syllabus. You'll see those listed at the end of the book. We also added references to some other books, papers and websites that we thought useful or which we referred to when writing. You do not need to read all referenced books for the exam! However, you may find some of them useful for further reading to increase your knowledge after the exam, and to help you apply some of the ideas you'll come across in the book.

5 When you get to the end of a chapter (for Chapters 1 to 6), answer the exam questions then turn to 'Answers to the Sample Exam Questions' to check if your answers were correct. After you have completed all of the six chapters, then take the exam in Chapter 7. If you would like the most realistic exam conditions, then allow yourself just an hour to take the exam in Chapter 7.

Digital Support Resources

All of our Higher Education textbooks are accompanied by a range of digital support resources.

- A password protected area for instructors
- An open-access area for students

Lecturers: to discover the lecturer digital support resources accompanying this textbook please register here for access: http://login.cengage.com.

Students: to discover the student digital support resources accompanying this textbook, please search for Foundations of Software Testing ISTQB Certification on: **www.cengagebrain.co.uk**

CHAPTER ONE
Fundamentals of testing

In this chapter, we will introduce you to the fundamentals of testing: why testing is needed; its limitations, objectives and purpose; the principles behind testing; the process that testers follow; and some of the psychological factors that testers must consider in their work. By reading this chapter you'll gain an understanding of the fundamentals of testing and be able to describe those fundamentals.

1.1 WHY IS TESTING NECESSARY?

SYLLABUS LEARNING OBJECTIVES FOR 1.1 WHY IS TESTING NECESSARY? (K2)

LO-1.1.1 Describe, with examples, the way in which a defect in software can cause harm to a person, to the environment or to a company. (K2)

LO-1.1.2 Distinguish between the root cause of a defect and its effects. (K2)

LO-1.1.3 Give reasons why testing is necessary by giving examples. (K2)

LO-1.1.4 Describe why testing is part of quality assurance and give examples of how testing contributes to higher quality. (K2)

LO-1.1.5 Explain and compare the terms error, defect, fault, failure and the corresponding terms mistake and bug, using examples. (K2)

In this section, we're going to kick off the book with a discussion on why testing matters. We'll describe and illustrate how software defects or bugs can cause problems for people, the environment or a company. We'll draw important distinctions between defects, their root causes and their effects. We'll explain why testing is necessary to find these defects, how testing promotes quality, and how testing fits into quality assurance.

As we go through this section, watch for the Syllabus terms **bug, defect, error, fails (false-fail result, false-positive result), failure, fault, mistake, passed (false-negative result, false-pass result), quality,** and **risk**. You'll find these terms defined in the glossary.

1.1.1 Software systems context

The last 100 years have seen an amazing human triumph of technology. Diseases that once killed and paralyzed are routinely treated or prevented – or even eradicated entirely, as with smallpox. Some children who stood amazed as they watched the first gasoline-powered automobile in their town are alive today, having seen people walk on the moon, an event that happened before a large percentage of today's workforce was even born.

Perhaps the most dramatic advances in technology have occurred in the arena of information technology. Software systems, in the sense that we know them, are a young innovation, less than 70 years old, but have already transformed daily life around the world. Thomas Watson, the one-time head of IBM, famously predicted that only about five computers were needed in the whole world. This vastly inaccurate prediction was based on the idea that information technology was useful only for business and government applications, such as banking, insurance, and conducting a census. (The Hollerith punch-cards used by computers at the time Watson made his prediction were developed for the United States census.) Now, everyone who drives a car is using a machine not only designed with the help of computers, but which also contains more computing power than the computers used by NASA to get Apollo missions to and from the moon. Billions of mobile phones exist, many of which are hand-held computers that get smarter and smarter with every new model.

However, in the software world, the technological triumph has not been perfect. Almost every living person has been touched by information technology, and most of us have dealt with the frustration and wasted time that occurs when software **fails** and exhibits unexpected behaviours. Some unfortunate individuals and companies have experienced financial loss or damage to their personal or business reputations as a result of defective software. A highly unlucky few have even been injured or killed by software failures.

False-fail result: A test result in which a defect is reported although no such defect actually exists in the test object.

False-positive result: See false-fail result.

1.1.2 The human (and other) causes of software defects

Why does software fail? Part of the problem is that, ironically, while computerization has allowed dramatic automation of many professions, software engineering remains a human-intensive activity. And humans are fallible beings. So, software is fallible because humans are fallible.

Error (mistake) A human action that produces an incorrect result.

Defect (bug, fault) A flaw in a component or system that can cause the component or system to fail to perform its required function, e.g. an incorrect statement or data definition. A defect, if encountered during execution, may cause a failure of the component or system.

Failure Deviation of the component or system from its expected delivery, service or result.

The precise chain of events goes something like this. A programmer makes a **mistake** (or **error**), such as forgetting about the possibility of inputting an excessively long string into a field on a screen. The programmer thus puts a **defect** (or **fault** or **bug**) into the program, such as forgetting to check input strings for length prior to processing them. When the program is executed, if the right conditions exist (or the wrong conditions, depending on how you look at it), the defect will result in unexpected behaviour; i.e. the system exhibits a **failure**, such as accepting an over-long input that it should reject.

Other sequences of events can result in eventual failures, too. A business analyst can introduce a defect into a requirement, which can escape into the design of the system and further escape into the code. For example, a business analyst might say that an e-commerce system should support 100 simultaneous users, but actually peak load should be 1000 users. If that defect is not detected in a requirements review (see Chapter 3), it could escape from the requirements phase into the design and implementation of the system. Once the load exceeds 100 users, resource utilization may eventually spike to dangerous levels, leading to reduced response time and reliability problems.

A technical writer can introduce a defect into the online help screens. For example, suppose that an accounting system is supposed to multiply two numbers together, but the help screens say that the two numbers should be added. In some cases, the system will appear to work properly, such as when the two numbers are both 0 or both 2. However, most frequently the program will exhibit unexpected results (at least based on the help screens).

So, human beings are fallible and thus, when they work, they sometimes introduce defects. It's important to point out that the introduction of defects is not a purely random accident, though some defects are introduced randomly, such as when a phone rings and distracts a systems engineer in the middle of a complex series of design decisions. The rate at which people make mistakes increases when they are under time pressure, when they are working with complex systems, interfaces, or code, and when they are dealing with changing technologies or highly interconnected systems.

While we commonly think of failures being the result of 'bugs in the code', a significant number of defects are introduced in work products such as requirements specifications and design specifications. Capers Jones reports that about 20% of defects are introduced in requirements, and about 25% in design. The remaining 55% are introduced during implementation or repair of the code, metadata, or documentation [Jones 2008]. Other experts and researchers have reached similar conclusions, with one organization finding that as many as 75% of defects originate in requirements and design. Figure 1.1 shows four typical scenarios, the upper stream being correct requirements, design, and implementation, the lower three streams showing defect introduction at some phase in the software lifecycle.

Ideally, defects are removed in the same phase of the lifecycle in which they are introduced. (Well, ideally defects aren't introduced at all, but this is not possible, for, as discussed before, people are fallible.) The extent to which defects are removed in the phase of introduction is called phase containment. Phase containment is important because the cost of finding and removing a defect increases each time that defect escapes to a later lifecycle phase. Multiplicative increases in cost, of the sort seen in

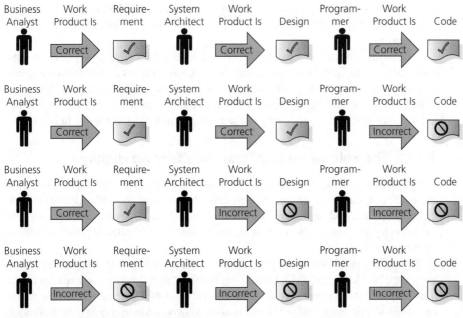

FIGURE 1.1   Four typical scenarios

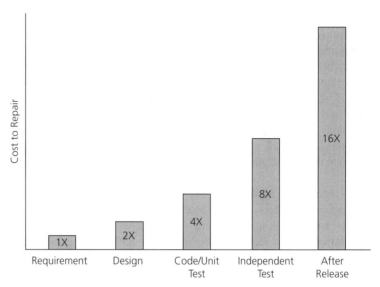

FIGURE 1.2   Multiplicative increases in cost

Figure 1.2, are not unusual. The specific increases vary considerably, with Boehm reporting cost increases of 1: 5 (from requirements to after release) for simple systems to as high as 1:100 for complex systems. If you are curious about the economics of software testing and other **quality**-related activities, you can see [Gilb and Graham 1993], [Black 2009] or [Black 2004].

Defects may result in failures, or they may not, depending on inputs and other conditions. In some cases, a defect can exist that will never cause a failure in actual use, because the conditions that could cause the failure can never arise. In other cases, a defect can exist that will not cause a failure during testing, but which always results in failures in production. This can happen with security, reliability, and performance defects especially, if the test environments do not closely replicate the production environment(s).

It can also happen that expected and actual results do not match for reasons other than a defect. In some cases, environmental conditions can lead to unexpected results that do not relate to a software defect. Radiation, magnetism, electronic fields, and pollution can damage hardware or firmware, or simply change the conditions of the hardware or firmware temporarily in a way that causes the software to fail.

1.1.3 The role of testing, and its effect on quality

Since software and the associated work products are written by fallible humans, all of these work products will always have defects. Where there are defects, there are **risks** of failure. While nothing can reduce the level of risk to zero, we certainly can – and should – try to reduce risk to an acceptable level prior to releasing the software to customers and users.

Testing is part of how these risks of failure can be reduced. If the software and its associated work products (including requirements specifications, design specifica- tions, documentation, etc.) are subjected to the kind of rigorous, systematic testing described in this book and in the Foundation syllabus, the testers are more likely to find defects in some areas, while reducing the risk in other areas by determining that

Quality The degree to which a component, system or process meets specified requirements and/or user/customer needs and expectations.

Risk A factor that could result in future negative consequences; usually expressed as impact and likelihood.

the software works properly under the tested conditions. Developers and others on the project teams can then debug the system, removing the defects found.

Testing does not change the quality of the system under test directly. When testing finds defects and those defects are repaired, the quality of the system is increased. However, debugging, not testing, is the activity that changed the quality of the system (see Section 1.2 below).

Testing does provide a way of measuring the system's quality. The rate of defect discovery, the number of known defects, the extent of test coverage, and the percentage of tests which have **passed** all reflect on the quality of the system. If the tests find few or no defects (assuming we followed proper testing approaches such as those described in this book), or if all of the defects found are resolved, then we can have confidence in the system. When a properly designed test is run, an unknown situation is changed into a known situation, which reduces the level of risk to the quality of the product.

At this juncture, let us point out that a properly designed set of tests should measure the quality of the system in terms of both functional and non-functional characteristics. The specific characteristics tested depend on what matters in terms of quality for the particular system under test. We'll discuss functional and non-functional test types further in Chapter 2. You can find more information on functional and non-functional quality characteristics in 'Software Engineering – Software Product Quality' [ISO 9126].

> **False-pass result:** A test result which fails to identify the presence of a defect that is actually present in the test object.
>
> **False-negative result:** See false-pass result.

Testing also provides a learning opportunity that allows for improved quality if lessons are learned from each project. If root cause analysis is carried out for the defects found on each project, the team can improve its software development processes to avoid the introduction of similar defects in future systems. Through this simple process of learning from past mistakes, organizations can continuously improve the quality of their processes and their software.

Testing thus plays an essential supporting role in delivering quality software. However, testing by itself is not sufficient. Testing should be integrated into a complete, team-wide and software process-wide set of activities for quality assurance. Proper application of standards, training of staff, the use of retrospectives to learn lessons from defects and other important elements of previous projects, rigorous and appropriate software testing: all of these activities and more should be deployed by organizations to assure acceptable levels of quality and quality risk upon release.

1.1.4 How much testing is enough?

Selecting which test conditions to cover is a fundamental problem of testing. As will be discussed later in this chapter and often in this book, the number of possible test cases is infinite for all but the simplest systems. Given immortality and unlimited resources, we *could* conceivably test forever. However, in the real world, we can only select a finite number of test cases for design, implementation, and execution.

Instead of trying to find every possible test case, an impossible ideal, we should focus on what tests give us the greatest value by covering the most important parts of the system. Coverage can be measured in a number of ways. In this book, we will talk about coverage of requirements, coverage of code structures, and coverage of risks to the quality of the product (including risks derived from technical, safety, and business considerations).

We could say that sufficient coverage is achieved when we balance what we should cover against project constraints such as time and budget. We should also ensure that testing provides sufficient information to the project and product stakeholders, so that they can decide whether to proceed with the project or with release. All three of these areas – our analysis of what should be covered, the limitations on what can be covered, and the stakeholders' specific needs for information – are to some extent in tension, in that we may have to give up something in one area in order to increase what we achieve in one or both of the other areas.

Testing always involves trade-offs. At some point, the various risks associated with the project will have reached some acceptable level, one understood by the various project stakeholders. We will discuss this issue of risk and how it influences testing in Chapter 5.

In some cases, software testing is not just a good way to reduce risks to the quality of the system to an acceptable level; testing can be required to meet contractual or legal requirements, or industry-specific standards. The authors have clients in the medical systems business, and those clients are subject to regulations that require a certain degree and rigor of testing. For companies writing software used on commercial aviation, the US Federal Aviation Administration requires a certain level of structural test coverage, a topic which we'll discuss in Chapter 4.

1.2 WHAT IS TESTING?

SYLLABUS LEARNING OBJECTIVES FOR 1.2 WHAT IS TESTING? (K2)

LO-1.2.1   Recall the common objectives of testing. (K1)

LO-1.2.2   Provide examples for the objectives of testing in different phases of the software life cycle. (K2)

LO-1.2.3   Differentiate testing from debugging. (K2)

In this section, we will review the common objectives of testing and the activities that allow us to achieve those objectives. We'll explain how testing helps us to find defects, provide confidence and information, and prevent defects.

As you read this section, you'll encounter the terms **confirmation testing, debugging, requirement, re-testing, review, test case, test control, test design specification, testing,** and **test objective.**

An ongoing misperception about testing is that it only involves running tests. Specifically, some people think that testing involves nothing beyond carrying out some sequence of actions on the system under test, submitting various inputs along the way, and evaluating the observed results. Certainly, these activities are one element of testing – specifically, these activities make up the bulk of the test execution activities – but there are other activities involved in the test process.

While we'll discuss the test process in more detail later in this chapter (in section 1.4), let's look briefly at some of the major activities in the test process:

● **Test planning**: In test planning, we establish (and update) the scope, approach, resources, schedule, and specific tasks in the intended test activities that comprise the rest of the test process. Test planning should identify test items, the features to be tested and not tested, the roles and responsibilities of the participants and stakeholders, the relationship between the testers and the developers of the test items, the extent to which testing is independent of development of these work items (see section 1.5 below), the test environments required, the appropriate **test design** techniques, entry, and exit criteria, and how we'll handle project risks related to testing. Test planning often produces, as a deliverable work product, a test plan. Test planning is discussed in Chapter 5.

- **Test control**: While test planning is essential, things don't always go according to plan. In **test control**, we develop and carry out corrective actions to get a test project back on track when we deviate from the plan. Test control is discussed in Chapter 5.

- **Test analysis**: In test analysis, we identify what to test, choosing the test conditions we need to cover. These conditions are any item or event that we can and should verify using one or more **test cases**. Test conditions can be functions, transactions, features, quality attributes, quality risks, or structural elements. Test analysis is discussed in Chapter 4.

- **Test design**: In test design, we determine how we will test what we decided to test during test analysis. Using test design techniques, we transform these general test conditions and the general **testing objectives** from the test plan into tangible test cases at the appropriate level of detail. Test design generally, and specific test design techniques, are discussed in Chapter 4.

- **Test implementation**: In test implementation, we carry out the remaining activities required to be ready for test execution, such as developing and prioritizing our test procedures, creating test data, and setting up test environments. These elements of test implementation are covered in Chapter 4. In many cases, we want to use automated test execution as part of our test process. In such cases, test implementation includes preparing test harnesses and writing automated test scripts. These elements of test implementation are covered in Chapter 6.

- **Test execution**: In test execution, we run our tests against the test object (also called the system under test).

- **Checking results**: As part test execution, we see the actual results of the test case, the consequences and outcomes. These include outputs to screens, changes to data, reports, and communication messages sent out. We must compare these actual results against expected results to determine the pass/fail status of the test. Defining expected results is discussed in Chapter 4, while managing test execution, including checking of results, is discussed in Chapter 5.

- **Evaluating exit criteria**: At a high level, exit criteria are a set of conditions that would allow some part of a process to complete. Exit criteria are usually defined during test planning by working with the project and product stakeholders to balance quality needs against other priorities and various project constraints. Such criteria ensure that everything that should be done has been done before we declare some set of activities finished. Specifically, test exit criteria help us report our results (as we can report progress against the criteria) as well as helping us plan when to stop testing. Establishing and evaluating exit criteria are discussed in Chapter 5.

- **Test results reporting**: In test results reporting, we want to report our progress against exit criteria, as described above. This often involves details related to the status of the test project, the test process, and quality of the system under test. We'll discuss test results reporting in Chapter 5.

- **Test closure**: Test closure involves collecting test process data related to the various completed test activities in order to consolidate our experience, re-useable testware, important facts, and relevant metrics. Test closure is discussed in section 1.4 below.

Test design specification A document specifying the test conditions (coverage items) for a test item, the detailed test approach and identifying the associated high level test cases.

Test control A test management task that deals with developing and applying a set of corrective actions to get a test project on track when monitoring shows a deviation from what was planned.

Test case A set of input values, execution preconditions, expected results and execution postconditions, developed for a particular objective or test condition, such as to exercise a particular program path or to verify compliance with a specific requirement.

Test objective A reason or purpose for designing and executing a test.

Testing The process consisting of all lifecycle activities, both static and dynamic, concerned with planning, preparation and evaluation of software products and related work products to determine that they satisfy specified requirements, to demonstrate that they are fit for purpose and to detect defects.

Requirement A condition or capability needed by a user to solve a problem or achieve an objective that must be met or possessed by a system or system component to satisfy a contract, standard, specification, or other formally imposed document.

Review An evaluation of a product or project status to ascertain discrepancies from planned results and to recommend improvements. Examples include management review, informal review, technical review, inspection, and walkthrough.

Notice that there are major test activities both before and after test execution. In addition, in the ISTQB definition of software **testing**, you'll see that testing includes both static and dynamic testing. Static testing is any evaluation of the software or related work products (such as **requirements** specifications or user stories) that occurs without executing the software itself. Dynamic testing is an evaluation of that software or related work products that does involve executing the software. As such, the ISTQB definition of testing not only includes a number of pre-execution and post-execution activities that non-testers often do not consider 'testing', but also includes software quality activities (e.g. requirements, **reviews** and static analysis of code) that non-testers (and even sometime testers) often do not consider 'testing' either.

The reason for this broad definition is that both dynamic testing (at whatever level) and static testing (of whatever type) often enable the achievement of similar project objectives. Dynamic testing and static testing also generate information that can help achieve an important process objective; that of understanding and improving the software development and testing processes. Dynamic testing and static testing are complementary activities, each able to generate information that the other cannot.

The following are some objectives for testing given in the Foundation Syllabus:

- Finding defects, such as the identification of failures during test execution that lead to the discovery of the underlying defects.
- Gaining confidence in the level of quality, such as when those tests considered highest risk pass and when the failures that are observed in the other tests are considered acceptable.
- Providing information for decision-making, such as satisfaction of entry or exit criteria.
- Preventing defects, such as when early test activities such as requirements reviews or early test design identify defects in requirements specifications that are removed before they cause defects in the design specifications and subsequently the code itself. Both reviews and test design serve as a verification of these test basis documents that will reveal problems that otherwise would not surface until test execution, potentially much later in the project.

These objectives are not universal. Different test viewpoints, test levels, and test stakeholders can have different objectives. While many levels of testing, such as component, integration and system testing, focus on discovering as many failures as possible in order to find and remove defects, in acceptance testing the main objective is confirmation of correct system operation (at least under normal conditions) along with building confidence that the system meets its requirements.

When done to evaluate a software package that might be purchased or integrated into a larger software system, the main objective of testing might be the assessment of the quality of the software. Defects found may not be fixed, but rather might support a conclusion that the software be rejected.

Testing can focus on providing stakeholders with an evaluation of the risk of releasing the system at a given time. Evaluating risk can be part of a mix of objectives, or can be an objective of a separate level of testing, as when testing a safety critical system.

During maintenance testing, our objectives often include checking whether developers have introduced any regressions (i.e. new defects not present in the previous version) while making changes. Some forms of testing, such as operational testing, focus on assessing system characteristics such as reliability, security, performance or availability.

Let's end this section by saying what testing is not, but is often thought to be. Testing is not **debugging**. While dynamic testing often locates failures which are caused by defects, and static testing often locates defects themselves, testing does not fix defects. It is during debugging, a development activity, that a member of the project team finds, analyzes and removes the defect, the underlying cause of the failure. After debugging, there is a further testing activity associated with the defect, which is called **confirmation testing** or **re-testing**. This activity ensures that the fix does indeed resolve the failure. In terms of roles, dynamic and static testing are testing roles, debugging is a development role, and confirmation testing is again a testing role.

1.3   SEVEN TESTING PRINCIPLES

> **SYLLABUS LEARNING OBJECTIVES FOR 1.3 SEVEN TESTING PRINCIPLES (K2)**
>
> **LO-1.3.1   Explain the seven principles in testing. (K2)**

> **Debugging** The process of finding, analyzing and removing the causes of failures in software.

> **Confirmation testing (re-testing)** Testing that runs test cases that failed the last time they were run, in order to verify the success of corrective actions. [Note: While the Glossary uses re-testing as the preferred term, this preference is out of step with ordinary usage and with the actual English-language definition of 're-testing'.]

In this section, we will review seven fundamental principles of testing which have been observed over the last 40 years. These principles, while not always understood or noticed, are in action on most if not all projects. Knowing how to spot these principles, and how to take advantage of them, will make you a better tester.

As you read this section, you'll encounter the terms **complete testing**, **exhaustive testing** and **test strategy**.

The following subsections will review each principle, using the principle name as the subsection title for easy correlation to the syllabus. In addition, you can refer to Table 1.1 for a quick reference of the principles and their text, as written in the syllabus.

1.3.1   Testing shows the presence of defects

As mentioned in the previous section, one typical objective of many testing efforts is to find defects. Many testing organizations that the authors have worked with are quite effective at doing so. One of our clients consistently finds, on average, 99.5% of the defects in the software it tests. In addition, the defects left undiscovered are less important and unlikely to happen frequently in production. Sometimes, it turns out that this test team has indeed found 100% of the defects that would matter to customers, as no previously-unreported defects are reported after release.

However, no test team, test technique, or **test strategy** can achieve 100% defect detection effectiveness. Thus, it is important to understand that, while testing can show that defects are present, it cannot prove that there are no defects left undiscovered. Of course, as testing continues, we reduce the likelihood of defects that remain undiscovered, but eventually a form of Zeno's paradox takes hold. Each additional test run may cut the risk of a remaining defect in half, but only an infinite number of tests can cut the risk down to zero with such a mathematical series.

That said, testers should not despair or let the perfect be the enemy of the good. While testing can never prove that the software works, it can reduce the remaining level of risk to product quality to an acceptable level, as mentioned before. In any endeavour worth doing, there is some risk. Software projects – and software testing – are endeavours worth doing.

> **Test strategy** A high-level description of the test levels to be performed and the testing within those levels for an organization or program (one or more projects).

TABLE 1.1   Testing principles

Principle 1:	Testing shows presence of defects	Testing can show that defects are present, but cannot prove that there are no defects. Testing reduces the probability of undiscovered defects remaining in the software but, even if no defects are found, it is not a proof of correctness.
Principle 2:	Exhaustive testing is impossible	Testing everything (all combinations of inputs and preconditions) is not feasible except for trivial cases. Instead of exhaustive testing, risk analysis and priorities should be used to focus testing efforts.
Principle 3:	Early testing	To find defects early, testing activities shall be started as early as possible in the software or system development life cycle, and shall be focused on defined objectives.
Principle 4:	Defect clustering	Testing effort shall be focused proportionally to the expected and later observed defect density of modules. A small number of modules usually contains most of the defects discovered during pre-release testing, or is responsible for most of the operational failures.
Principle 5:	Pesticide paradox	If the same tests are repeated over and over again, eventually the same set of test cases will no longer find any new defects. To overcome this 'pesticide paradox', test cases need to be regularly reviewed and revised, and new and different tests need to be written to exercise different parts of the software or system to find potentially more defects.
Principle 6:	Testing is context dependent	Testing is done differently in different contexts. For example, safety-critical software is tested differently from an e-commerce site.
Principle 7:	Absence-of-errors fallacy	Finding and fixing defects does not help if the system built is unusable and does not fulfil the users' needs and expectations.

Exhaustive testing (complete testing) A test approach in which the test suite comprises all combinations of input values and preconditions.

1.3.2 Exhaustive testing is impossible

This principle is closely related to the previous principle. For any real-sized system, anything beyond the trivial software constructed in first-year software engineering courses, the number of possible test cases is either infinite or so close to infinite as to be practically innumerable.

Infinity is a tough concept for the human brain to comprehend or accept, so let's use a couple of examples. One of our clients mentioned that they had calculated the number of possible internal data value combinations in the Unix operating system as greater than the number of known molecules in the universe by four orders of magnitude. They further calculated that, even with their fastest automated tests, just to test all of these internal state combinations would require more time than the current age of the universe. Even that would not be a complete test of the operating system; it would only cover all the possible data value combinations.

So, as mentioned in section 1.1, we are confronted with a big, infinite cloud of possible tests; we must select a subset from it. One way to select tests is to wander aimlessly in the cloud of tests, selecting at random, until we run out of time. While there is a place for automated random testing, by itself it is a poor strategy. We'll discuss testing strategies further in Chapter 5, but for the moment let's look at two.

One strategy for selecting tests is risk based testing. In risk based testing, we have a cross-functional team of project and product stakeholders perform a special type of risk analysis. In this analysis, stakeholders identify risks to the quality of the system, and assess the level of risk (often using likelihood and impact) associated with each risk item. We focus the test effort based on the level of risk, using the level of risk to determine the appropriate number of test cases for each risk item, and also to sequence the test cases.

Another strategy for selecting tests is requirements based testing. In requirements based testing, testers analyze the requirements specification to identify test conditions. These test conditions inherit the priority of the requirement they derive from. We focus the test effort based on the priority to determine the appropriate number of test cases for each requirement, and also to sequence the test cases.

1.3.3 Early testing

This principle tells us that we should start testing as early as possible in order to find as many defects as possible. In addition, since the cost of finding and removing a defect increases the longer that defect is in the system, early testing also means we should minimize the cost of removing defects.

So, the first principle tells us that we can't find all the bugs, but rather can only find some percentage of them. The second principle tells us that we can't run every possible test. The third principle tells us to start testing early. What can we conclude when we put these three principles together?

Imagine that you have a system with 1000 defects. Suppose we wait until the very end of the project and run one level of testing, system test. You find and fix 90% of the defects. That still leaves 100 defects, which presumably will escape to the customers or users.

Instead, suppose that you start testing early and continue throughout the lifecycle. You perform requirements reviews, design reviews, and code reviews. You perform unit testing, integration testing, and system testing. Suppose that, during each test activity, you find and remove only 45% of the defects, half as effective as the previous system test level. Nevertheless, at the end of the process, less than 30 defects remain. Even though each test activity was only 45% effective at finding defects, the overall sequence of activities was 97% effective.

In addition, defects removed early cost less to remove. Further, since much of the cost in software engineering is associated with human effort, and since the size of a project team is relatively inflexible once that project is underway, reduced cost of defects also means reduced duration of the project. That situation is shown graphically in Figure 1.3.

Now, this type of cumulative and highly efficient defect removal only works if each of the test activities in the sequence is focused on different, defined objectives. If we simply test the same test conditions over and over, we won't achieve the cumulative effect, for reasons we'll discuss in a moment.

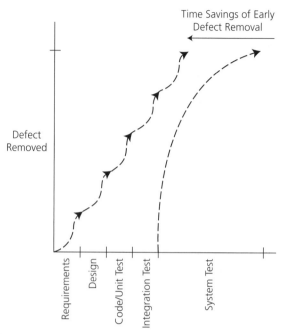

FIGURE 1.3   Time savings of early defect removal

1.3.4 Defect clustering

This principle relates to something we discussed previously, that relying entirely on the testing strategy of a random walk in the infinite cloud of possible tests is relatively weak. Defects are not randomly and uniformly distributed throughout the software under test. Rather, defects tend to be found in clusters, with 20% (or less) of the modules accounting for 80% (or more) of the defects. In other words, the defect density of modules varies considerably. While controversy exists about why defect clustering happens, the reality of defect clustering is well-established. It was first demonstrated in studies performed by IBM in the 1960s [Jones 2008]. We continue to see evidence of defect clustering in our work with clients.

Defect clustering is helpful to us as testers, because it provides a useful guide. If we focus our test effort (at least in part) based on the expected (and ultimately observed) likelihood of finding a defect in a certain area, we can make our testing more effective and efficient, at least in terms of our objective of finding defects. Knowledge of and predictions about defect clusters are important inputs to the risk based testing strategy discussed earlier. In a metaphorical way, we can imagine that bugs are social creatures, who like to hang out together in the dark corners of the software.

1.3.5 Pesticide paradox

This principle was coined by Boris Beizer [Beizer 1990]. He observed that, just as a pesticide repeatedly sprayed on a field will kill fewer and fewer bugs each time it's used, so too a given set of tests will eventually stop finding new defects when it's re-run against a system under development or maintenance. If the tests don't provide adequate coverage, this slowdown in defect finding will result in a level of false confidence and excessive optimism among the project team. The air will be let out of the balloon once the system is released to customers and users, though.

Using the right test strategies is the first step towards achieving adequate coverage. However, no strategy is perfect. You should plan to regularly review the test results during the project, and revise the tests based on your findings. In some cases, you need to write new and different tests to exercise different parts of the software or system. These new tests can lead to discovery of previously-unknown defect clusters, which is a good reason not to wait until the end of the test effort to review your test results and evaluate the adequacy of test coverage.

The pesticide paradox is important when implementing the multilevel testing discussed previously in regards to the principle of early testing. Simply repeating our tests of the same conditions over and over will not result in good cumulative defect detection. However, when used properly, each type and level of testing has its own strengths and weaknesses in terms of defect detection, and collectively we can assemble a very effective sequence of defect filters from them. After such a sequence of complementary test activities, we can be confident that the test coverage set is adequate, and that the remaining level of risk is acceptable.

1.3.6 Testing is context dependent

Our safety-critical clients test with a great deal of rigor and care – and cost. When lives are at stake, we must be extremely careful to minimize the risk of undetected defects. Our clients who release software on the web, such as e-commerce sites, can take advantage of the possibility to quickly change the software when necessary, leading to a different set of testing challenges – and opportunities. If you tried to apply safety-critical approaches to an e-commerce site, you might put the company out of business; if you tried to apply e-commerce approaches to safety-critical software, you could put lives in danger. So the context of the testing influences how much testing we do and how the testing is done.

1.3.7 Absence-of-errors fallacy

Throughout this section, we've expounded the idea that a sequence of test activities, started early, targeting specific and diverse objectives and areas of the system, can effectively and efficiently find – and help a project team to remove – a large percentage of the defects. Surely that's all which is required to achieve project success?

Sadly, it is not. Many systems have been built which failed in user acceptance testing or in the marketplace. Some of these systems failed due to a high level of defects, such as the Apple Newton. However, some systems had very low levels of defects, yet still failed.

Consider desktop computer operating systems. In the 1990s, as competition peaked for dominance of the PC operating system market, Unix and its variants had higher levels of quality than DOS and Windows. However, 20 years on, Windows dominates the desktop marketplace. One major reason is that Unix and its variants were too difficult for most users in the early 1990s.

Perhaps you are wondering where this leaves Apple. If usability is important, why is the Mac's share of the desktop marketplace so low, given the MacOS reputation for ease-of-use? The problem lies in Apple's failure to optimize MacOS for enterprise and large-company use. Certain features treasured by system administrators are not present in MacOS.

Macs also suffer from a major problem, which, while not related to software quality, creates an insurmountable obstacle for many CIOs and CFOs: unit price. With organizations forced to refresh their desktop systems anywhere from two to three times a decade, and with many large enterprises owning thousands upon thousands of desktop systems, spending even $100 more than necessary on commoditized computer hardware is simply a non-starter, no matter how well the system works.

1.4 FUNDAMENTAL TEST PROCESS

**SYLLABUS LEARNING OBJECTIVES FOR
1.4 FUNDAMENTAL TEST PROCESS (K1)**

LO-1.4.1   **Recall the five fundamental test activities and respective tasks
from planning to closure (K1)**

In this section, we will describe the fundamental test process and activities. These start with test planning and continue through to test closure. For each part of the test process, we'll discuss the main tasks of each test activity.

In this section, you'll also encounter the glossary terms **coverage (test coverage), exit criteria, incident, regression testing, test approach, test basis, test condition, test data, test execution, test log, test monitoring, test plan, test procedure, test suite, test summary report,** and **testware.**

In section 1.2, we had an overview of testing activities throughout the lifecycle, going beyond the usual understanding of testing as consisting simply of **test execution**. Certainly, test execution is the most visible testing activity. However, as we saw in section 1.3, effective and efficient testing requires properly planned and executed **test approaches**, with tests designed and implemented to cover the proper areas of the system, executed in the right sequence, and with their results reviewed regularly.

To help testers maximize the likelihood of such effective and efficient software testing, the ISTQB has defined and published a fundamental test process consisting of the following main activities:

- Planning and control
- Analysis and design
- Implementation and execution
- Evaluating exit criteria and reporting
- Test closure activities

These activities are logically sequential, in the sense that tasks within each activity often create the pre-conditions or precursor work products for tasks in subsequent activities. However, in many cases, the activities in the process may overlap or take place concurrently, provided that these dependencies are fulfilled.

You should not mistake the name given above, fundamental test process, to mean 'the one and only way to test which never alters from one project to another and always contains these and only these test tasks'. We have found that most of these activities, and many of the tasks within these activities, are carried out in some form or another on most successful test efforts. However, you should expect to have to tailor

Test execution The process of running a test on the component or system under test, producing actual result(s).

Test approach The implementation of the test strategy for a specific project. It typically includes the decisions made that follow based on the (test) project's goal and the risk assessment carried out, starting points regarding the test process, the test design techniques to be applied, exit criteria and test types to be performed.

the fundamental test process, its main activities, and the constituent tasks, based on the organizational, project, process, and product needs, constraints, and other contextual realities.

1.4.1 Test planning and control

As mentioned in section 1.2, planning involves defining the overall strategic and tactical objectives of testing, as well as discovering and specifying the specific test activities required to satisfy those objectives and the general mission of testing. Metaphorically, you can think of **test planning** as similar to figuring out how to get from one place to another. For small, simple, and familiar projects, finding the route merely involves taking an existing map, highlighting the route, and jotting down the specific directions. For large, complex, or new projects, finding the route can involve a sophisticated process of creating a new map, exploring unknown territory, and blazing a fresh trail.

To continue our metaphor, even with the best map and the clearest directions, getting from one place to another involves careful attention, watching the dashboard, minor (and sometimes major) course corrections, talking with our companions about the journey, looking ahead for trouble, tracking progress towards the ultimate destination, and coping with finding an alternate route if the road we wanted is blocked. So, in test control we continuously compare actual progress against the plan, adjust the plan, report the test status and any necessary deviations from the plan, monitor test activities, and take whatever actions are necessary to meet the mission and objectives of the project. To some extent, test control involves re-planning, which should take into account the feedback from these **test monitoring** and control activities.

We'll discuss test planning and control tasks in more detail in Chapter 5.

1.4.2 Test analysis and design

In test analysis and design, we transform the more general testing objectives defined in the test plan into tangible **test conditions** and test cases. The way in which and degree to which the test conditions and test cases are made tangible – that is to say, specifically documented – depends on the needs of the testers, the expectations of the project team, any applicable regulations, and other considerations. Test analysis and design is discussed in more detail in Chapter 4.

During test analysis and design activities, we may have to perform the following major tasks:

- Review the **test basis**. We can say colloquially that the test bases are those documents upon which we base our tests. The test basis can include requirements and design specifications, risk analysis reports, the system design and architecture, and interface specifications. The Foundation syllabus also defines the software integrity level as a possible test basis. The software integrity level is the degree to which software must comply with a set of stakeholder-selected characteristics, such as software complexity, the risk assessment, the required safety and security levels, desired performance and reliability, or cost, which reflect the importance of the software to its stakeholders.

- Evaluate the testability of the test basis and test objects, which can result in reporting on any issues that might impede testing and adjusting the test plan to deal with these issues. This task often occurs as part of or in parallel with the

Test plan A document describing the scope, approach, resources and schedule of intended test activities. It identifies among others test items, the features to be tested, the testing tasks, who will do each task, degree of tester independence, the test environment, the test design techniques and entry and exit criteria to be used, and the rationale for their choice, and any risks requiring contingency planning. It is a record of the test planning process.

Test monitoring A test management task that deals with the activities related to periodically checking the status of a test project. Reports are prepared that compare the actuals to that which was planned.

Test condition An item or event of a component or system that could be verified by one or more test cases, e.g. a function, transaction, feature, quality attribute, or structural element.

Test basis All documents from which the requirements of a component or system can be inferred. The documentation on which the test cases are based. If a document can be amended only by way of formal amendment procedure, then the test basis is called a frozen test basis.

review of the test basis, but it's important to see these as distinct so that this important task is not forgotten.

● Identify and prioritize specific test conditions based on analysis of the risks, test items, the requirements and design specifications, and the behaviour and structure of the software.

● Design and prioritize high level (i.e. abstract or logical) test cases. Such test cases give general guidance on inputs and expected results, but do not include the specific inputs or expected results. For example, a high level test case might specify testing the checkout function of an e-commerce application, but would not include the particular inputs for specific fields or the exact appearance of screens after the inputs are submitted.

Test data Data that exists (for example, in a database) before a test is executed, and that affects or is affected by the component or system under test.

● Identify the necessary **test data** to support the test conditions and test cases as they are identified and designed.

● Design the test environment, including the set-up and any required infrastructure and tools.

● Create traceability between the test basis documents and the test cases. This traceability should be bi-directional so that we can check which test basis elements go with which test cases (and vice versa) and determine the degree of **coverage** of the test basis by the test cases. Traceability is also very important for maintenance testing, as we'll discuss in Chapter 2.

Coverage (test coverage) The degree, expressed as a percentage, to which a specified coverage item has been exercised by a test suite.

Which of these specific tasks applies to a particular project depends on various contextual issues relevant to the project, which are discussed further in Chapter 5.

1.4.3 Test implementation and execution

Test procedure specification (test procedure, test script, manual test script) A document specifying a sequence of actions for the execution of a test.

In test implementation and execution, we specify **test procedures** (or test scripts). This involves combining the test cases in a particular order, as well as including any other information needed for test execution. This involves transforming the high level (or abstract or logical) test cases into low level (concrete) test cases, which may be done more formally and written into a test script, or it may be done 'on the fly' as a tester is executing tests from a list of high level test conditions. Test implementation also involves setting up the test environment. During test execution, of course, we run the tests.

During test implementation, we may have to perform the following major tasks:

● Finalize, implement and prioritize the test cases.

● Identify and create specific test data, which can take the form of inputs, data resident in databases and other data repositories, and system configuration data.

● Develop and prioritize test procedures, often using the test basis and test project constraints to achieve the optimal order of test execution. Once we have prioritized test procedures, we may need to create **test suites** from the test procedures for efficient test execution.

Test suite A set of several test cases for a component or system under test, where the post condition of one test is often used as the precondition for the next one.

● If automation is to occur, prepare test harnesses and write automated test scripts. Test automation is discussed in Chapter 6.

● Verify that the test environment has been set up correctly, ideally before test execution starts so that test environment issues do not impede test progress.

● Verify and update the bi-directional traceability prepared previously, to make certain that adequate coverage exists.

Ideally, all of these tasks are completed before test execution begins, because otherwise precious, limited test execution time can be lost on these types of preparatory tasks. One of our clients reported losing as much as 25% of the test execution period to what they called 'environmental shakedown', which turned out to be comprised almost entirely of test implementation activities that could have been completed before the software was delivered.

During test execution, we may have to perform the following major tasks:

- Execute the test procedures manually or with the use of automated test execution tools, according to the planned sequence.

- Compare actual results with expected results, observing where the actual and expected results differ. These anomalies should be logged as **incidents** for further investigation.

- Log the outcome of test execution. This includes not only the anomalies observed and the pass/fail status of the test cases, but also the identities and versions of the software under test, test tools and **testware**.

- Analyze the incidents in order to establish their cause. Causes of incidents can include defects in the code, in which case we have a failure. Other incidents result from defects in specified test data, in the test document, or simply a mistake in the way the test was executed. Report the incidents as appropriate. Some organizations track test defects (i.e. defects in the tests themselves) as incidents, while others do not. Incident analysis and reporting is discussed in Chapter 5.

- As necessary, repeat test activities when actions are taken to resolve discrepancies. For example, we might need to re-run a test that previously failed in order to confirm a fix (confirmation testing). We might need to run a corrected test. We might also need to run additional, previously-executed tests to see whether defects have been introduced in unchanged areas of the software or to see whether a fixed defect now makes another defect apparent (**regression testing**).

As before, which of these specific tasks applies to a particular project depends on various contextual issues relevant to the project, which are discussed further in Chapter 5.

1.4.4 Evaluating exit criteria and reporting

In evaluating **exit criteria** and reporting, we assess test execution against the objectives which we defined in the test plan. We should do so for each test level (as discussed in Chapter 2, Section 2).

During evaluation of exit criteria and reporting, we may have to perform the following major tasks:

- Check the **test logs** gathered during test execution against the exit criteria specified in test planning.

- Assess if more tests are needed or if the exit criteria specified should be changed.

- Write a **test summary report** for stakeholders, as discussed in Chapter 5.

The specific evaluation and reporting tasks and deliverables that apply to a particular project depends on various contextual issues relevant to the project, which are discussed further in Chapter 5.

Incident Any event occurring that requires investigation.

Testware Artifacts produced during the test process required to plan, design, and execute tests, such as documentation, scripts, inputs, expected results, set-up and clear-up procedures, files, databases, environment, and any additional software or utilities used in testing.

Regression testing Testing of a previously tested program following modification to ensure that defects have not been introduced or uncovered in unchanged areas of the software, as a result of the changes made. It is performed when the software or its environment is changed.

Exit criteria The set of generic and specific conditions, agreed upon with the stakeholders, for permitting a process to be officially completed. The purpose of exit criteria is to prevent a task from being considered completed when there are still outstanding parts of the task which have not been finished. Exit criteria are used to report against and to plan when to stop testing.

Test log A chronological record of relevant details about the execution of tests.

Test summary report A document summarizing testing activities and results. It also contains an evaluation of the corresponding test items against exit criteria.

1.4.5 Test closure activities (K1)

In test closure, we collect data from completed test activities to consolidate experience, testware, facts and numbers. Test closure activities should occur at major project milestones. These can include when a software system is released, a test project is completed (or cancelled), a milestone has been achieved, or a maintenance release has been completed, though the specific milestones that involve closure activities should be specified in the test plan.

During test closure, we may have to perform the following major tasks:

- Check which planned deliverables have been delivered, and possibly create any deliverables we might have missed.
- Ensure that all incident reports are resolved, and possibly log change requests for any that remain open.
- Document the acceptance of the system, particularly as part of the closure of the user acceptance test level.
- Finalize and archive testware, the test environment and the test infrastructure for later reuse.
- Hand over the testware to the maintenance organization, if that is a different group.
- Analyze lessons learned to determine changes needed for future releases and projects (i.e. perform a retrospective).
- Use the information gathered to improve test maturity, especially as an input to test planning for future projects.

The degree and extent to which test closure activities occur, and which specific test closure activities do occur, depends on various contextual issues relevant to the project, which are discussed further in Chapter 5.

1.5 THE PSYCHOLOGY OF TESTING

> **SYLLABUS LEARNING OBJECTIVES FOR 1.5 THE PSYCHOLOGY OF TESTING (K2)**
>
> **LO-1.5.1** Recall the psychological factors that influence the success of testing (K1)
>
> **LO-1.5.2** Contrast the mindset of a tester and of a developer (K2)

In this section, we'll discuss the various psychological factors that influence testing and its success. These include clear objectives for testing, the proper roles and balance of self-testing and independent testing, clear, courteous communication and feedback on defects. We'll also contrast the mindset of a tester and of a developer.

You'll find a few syllabus terms in this section, **error guessing**, **independence of testing** and **test policy**.

As mentioned earlier, the ISTQB definition of software testing includes both dynamic testing and static testing. Let's review the distinction again. Dynamic software testing involves actually executing the software or some part of it, such as checking an application-produced report for accuracy or checking response time to user input. Static software testing does not execute the software but uses two possible approaches: automated static analysis on the code (e.g. evaluating its complexity) or on a document (e.g. to evaluate the readability of a use case) or reviews of code or documents (e.g. to evaluate a requirement specification for consistency, ambiguity and completeness).

While these are very different types of activities, they have in common their ability to find defects. Static testing finds defects directly, while dynamic testing finds evidence of a defect through a failure of the software to behave as expected. Either way, people carrying out static or dynamic tests must be focused on the possibility – indeed, the high likelihood in many case – of finding defects. Indeed many times finding defects is a primary objective of static and dynamic testing activities.

That mindset is quite different from the mindset that a business analyst, system design, architect, database administrator, or programmer must bring to creating the work products involved in developing software. While the testers (or reviewers) must assume that the work product under review or test is defective in some way – and it is their job to find those defects – the people developing that work product must have confidence that they understand how to do so properly.

This confidence in their understanding is in some sense necessary for developers. They cannot proceed without it, but at the same time this confidence creates what the Foundation syllabus refers to as the author bias. Simply put, the author of a work product has confidence that they have solved the requirements, design, metadata or code problem, at least in an acceptable fashion; however, strictly speaking, that is false confidence. As we saw earlier, because human beings are fallible, all software work products contain defects when initially created, and any one of those defects could render the work product unfit for use.

While some developers are aware of their author bias when they participate in reviews and perform unit testing of their own work products, that author bias acts to impede their effectiveness at finding their own defects. The mental mistakes that caused them to create the defects remain in their minds in most cases. When proof-reading our own work, for example, we see what we meant, not what we put!

In addition, many business analysts, system designers, architects, database admin-istrators, and programmers do not know the review, static analysis, and dynamic testing techniques discussed in the Foundation syllabus and this book. While that situation is gradually changing, much of the self-testing by software work product devel-opers is either not done or is not done as effectively as it could be. The principles and techniques in the Foundation syllabus and this book are intended to help either testers or others to be more effective at finding defects, both their own and those of others.

A trained independent tester – or better yet a trained, certified, independent test team – can overcome both of these limitations. Independent test teams tend to be more effective at finding defects and failures. Capers Jones reports that unit testing by developers tops out at 40 to 50% defect detection effectiveness, while we regularly find independent test teams scoring 85% defect detection effectiveness. Indeed, some of our best clients, those with trained, certified, independent test teams, regularly score defect detection effectiveness of 95% and above.

To be most effective at finding defects, a tester needs the right mindset. Looking for defects and failures in a system calls for people with the following traits:

● Curiosity. Good testers are curious about why systems behave the way they do and how systems are built. When they see unexpected behaviour, they have a natural urge to explore further, to isolate the failure, to look for more generalized problems, and to gain deeper understanding.

● Professional pessimism. Good testers expect to find defects and failures. They understand human fallibility and its implications for software development. (However, this is not to say that they are negative or adversarial, as we'll discuss in a moment.)

● A critical eye. Good testers couple this professional pessimism with a natural inclination to doubt the correctness of software work products and their behaviours as they look at them. A good tester has, as her personal slogan, 'If in doubt, it's a bug'.

● Attention to detail. Good testers notice everything, even the smallest details. Sometimes these details are cosmetic problems like font-size mismatches, but sometimes these details are subtle clues that a serious failure is about to happen. This trait is both a blessing and a curse. Some testers find that they cannot turn this trait off, so they are constantly finding defects in the real world – even when not being paid to find them.

● Experience. Good testers not only know a defect when they see one, they also know where to look for defects. Experienced testers have seen a veritable parade of bugs in their time, and they leverage this experience during all types of testing, especially experience-based testing such as **error guessing** (see Chapter 4).

● Good communication skills. All of these traits are essential, but, without the ability to effectively communicate their findings, testers will produce useful information that will – alas – be put to no use. Good communicators know how to explain the test results, even negative results such as serious defects and quality risks, without coming across as preachy, scolding or defeatist.

Error guessing A test design technique where the experience of the tester is used to anticipate what defects might be present in the component or system under test as a result of errors made, and to design tests specifically to expose them.

A good independent tester has the skills, the training, the certification, and the mindset of a professional tester, and of these four the most important – and perhaps the most elusive – is the mindset. The best testers continuously strive to attain a more professional mindset, and it is a lifelong journey.

All of this is not to say that software work product developers – business analysts, system designers, architects, database administrators, and programmers – should not review and test their own work. They certainly should. Quality is everyone's responsibility. The presence of an independent test team or single tester is not a signal to developers to abdicate their professional responsibilities to produce the best quality work products they can. Abdicating responsibility for quality and saying, 'Hurrah, we have an independent test team now, so we don't have to test our own work, we can just let the testers find all the bugs', is a known worst-practice of software development.

When highly-defective, barely functioning software is delivered to independent test teams in higher levels of testing such as system test or system integration test, such a level of bugginess often overwhelms the testing process and results in defect detection effectiveness much lower than 85%. Since more defects are delivered in the first place, this situation results in a much higher number of defects delivered to users and customers.

So, developer self-testing has an important role to play. Business analysts have a deep understanding of the problem the software is to solve. Designers, system architects, and database administrators have a deep understanding of how the system fits together, and fits with other important systems such as databases. Programmers have a deep understanding of the implementation and low-level design of the software. For this reason, business analysts, system designers, architects, database administrators, and programmers should participate in reviews of their work products and carry out static analysis of their work products. In addition, unit and component integration testing is usually carried out by programmers, though independent testers can play a role in these test levels.

It's also important to understand that **independence of testing** exists on a spectrum running from lower to higher:

- When tests are designed and possibly even executed by the software work product developer who wrote the work product, this is a low level of independence. As mentioned above, this kind of testing is necessary, but we should have no illusions about achieving a high level of defect detection effectiveness with such tests.

- When tests are designed by someone other than the author, but someone from within the development team, this does reduce the author bias to some extent. However, group-think can exist within such teams, limiting the independence of thought and the effectiveness of test design. In addition, as noted above, there may be a lack of knowledge about how to test well.

- When tests are designed by people from a different organizational group, such as an independent test team or tester who specialize in usability or performance testing, this is a high level of independence. As mentioned earlier, such test teams can be highly effective defect detectors.

- When tests are designed and executed by people from a different organization or company, such as an outsource testing service provider or system certification body (e.g. the FDA for pharmaceutical systems), this provides the highest level of independence.

We'll revisit this issue of tester independence in Chapter 5.

Independence by itself doesn't guarantee successful testing. Testing activities need clearly defined objectives, too, as people involved in testing will tend to look to such objectives for direction during planning and other activities in the test process. For example, if the main objective of user acceptance testing is to gain confidence that the most-used business processes are working smoothly, a tester who thinks the main objective is to find defects may concentrate on obscure areas of the system instead of the main user paths. The tester may think they are doing the right thing, but in fact they are not. This is why test objectives should be clearly defined in a **testing policy**, ideally with effectiveness and efficiency measures and goals for each objective, and these goals clearly communicated to the testers.

Now, as we mentioned earlier, independence from the developers doesn't mean an adversarial relationship with them. In fact, such a relationship is toxic – often fatally so – to a test team's effectiveness. For example, if testers are not careful about the way they communicate, developers may perceive the identification of defects

Independence of testing Separation of responsibilities, which encourages the accomplishment of objective testing.

Test policy A high level document describing the principles, approach and major objectives of the organization regarding testing.

(in reviews) and failures (during test execution) as a criticism of their work and in fact of them personally. This can result in a perception that testing is a destructive activity.

It is a particular problem when testers revel in being the bearer of bad news. For example, one tester made a revealing – and not very flattering – remark during an interview with one of the authors. When asked what he liked about testing, he responded, 'I like to catch the developers'. He went on to explain that, when he found a defect in someone's work, he would go and demonstrate the failure on the programmer's work-station. He said that he made sure that he found at least one defect in everyone's work on a project, and went through this process of ritually humiliating the programmer with each and every one of his colleagues. When asked why, he said, 'I want to prove to everyone that I am their intellectual equal'. This person, while possessing many of the skills and traits one would want in a tester, had exactly the wrong personality to be a truly professional tester.

Instead of seeing themselves as their colleagues' adversaries or social inferiors out to prove their equality, testers must see themselves as teammates. In their special role, testers provide essential services within the development organization. They should ask themselves, 'Who are the stakeholders in the work that I do as a tester?' Having identified these stakeholders, they should ask each stakeholder group, 'What services do you want from the testing team, and how well are we doing?'

While the specific services are not always defined, it is common that mature development team members see testing as a constructive activity that helps the organization manage its quality risks. In addition, wise developers know that study-ing their mistakes and the defects they have introduced is the key to learning how to get better. Further, smart software development managers understand that finding and fixing defects during testing not only reduces the level of risk to the quality of the product, it also saves time and money when compared to finding defects in production. Working with stakeholders to define these services is an essential part of defining the objectives, measures and goals for the test policy document mentioned earlier.

Such clearly defined objectives and goals, combined with constructive styles of communication on the part of test professionals, will help to avoid any negative personal or group dynamics between testers and their colleagues in the development team. Whenever defects are found by independent testers, whether during reviews, static analysis, or dynamic testing, true testing professionals distinguish themselves by demonstrating good interpersonal skills. True testing professionals communicate facts about defects, progress and risks in a constructive way. While this is not necessary, we have noticed that many of consummate testing professionals have business analysts, system designers, architects, programmers, and other developers with whom they work as close personal friends.

Certainly, having good communication skills is a complex topic, well beyond the scope of a book on fundamental testing techniques. However, we can give you some basics for good communication with your development teammates:

● First of all, remember to think of your colleagues as teammates, not as opponents or adversaries. The way you regard people has a profound effect on the way you treat them. You don't have to think in terms of kinship or achieving world peace, but you should keep in mind that everyone on the development team has the common goal of delivering a quality system, and must work together to accomplish that.

- Next, recognize that your colleagues have pride in their work, just as you do, and as such you owe them a tactful communication about defects you have found. It's not really any harder to communicate your findings, especially the potentially embarrassing findings, in a neutral, fact-focused way. In fact, you'll find that, if you avoid criticizing people and their work products, but instead keep your written and verbal communications objective and factual, you also will avoid a lot of unnecessary conflict and drama with your colleagues.

- In addition, before you communicate these potentially embarrassing findings, mentally put yourself in the position of the person who created the work product. How are they going to feel about this information? How might they react? What can you do to help them get the essential message that they need to receive without provoking a negative emotional reaction from them?

- Finally, keep in mind the psychological element of cognitive dissonance. Cognitive dissonance is a defect – or perhaps a feature – in the human brain that makes it difficult to process unexpected information, especially bad news. So, while you might have been clear in what you said or wrote, the person on the receiving end might not have clearly understood. Cognitive dissonance is a two-way street, too, and it's quite possible that you are misunderstanding someone's reaction to your findings. So, before assuming the worst about someone and their motivations, instead confirm that the other person has understood what you have said and vice versa.

The softer side of software testing is often the harder side to master. A tester may have adequate or even excellent technique skills and certifications, but if they do not have adequate interpersonal and communication skills, they will not be an effective tester. Such soft skills can be improved with training and practice.

1.6 CODE OF ETHICS

SYLLABUS LEARNING OBJECTIVES FOR 1.6 CODE OF ETHICS

Note: At this time, no learning objectives are provided for this section, nor is an overall section K-level defined. You should remember the code of ethics.

In this section, we'll briefly introduce you to the ISTQB code of ethics. There are no Syllabus terms for this section.

As a software tester, as in any other profession, you will from time to time encounter ethical challenges. On the one hand, you are likely to have access to confidential and privileged information, or to be in the position to harm someone's interests. On the other hand, you are likely to have opportunities to advance good causes. So, a code of ethics will help guide your decisions and choose the best-possible outcome.

The ISTQB has derived its code of ethics from the ACM and IEEE code of ethics. The ISTQB code of ethics is shown in Table 1.2.

TABLE 1.2 ISTQB Code of Ethics

PUBLIC	Certified software testers shall act consistently with the public interest.
CLIENT AND EMPLOYER	Certified software testers shall act in a manner that is in the best interests of their client and employer, consistent with the public interest.
PRODUCT	Certified software testers shall ensure that the deliverables they provide (on the products and systems they test) meet the highest professional standards possible.
JUDGMENT	Certified software testers shall maintain integrity and independence in their professional judgment.
MANAGEMENT	Certified software test managers and leaders shall subscribe to and promote an ethical approach to the management of software testing.
PROFESSION	Certified software testers shall advance the integrity and reputation of the profession consistent with the public interest.
COLLEAGUES	Certified software testers shall be fair to and supportive of their colleagues, and promote cooperation with software developers.
SELF	Certified software testers shall participate in lifelong learning regarding the practice of their profession and shall promote an ethical approach to the practice of the profession.

CHAPTER REVIEW

Let's review what you have learned in this chapter.

From Section 1.1, you should now be able to explain why testing is necessary and support that explanation with examples and evidence. You should be able to give examples of negative consequences of a software defect or bug for people, companies, and the environment. You should be able to contrast a defect with its symptoms, the anomalies caused by defects. You should be able to discuss the ways in which testing fits into and supports higher quality. You should know the glossary terms **bug, defect, error, fails (false-fail result, false-positive result), failure, fault, mistake, passed (false-negative result, false-pass result), quality** and **risk**.

From Section 1.2, you should now know what testing is. You should be able to remember the common objectives of testing. You should be able to describe how testing can find defects, provide confidence and information and prevent defects. You should know the glossary terms **confirmation testing, debugging, re-testing, requirement, review, test case, test control, test design specification, testing** and **test objective.**

You should be able to explain the fundamental principles of testing, discussed in Section 1.3. You should know the glossary terms **complete testing, exhaustive testing** and **test strategy**.

From Section 1.4, you should now recognize the fundamental test process. You should be able to recall the main testing activities related to test planning and control, analysis and design, implementation and execution, evaluating exit criteria and reporting, and test closure. You should know the glossary terms **coverage (test coverage), exit criteria, incident, regression testing, test approach, test basis, test condition, test data, test execution, test log, test monitoring, test plan, test procedure, test suite, test summary report** and **testware**.

From Section 1.5, you now should be able to explain the psychology of testing and how people influence testing success. You should recall the importance of clear objectives, the right mix of self-testing and independent testing and courteous, respectful communication between testers and others on the project team, especially about defects. You should be able to explain and contrast the mindsets of testers and programmers and why these differences can lead to conflicts. You should know the glossary terms **error guessing, independence of testing** and **test policy**.

Finally, from section 1.6, you should understand the ISTQB Code of Ethics.

SAMPLE EXAM QUESTIONS

Question 1   A company recently purchased a commercial off-the-shelf application to automate their bill-paying process. They now plan to run an acceptance test against the package prior to putting it into production. Which of the following is their most likely reason for testing?

a. To build confidence in the application.

b. To detect bugs in the application.

c. To gather evidence for a lawsuit.

d. To train the users.

Question 2   According to the ISTQB Glossary, the word 'bug' is synonymous with which of the following words?

a. Incident.

b. Defect.

c. Mistake.

d. Error.

Question 3   According to the ISTQB Glossary, a risk relates to which of the following?

a. Negative feedback to the tester.

b. Negative consequences that will occur.

c. Negative consequences that could occur.

d. Negative consequences for the test object.

Question 4   Ensuring that test design starts during the requirements definition phase is important to enable which of the following test objectives?

a. Preventing defects in the system.

b. Finding defects through dynamic testing.

c. Gaining confidence in the system.

d. Finishing the project on time.

Question 5   A test team consistently finds between 90% and 95% of the defects present in the system under test. While the test manager understands that this is a good defect-detection percentage for her test team and industry, senior management and executives remain disappointed in the test group, saying that the test team misses too many bugs. Given that the users

are generally happy with the system and that the failures which have occurred have generally been low impact, which of the following testing principles is most likely to help the test manager explain to these managers and executives why some defects are likely to be missed?

a. Exhaustive testing is impossible.

b. Defect clustering.

c. Pesticide paradox.

d. Absence-of-errors fallacy.

Question 6   According to the ISTQB Glossary, regression testing is required for what purpose?

a. To verify the success of corrective actions.

b. To prevent a task from being incorrectly considered completed.

c. To ensure that defects have not been introduced by a modification.

d. To motivate better unit testing by the programmers.

Question 7   Which of the following is most important to promote and maintain good relationships between testers and developers?

a. Understanding what managers value about testing.

b. Explaining test results in a neutral fashion.

c. Identifying potential customer work-arounds for bugs.

d. Promoting better quality software whenever possible.

Question 8   Which of the statements below is the best assessment of how the test principles apply across the test life cycle?

a. Test principles only affect the preparation for testing.

b. Test principles only affect test execution activities.

c. Test principles affect the early test activities such as review.

d. Test principles affect activities throughout the test life cycle.

CHAPTER TWO

Testing throughout the software life cycle

Testing is not a stand-alone activity. It has its place within a software development life cycle model and therefore the life cycle applied will largely determine how testing is organized. There are many different forms of testing. Because several disciplines, often with different interests, are involved in the development life cycle, it is important to clearly understand and define the various test levels and types. This chapter discusses the most commonly applied software development models, test levels and test types. Maintenance can be seen as a specific instance of a development process. The way maintenance influences the test process, levels and types and how testing can be organized is described in the last section of this chapter.

2.1 SOFTWARE DEVELOPMENT MODELS

SYLLABUS LEARNING OBJECTIVES FOR 2.1 SOFTWARE DEVELOPMENT MODELS (K2)

LO-2.1.1 Explain the relationship between development, test activities and work products in the development life cycle, by giving examples using project and product types. (K2)

LO-2.1.2 Recognize the fact that software development models must be adapted to the context of project and product characteristics. (K1)

LO-2.1.3 Recall characteristics of good testing that are applicable to any life cycle model. (K1)

In this section, we'll discuss software development models and how testing fits into them. We'll discuss sequential models, focusing on the V-model approach rather than the flawed 'test at the end' waterfall. We'll discuss iterative and incremental types of models such as prototyping, Rapid Application Development (RAD), Rational Unified Process (RUP) and agile development. We'll finish with a discussion of the common aspects of fitting testing into a lifecycle.

As we go through this section, watch for the Syllabus terms **agile manifesto, agile software development, Commercial Off-The-Shelf (COTS), incremental development model, integration, iterative development model, performance, requirement, test level, validation, verification,** and **V-model.** You'll find these terms defined in the glossary.

The development process adopted for a project will depend on the project aims and goals. There are numerous development life cycles that have been developed in order to achieve different required objectives. These life cycles range from lightweight and fast methodologies, where time to market is of the essence, through to fully controlled and documented methodologies where quality and reliability are key drivers. Each of these methodologies has its place in modern software development and the most appropriate development process should be applied to each project. The models specify the various stages of the process and the order in which they are carried out.

The life cycle model that is adopted for a project will have a big impact on the testing that is carried out. Testing does not exist in isolation; test activities are highly related to software development activities. It will define the what, where, and when of our planned testing, influence regression testing, and largely determine which test techniques to use. The way testing is organized must fit the development life cycle or it will fail to deliver its benefit. If time to market is the key driver, then the testing must be fast and efficient. If a fully documented software development life cycle, with an audit trail of evidence, is required, the testing must be fully documented.

In every development life cycle, a part of testing is focused on **verification** testing and a part is focused on **validation** testing. Verification is concerned with evaluating a work product, component or system to determine whether it meets the requirements set. In fact, verification focuses on the question 'Is the deliverable built according to the specification?'. Validation is concerned with evaluating a work product, component or system to determine whether it meets the user needs and requirements. Validation focuses on the question 'Is the deliverable fit for purpose, e.g. does it provide a solution to the problem?'.

2.1.1 V-model

Before discussing the **V-model**, we will look at the model which came before it. The waterfall model (in Figure 2.1) was one of the earliest models to be designed. It has a natural timeline where tasks are executed in a sequential fashion. We start at the top of the waterfall with a feasibility study and flow down through the various project tasks finishing with implementation into the live environment. Design flows through into development, which in turn flows into build, and finally on into test. Testing tends to happen towards the end of the project life cycle so defects are detected close to the live implementation date. With this model it has been difficult to get feedback passed backwards up the waterfall and there are difficulties if we need to carry out numerous iterations for a particular phase.

The V-model was developed to address some of the problems experienced using the traditional waterfall approach. Defects were being found too late in the life cycle, as testing was not involved until the end of the project. Testing also added lead time due to its late involvement. The V-model provides guidance that testing needs to begin as early as possible in the life cycle, which, as we've seen in Chapter 1, is one of the fundamental principles of structured testing. It also shows that testing is not only an execution-based activity. There are a variety of activities that need to be performed before the end of the coding phase. These activities should be carried out in *parallel* with development activities, and testers need to work with developers and business analysts so they can perform these activities and tasks and produce a set of test deliverables. The work products produced by the developers and business analysts during development are the basis of testing in one or more levels. By starting test design early, defects are often found in the test basis documents. A good practice is to have testers involved even earlier, during the review of the (draft) test

---

Verification
Confirmation by examination and through provision of objective evidence that specified requirements have been fulfilled.

Validation
Confirmation by examination and through provision of objective evidence that the requirements for a specific intended use or application have been fulfilled.

V-model A framework to describe the software development lifecycle activities from requirements specification to maintenance. The V-model illustrates how testing activities can be integrated into each phase of the software development lifecycle.

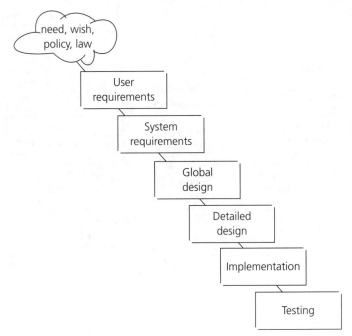

FIGURE 2.1 Waterfall model

basis documents. The V-model is a model that illustrates how testing activities (verification and validation) can be integrated into each phase of the life cycle. Within the V-model, validation testing takes place especially during the early stages, e.g. reviewing the user requirements, and late in the life cycle, e.g. during user acceptance testing.

Although variants of the V-model exist, a common type of V-model uses four **test levels**. The four test levels used, each with their own objectives, are:

- component testing: searches for defects in and verifies the functioning of software components (e.g. modules, programs, objects, classes, etc.) that are separately testable;

- **integration** testing: tests interfaces between components, interactions to different parts of a system such as an operating system, file system and hardware or interfaces between systems;

- system testing: concerned with the behaviour of the whole system/product as defined by the scope of a development project or product. The main focus of system testing is verification against specified requirements;

- acceptance testing: validation testing with respect to user needs, requirements, and business processes conducted to determine whether or not to accept the system.

The various test levels are explained and discussed in detail in Section 2.2.

In practice, a V-model may have more, fewer or different levels of development and testing, depending on the project and the software product. For example, there may be component integration testing after component testing and system integration testing after system testing. Test levels can be combined or reorganized depending on the nature of the project or the system architecture. For the integration

Test level A group of test activities that are organized and managed together. A test level is linked to the responsibilities in a project. Examples of test levels are component test, integration test, system test and acceptance test.

Integration The process of combining components or systems into larger assemblies.

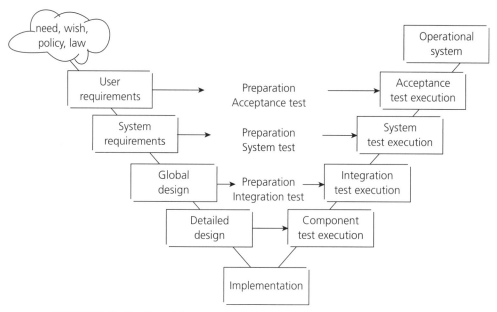

FIGURE 2.2 V-model

of a **commercial off-the-shelf (COTS) software** product into a system, a purchaser may perform only integration testing at the system level (e.g. integration to the infrastructure and other systems) and at a later stage acceptance testing. This acceptance testing can include both testing of system functions but also testing of quality attributes such as **performance** and other non-functional tests. The acceptance testing may be done from the perspective of the end user and may also be done from an operation point of view.

Note that the types of work products mentioned in Figure 2.2 on the left side of the V-model are just an illustration. In practice they come under many different names. References for generic work products include the Capability Maturity Model Integration (CMMi) or the 'Software life cycle processes' from ISO/IEC 12207. The CMMi is a framework for process improvement for both system engineering and software engineering. It provides guidance on where to focus and how, in order to increase the level of process maturity [Chrissis et al. 2004]. ISO/IEC 12207 is an integrated software life cycle process standard.

2.1.2 Iterative life cycles

Not all life cycles are sequential. There are also iterative or incremental life cycles where, instead of one large development time line from beginning to end, we cycle through a number of smaller self-contained life cycle phases for the same project. As with the V-model, there are many variants of iterative life cycles.

A common feature of iterative approaches is that the delivery is divided into increments or builds with each increment adding new functionality. The initial increment will contain the infrastructure required to support the initial build functionality. The increment produced by an iteration may be tested at several levels as part of its development. Subsequent increments will need testing for the new functionality, regression testing of the existing functionality, and integration testing

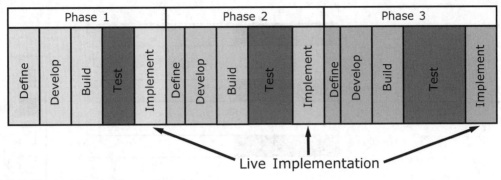

Phase 1					Phase 2					Phase 3				
Define	Develop	Build	Test	Implement	Define	Develop	Build	Test	Implement	Define	Develop	Build	Test	Implement

Live Implementation

FIGURE 2.3   Iterative development model

of both new and existing parts. Regression testing is increasingly important on all iterations after the first one. This means that more testing will be required at each subsequent delivery phase which must be allowed for in the project plans. This life cycle can give early market presence with critical functionality, can be simpler to manage because the workload is divided into smaller pieces, and can reduce initial investment although it may cost more in the long run. Also early market presence will mean validation testing is carried out at each increment, thereby giving early feedback on the business value and fitness-for-use of the product.

Examples of iterative or **incremental development models** are prototyping, Rapid Application Development (RAD), Rational Unified Process (RUP) and agile development (e.g. Scrum). For the purpose of better understanding **iterative development models** shown in Figure 2.3 and the changing role of testing a short explanation of both RAD and agile development is provided.

Rapid Application Development

Rapid Application Development (RAD) is formally a parallel development of functions and subsequent integration.

Components/functions are developed in parallel as if they were mini projects, the developments are time-boxed, delivered, and then assembled into a working prototype. This can very quickly give the customer something to see and use and to provide feedback regarding the delivery and their requirements. Rapid change and development of the product is possible using this methodology. However the product specification will need to be developed for the product at some point, and the project will need to be placed under more formal controls prior to going into production. This methodology allows early validation of technology risks and a rapid response to changing customer requirements.

Dynamic System Development Methodology [DSDM] is a refined RAD process that allows controls to be put in place in order to stop the process from getting out of control. Remember we still need to have the essentials of good development practice in place in order for these methodologies to work. We need to maintain strict configuration management of the rapid changes that we are making in a number of parallel development cycles. From the testing perspective we need to plan this very carefully and update our plans regularly as things will be changing very rapidly (see Chapter 5 for more on test plans).

The RAD development process shown in Figure 2.4, encourages active customer feedback. The customer gets early visibility of the product, can provide feedback on the design and can decide, based on the existing functionality, whether to proceed with the development, what functionality to include in the next delivery cycle or even

Incremental development model A development lifecycle where a project is broken into a series of increments, each of which delivers a portion of the functionality in the overall project requirements. The requirements are prioritized and delivered in priority order in the appropriate increment. In some (but not all) versions of this lifecycle model, each subproject follows a 'mini V-model' with its own design, coding and testing phases.

Iterative development model A development lifecycle where a project is broken into a usually large number of iterations. An iteration is a complete development loop resulting in a release (internal or external) of an executable product, a subset of the final product under development, which grows from iteration to iteration to become the final product.

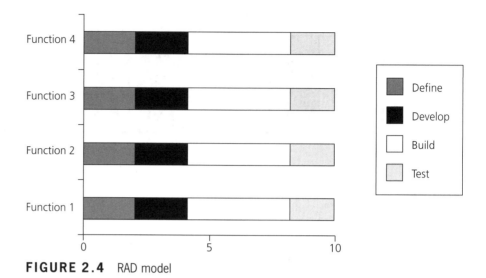

FIGURE 2.4 RAD model

to halt the project if it is not delivering the expected value. An early business-focused solution in the market place gives an early return on investment (ROI) and can provide valuable marketing information for the business. Validation with the RAD development process is thus an early and major activity.

Agile development

In this section, we will describe what agile development is and then cover the changes that this way of working brings to testing. **Agile software development** is a group of software development methodologies based on iterative incremental development, where requirements and solutions evolve through collaboration between self-organizing cross-functional teams. Most agile teams use Scrum, a management framework for iterative incremental development projects. Typical agile teams are 5 to 9 people, and the **agile manifesto** describes ways of working that are ideal for small teams, and that counteract problems prevalent in the late 1990s with its emphasis on process and documentation. The agile manifesto consists of four statements describing what is valued in this way of working:

- individuals and interactions over processes and tools
- working software over comprehensive documentation
- customer collaboration over contract negotiation
- responding to change over following a plan.

While there are a number of agile methodologies in practice, the industry seems to have settled on the use of Scrum as an agile management approach, and Extreme Programming (XP) as the main source of agile development ideas. Some characteristics of project teams using Scrum and XP are:

- The generation of business stories (a form of lightweight use cases) to define the functionality, rather than highly detailed requirements specifications.
- The incorporation of business representatives into the development process, as part of each iteration (called a 'sprint' and typical lasting 2 to 4 weeks), providing continual feedback and to define and carry out functional acceptance testing.

Agile software development A group of software development methodologies based on iterative incremental development, where requirements and solutions evolve through collaboration between self-organizing cross-functional teams.

Agile manifesto A statement on the values that underpin agile software development. The values are:
– individuals and interactions over processes and tools
– working software over comprehensive documentation
– customer collaboration over contract negotiation
– responding to change over following a plan.

- The recognition that we can't know the future, so changes to requirements are welcomed throughout the development process, as this approach can produce a product that better meets the stakeholders' needs as their knowledge grows over time.
- The concept of shared code ownership among the developers, and the close inclusion of testers in the sprint teams.
- The writing of tests as the first step in the development of a component, and the automation of those tests before any code is written. The component is complete when it then passes the automated tests. This is known as Test-Driven Development.
- Simplicity: building only what is necessary, not everything you can think of.
- The continuous integration and testing of the code throughout the sprint, at least once a day.

Proponents of the Scrum and XP approaches emphasize testing throughout the process. Each iteration (sprint) culminates in a short period of testing, often with an independent tester as well as a business representative. Developers are to write and run test cases for their code, and leading practitioners use tools to automate those tests and to measure structural coverage of the tests (see Chapters 4 and 6). Every time a change is made in the code, the component is tested and then integrated with the existing code, which is then tested using the full set of automated component test cases. This gives continuous integration, by which we mean that changes are incorporated continuously into the software build.

Agile development provides both benefits and challenges for testers. Some of the benefits are:

- the focus on working software and good quality code;
- the inclusion of testing as part of and the starting point of software development (test-driven development);
- accessibility of business stakeholders to help testers resolve questions about expected behaviour of the system;
- self-organizing teams where the whole team is responsible for quality and giving testers more autonomy in their work; and
- simplicity of design that should be easier to test.

There are also some significant challenges for testers when moving to an agile development approach.

- Testers used to working with well-documented requirements will be designing tests from a different kind of test basis: less formal and subject to change. The manifesto does not say that documentation is no longer necessary or that it has no value, but it is often interpreted that way.
- Because developers are doing more component testing, there may be a perception that testers are not needed. But component testing and confirmation-based acceptance testing by only business representatives may miss major problems. System testing, with its wider perspective and emphasis on non-functional testing as well as end to end functional testing is needed, even if it doesn't fit comfortably into a sprint.
- The tester's role is different: since there is less documentation and more personal interaction within an agile team, testers need to adapt to this style of working, and

this can be difficult for some testers. Testers may be acting more as coaches in testing to both stakeholders and developers, who may not have a lot of testing knowledge.

● Although there is less to test in one iteration than a whole system, there is also a constant time pressure and less time to think about the testing for the new features.

● Because each increment is adding to an existing working system, regression testing becomes extremely important, and automation becomes more beneficial. However, simply taking existing automated component or component integration tests may not make an adequate regression suite.

Software engineering teams are still learning how to apply agile approaches. Agile approaches cannot be applied to all projects or products, and some testing challenges remain to be surmounted with respect to agile development. However, agile methodologies are starting to show promising results in terms of both development efficiency and quality of the delivered code.

2.1.3 Testing within a life cycle model

In summary, whichever life cycle model is being used, there are several characteristics of good testing:

● for every development activity there is a corresponding testing activity;

● each test level has test objectives specific to that level;

● the analysis and design of tests for a given test level should begin during the corresponding development activity;

● testers should be involved in reviewing documents as soon as drafts are available in the development cycle.

2.2 TEST LEVELS

SYLLABUS LEARNING OBJECTIVES FOR 2.2 TEST LEVELS (K2)

LO-2.2.1 Compare the different levels of testing: major objectives, typical objects of testing, typical targets of testing (e.g. functional or structural) and related work products, people who test, types of defects and failures to be identified. (K2)

The V-model for testing was introduced in Section 2.1. In this section, we'll look in more detail at the various test levels. The key characteristics for each test level are discussed and defined to be able to more clearly separate the various test levels. A thorough understanding and definition of the various test levels will identify missing areas and prevent overlap and repetition. Sometimes we may wish to introduce deliberate overlap to address specific risks. Understanding whether we want overlaps and removing the gaps will make the test levels more complementary thus leading to more effective and efficient testing.

While the specific test levels required for – and planned for – a particular project can vary, testing best practices suggest that each test level have the following clearly identified:

- The process, product and project objectives, ideally with measurable effectiveness and **efficiency** metrics and targets.
- The test basis, which are the work products used to derive the test cases.
- The item, build, or system under test (also called the test object).
- The typical defects and failures that we are looking for.
- Any applicable requirements for test harnesses and tool support.
- The approaches we intend to use.
- The individuals who are responsible for the activities required to carry out the fundamental test process for the test level.

When these topics are clearly understood and defined for the entire project team, this contributes to the success of the project. In addition, during test planning, the managers responsible for the test levels should consider how they intend to test a system's configuration, if such data is part of a system.

As we go through this section, watch for the Syllabus terms **acceptance testing, alpha testing, beta testing, component testing, driver, efficiency testing, field testing, functional requirement, integration testing, maintenance, non-functional requirement, robustness testing, stub, system testing, test environment, test-driven development,** and **user acceptance testing.** You'll find these terms defined in the glossary.

2.2.1 Component testing

Component testing, also known as unit, module and program testing, searches for defects in, and verifies the functioning of software items (e.g. modules, programs, objects, classes, etc.) that are separately testable. Component tests are typically based on the requirements and detailed design specifications applicable to the component under test, as well as the code itself (which we'll discuss in Chapter 4 when we talk about white box testing). The component under test, the test object, includes the individual components (or even entire programs when the definition of components is sufficiently broad), the data conversion and migration programs used to enable the new release, and database tables, joins, views, modules, procedures, integrity and field constraints, and even whole databases.

Component testing may be done in isolation from the rest of the system depending on the context of the development life cycle and the system. Most often **stubs** and **drivers** are used to replace the missing software and simulate the interface between the software components in a simple manner. A stub is called from the software component to be tested; a driver calls a component to be tested (see Figure 2.5).

Component testing may include testing of functionality and specific non-functional characteristics such as resource-behaviour (e.g. memory leaks), performance or **robustness testing**, as well as structural testing (e.g. decision coverage). Test cases are derived from work products such as the software design or the data model.

Typically, component testing occurs with access to the code being tested and with the support of the development environment, such as a unit test frame-work or debugging tool, and in practice usually involves the programmer who wrote the

Efficiency testing The process of testing to determine the efficiency of a software product.

Component testing (unit testing, module testing) The testing of individual software components. Note: the ISTQB Glossary also lists **program testing** as a synonym, which is somewhat confusing, but consistent with the definition given.

Stub A skeletal or special-purpose implementation of a software component, used to develop or test a component that calls or is otherwise dependent on it. It replaces a called component.

Driver (test driver) A software component or test tool that replaces a component that takes care of the control and/or the calling of a component or system.

Robustness testing Testing to determine the robustness of the software product.

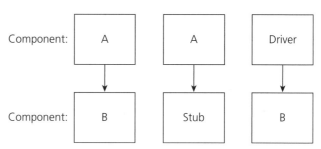

FIGURE 2.5 Stubs and drivers

code. Sometimes, depending on the applicable level of risk, component testing is carried out by a different programmer thereby introducing independence. Defects are typically fixed as soon as they are found, without formally recording the incidents found.

One approach in component testing, used in Extreme Programming (XP), is to prepare and automate test cases before coding. This is called a test-first approach or **test-driven development**. This approach is highly iterative and is based on cycles of developing test cases, then building and integrating small pieces of code, and executing the component tests until they pass.

2.2.2 Integration testing

Integration testing tests interfaces between components, interactions to different parts of a system such as an operating system, file system and hardware or interfaces between systems. Integration tests are typically based on the software and system design (both high-level and low-level), the system architecture (especially the relationships between components or objects), and the workflows or use cases by which the stakeholders will employ the system. The item under test, the test object, includes the following: builds including some or all of the components or objects in the system, the database elements applicable to the item under test, the system infrastructure, the interfaces between components or objects, the system configuration, and configuration data.

Note that integration testing should be differentiated from other integration activities. Integration testing is often carried out by the integrator, but preferably by a specific integration tester or test team.

There may be more than one level of integration testing and it may be carried out on test objects of varying size. For example:

- component integration testing tests the interactions between software components and is done after component testing;
- system integration testing tests the interactions between different systems and may be done after system testing. In this case, the developing organization may control only one side of the interface, so changes may be destabilizing. Business processes implemented as workflows may involve a series of systems that can even run on different platforms.

The greater the scope of integration, the more difficult it becomes to isolate failures to a specific interface, which may lead to an increased risk. This leads to varying approaches to integration testing. One extreme is that all components or systems are

Test-driven development A way of developing software where the test cases are developed, and often automated, before the software is developed to run those test cases.

Integration testing Testing performed to expose defects in the interfaces and in the interactions between integrated components or systems.

integrated simultaneously, after which everything is tested as a whole. This is called 'big-bang' integration testing. Big-bang testing has the advantage that everything is finished before integration testing starts. There is no need to simulate (as yet unfinished) parts. The major disadvantage is that in general it is time-consuming and difficult to trace the cause of failures with this late integration. So big-bang integration may seem like a good idea when planning the project, being optimistic and expecting to find no problems. If one thinks integration testing will find defects, it is a good practice to consider whether time might be saved by breaking the down the integration test process.

Another extreme is that all programs are integrated one by one, and a test is carried out after each step (incremental testing). Between these two extremes, there is a range of variants. The incremental approach has the advantage that the defects are found early in a smaller assembly when it is relatively easy to detect the cause. A disadvantage is that it can be time-consuming since stubs and drivers have to be developed and used in the test. Within incremental integration testing a range of possibilities exist, partly depending on the system architecture:

- Top-down: testing takes place from top to bottom, following the control flow or architectural structure (e.g. starting from the GUI or main menu). Components or systems are substituted by stubs.

- Bottom-up: testing takes place from the bottom of the control flow upwards. Components or systems are substituted by drivers.

- Functional incremental: integration and testing takes place on the basis of the functions or functionality, as documented in the functional specification.

The preferred integration sequence and the number of integration steps required depend on the location in the architecture of the high-risk interfaces. The best choice is to start integration with those interfaces that are expected to cause most problems. Doing so prevents major defects at the end of the integration test stage. In order to reduce the risk of late defect discovery, integration should normally be incremental rather than 'big-bang'. Ideally testers should understand the architecture and influence integration planning. If integration tests are planned before components or systems are built, they can be developed in the order required for most efficient testing.

At each stage of integration, testers concentrate solely on the integration itself. For example, if they are integrating component A with component B they are interested in testing the communication between the components, not the functionality of either one. Both functional and structural approaches may be used. Testing of specific non-functional characteristics (e.g. performance) may also be included in integration testing. Integration testing may be carried out by the developers, but can be done by a separate team of specialist integration testers, or by a specialist group of developers/integrators including non-functional specialists.

2.2.3 System testing

System testing is concerned with the behaviour of the whole system/product as defined by the scope of a development project or product. It may include tests based on risk analysis reports, system, functional, or software requirements specification, business processes, use cases, or other high level descriptions of system behaviour, interactions with the operating system, and system resources.

System testing The process of testing an integrated system to verify that it meets specified requirements. Note: The ISTQB Glossary derives from Hetzel's book *The Complete Guide to Software Testing*, and the implied objective of verification might not be adequate (or even appropriate) for all projects when doing system testing.

The system under test, the test object, includes the following: the entire integrated system, system, user and operation manuals, system configuration information, and configuration data.

System testing is most often the final test on behalf of development to verify that the system to be delivered meets the specification and its purpose may be to find as many defects as possible. Most often it is carried out by specialist testers that form a dedicated, and sometimes independent, test team within development, reporting to the development manager or project manager. In some organizations system testing is carried out by a third party team or by business analysts. Again the required level of independence is based on the applicable risk level and this will have a high influence on the way system testing is organized.

System testing should investigate both **functional** and **non-functional requirements** of the system. Typical non-functional tests include performance and reliability. Testers may also need to deal with incomplete or undocumented requirements. System testing of functional requirements starts by using the most appropriate specification-based (black-box) techniques for the aspect of the system to be tested. For example, a decision table may be created for combinations of effects described in business rules. Structure-based (white-box) techniques may also be used to assess the thoroughness of testing elements such as menu dialog structure or web page navigation (see Chapter 4 for more on the various types of technique).

System testing requires a controlled **test environment** with regard to, among other things, control of the software versions, testware and the test data (see Chapter 5 for more on configuration management). A system test is executed by the development organization in a (properly controlled) environment. The test environment should correspond to the final target or production environment as much as possible in order to minimize the risk of environment-specific failures not being found by testing.

2.2.4 Acceptance testing

When the development organization has performed its system test and has corrected all or most defects, the system will be delivered to the user or customer for **acceptance testing** (or **user acceptance testing**). Acceptance tests are typically based on user requirements, system requirements, use cases, business processes, and risk analysis reports. The system under test, the test object, includes the following: the business, operational, and **maintenance** processes (evaluated on a fully integrated system), user procedures, applicable forms, reports, and configuration data.

The acceptance test should answer questions such as: 'Can the system be released?', 'What, if any, are the outstanding (business) risks?' and 'Has development met their obligations?'. Acceptance testing is most often the responsibility of the user or customer, although other stakeholders may be involved as well. The execution of the acceptance test requires a test environment that is for most aspects, representative of the production environment ('as-if production').

The goal of acceptance testing is to establish confidence in the system, part of the system or specific non-functional characteristics, e.g. usability, of the system. Acceptance testing is most often focused on a validation type of testing, whereby we are trying to determine whether the system is fit for purpose. Finding defects should not be the main focus in acceptance testing. Although it assesses the system's readiness for deployment and use, it is not necessarily the final level of

Functional requirement A requirement that specifies a function that a component or system must perform.

Non-functional requirement A requirement that does not relate to functionality, but to attributes such as reliability, efficiency, usability, maintainability and portability.

Test environment (test bed) An environment containing hardware, instrumentation, simulators, software tools, and other support elements needed to conduct a test.

Acceptance testing (acceptance, user acceptance testing) Formal testing with respect to user needs, requirements, and business processes conducted to determine whether or not a system satisfies the acceptance criteria and to enable the user, customers or other authorized entity to determine whether or not to accept the system.

Maintenance Modification of a software product after delivery to correct defects, to improve performance or other attributes, or to adapt the product to a modified environment.

testing. For example, a large-scale system integration test may come after the acceptance of a system.

Acceptance testing may occur at more than just a single level, for example:

- A Commercial Off The Shelf (COTS) software product may be acceptance tested when it is installed or integrated.
- Acceptance testing of the usability of a component may be done during component testing.
- Acceptance testing of a new functional enhancement may come before system testing.

Within the acceptance test for a business-supporting system, two main test types can be distinguished; as a result of their special character, they are usually prepared and executed separately. The user acceptance test focuses mainly on the functionality thereby validating the fitness-for-use of the system by the business user, while the operational acceptance test (also called production acceptance test) validates whether the system meets the requirements for operation. The user acceptance test is performed by the users and application managers. In terms of planning, the user acceptance test usually links tightly to the system test and will, in many cases, be organized partly overlapping in time. If the system to be tested consists of a number of more or less independent subsystems, the acceptance test for a subsystem that complies to the exit criteria of the system test can start while another subsystem may still be in the system test phase. In most organizations, system administration will perform the operational acceptance test shortly before the system is released. The operational acceptance test may include testing of backup/restore, data load and migration tasks, disaster recovery, user management, maintenance tasks and periodic check of security vulnerabilities.

Other types of acceptance testing that exist are contract acceptance testing and regulatory acceptance testing. Contract acceptance testing is performed against a contract's acceptance criteria for producing custom-developed software. Acceptance should be formally defined when the contract is agreed. Regulatory acceptance testing or regulation acceptance testing is performed against the regulations which must be adhered to, such as governmental, legal or safety regulations.

If the system has been developed for the mass market, e.g. commercial off-the-shelf software (COTS), then testing it for individual users or customers is not practical or even possible in some cases. Feedback is needed from potential or existing users in their market before the software product is put out for sale commercially. Very often this type of system undergoes two stages of acceptance test. The first is called **alpha testing**. This test takes place at the developer's site. A cross-section of potential users and members of the developer's organization are invited to use the system. Developers observe the users and note problems. Alpha testing may also be carried out by an independent test team. **Beta testing**, or **field testing**, sends the system to a cross-section of users who install it and use it under real-world working conditions. The users send records of incidents with the system to the development organization where the defects are repaired.

Note that organizations may use other terms, such as factory acceptance testing and site acceptance testing for systems that are tested before and after being moved to a customer's site.

Alpha testing
Simulated or actual operational testing by potential users/customers or an independent test team at the developers' site, but outside the development organization. Alpha testing is often employed for off-the-shelf software as a form of internal acceptance testing.

Beta testing (field testing) Operational testing by potential and/or existing users/customers at an external site not otherwise involved with the developers, to determine whether or not a component or system satisfies the user/customer needs and fits within the business processes. Beta testing is often employed as a form of external acceptance testing for off-the-shelf software in order to acquire feedback from the market.

2.3 TEST TYPES

**SYLLABUS LEARNING OBJECTIVES FOR
2.3 TEST TYPES: (K2)**

LO-2.3.1   Compare four software test types (functional, non-functional, structural and change related) by example. (K2)

LO-2.3.2   Recognize that functional and structural tests occur at any test level. (K1)

LO-2.3.3   Identify and describe non-functional test types based on non-functional requirements. (K2)

LO-2.3.4   Identify and describe test types based on the analysis of a software system's structure or architecture. (K2)

LO-2.3.5   Describe the purpose of confirmation testing and regression testing. (K2)

In this section, we'll look at different test types. We'll discuss tests that focus on the functionality of a system, which informally is *testing what the system does*. We'll also discuss tests that focus on non-functionality attributes of a system, which informally are *testing how the system does what it does*. We'll introduce testing based on the system's structure. Finally, we'll look at testing of changes to the system, both confirmation testing (testing that the changes succeeded) and regression testing (testing that the changes didn't affect anything unintentionally).

The test types discussed here can involve the development and use of a model of the software or its behaviours. Such models can occur in structural testing when we use control flow models or menu structure models. Such models in non-functional testing can involve performance models, usability models, and security threat models. Such models can also arise in functional testing, such as the use of process flow models, state transition models, or plain language specifications. Examples of such models will be found in Chapter 4.

As we go through this section, watch for the Syllabus terms **black box text design technique, black box testing, code coverage, efficiency, functional testing, functionality, functionality testing, interoperability testing, load testing, maintainability, maintainability testing, performance testing, portability, portability testing, reliability, reliability testing, robustness, security, security testing, specification based testing, stress testing, structural based testing, structural testing, test type, usability, usability testing, white-box test design techniques** and **white-box testing**. You'll find these terms defined in the glossary.

Test types are introduced as a means of clearly defining the objective of a certain test level for a program or project. We need to think about different types of testing because testing the functionality of the component or system may not be sufficient at each level to meet the overall test objectives. Focusing the testing on a specific test objective and, therefore, selecting the appropriate type of test helps make it easier to make and communicate decisions about test objectives.

A **test type** is focused on a particular test objective, which could be the testing of a function to be performed by the component or system; a non-functional quality characteristic, such as reliability or usability; the structure or architecture of the component or system; or related to changes, i.e. confirming that defects have been fixed (confirmation testing, or re-testing) and looking for unintended changes (regression testing). Depending on its objectives, testing will be organized differently. For example, component testing aimed at performance would be quite different to component testing aimed at achieving decision coverage.

> **Test type** A group of test activities aimed at testing a component or system focused on a specific test objective, i.e. functional test, usability test, regression test etc. A test type may take place on one or more test levels or test phases.

2.3.1 Testing of function (functional testing)

The function of a system (or component) is 'what it does'. This is typically described in a requirements specification, a functional specification, in use cases, or, in agile teams, in user stories. There may be some functions that are 'assumed' to be provided that are not documented that are also part of the requirement for a system, though it is difficult to test against undocumented and implicit requirements. Functional tests are based on these functions, described in documents or understood by the testers and may be performed at all test levels (e.g. test for components may be based on a component specification).

Functional testing considers the specified behaviour and is often also referred to as **black-box testing (specification based testing)**. This is not entirely true, since black-box testing also includes non-functional testing (see Section 2.3.2).

Function (or **functionality**) **testing** can, based upon ISO 9126, be done focusing on suitability, **interoperability testing, security**, accuracy and compliance. **Security testing**, for example, investigates the functions (e.g. a firewall) relating to detection of threats, such as viruses, from malicious outsiders.

Testing functionality can be done from two perspectives: requirements-based or business-process-based.

Requirements-based testing uses a specification of the functional requirements for the system as the basis for designing tests. A good way to start is to use the table of contents of the requirements specification as an initial test inventory or list of items to test (or not to test). We should also prioritize the requirements based on risk criteria (if this is not already done in the specification) and use this to prioritize the tests. This will ensure that the most important and most critical tests are included in the testing effort.

Business-process-based testing uses knowledge of the business processes. Business processes describe the scenarios involved in the day-to-day business use of the system. For example, a personnel and payroll system may have a business process along the lines of: someone joins the company, he or she is paid on a regular basis, and he or she finally leaves the company. Use cases originate from object-oriented development, but are nowadays popular in many development life cycles. They also take the business processes as a starting point, although they start from tasks to be performed by users. Use cases are a very useful basis for test cases from a business perspective.

The techniques used for functional testing are often **specification-based**, but experienced-based techniques can also be used (see Chapter 4 for more on test techniques). Test conditions and test cases are derived from the functionality of the component or system. As part of test designing, a model may be developed, such as a process model, state transition model or a plain-language specification.

> **Functional testing** Testing based on an analysis of the specification of the functionality of a component or system.
>
> **Black-box testing (specification based testing)** Testing, either functional or non-functional, without reference to the internal structure of the component or system.
>
> **Functionality testing** The process of testing to determine the functionality of a software product.
>
> **Interoperability testing** The process of testing to determine the interoperability of a software product.
>
> **Security** Attributes of software products that bear on its ability to prevent unauthorized access, whether accidental or deliberate, to programs and data.
>
> **Security testing** Testing to determine the security of the software product.

2.3.2 Testing of software product characteristics (non-functional testing)

Performance testing The process of testing to determine the performance of a software product.

Load testing A type of performance testing conducted to evaluate the behaviour of a component or system with increasing load, e.g. numbers of parallel users and/or numbers of transactions, to determine what load can be handled by the component or system.

Stress testing A type of performance testing conducted to evaluate a system or component at or beyond the limits of its anticipated or specified work loads, or with reduced availability of resources such as access to memory or servers.

Usability testing Testing to determine the extent to which the software product is understood, easy to learn, easy to operate and attractive to the users under specified conditions.

Maintainability testing The process of testing to determine the maintainability of a software product.

Reliability testing The process of testing to determine the reliability of a software product.

Portability testing The process of testing to determine the portability of a software product.

A second target for testing is the testing of the quality characteristics, or non-functional attributes of the system (or component or integration group). Here we are interested in how well or how fast something is done. We are testing something that we need to measure on a scale of measurement, for example time to respond.

Non-functional testing, as functional testing, is performed at all test levels. Non-functional testing includes, but is not limited to, **performance testing, load testing, stress testing**, **usability testing**, **maintainability testing**, **reliability testing** and **portability testing**. It is the testing of 'how well' the system works.

Many have tried to capture software quality in a collection of characteristics and related sub-characteristics. In these models some elementary characteristics keep on reappearing, although their place in the hierarchy can differ. The International Organization for Standardization (ISO) has defined a set of quality characteristics [ISO/IEC 9126 2001]. This set reflects a major step towards consensus in the IT industry and thereby addresses the general notion of software quality. The ISO 9126 standard defines six quality characteristics and the subdivision of each quality characteristic into a number of sub-characteristics. This standard is getting more and more recognition in the industry, enabling development, testing and their stakeholders to use a common terminology for quality characteristics and thereby for non-functional testing.

The characteristics and their sub-characteristics are, respectively:

- **functionality**, which consists of five sub-characteristics: suitability, accuracy, security, interoperability and compliance; this characteristic deals with functional testing as described in Section 2.3.1;

- **reliability**, which is defined further into the sub-characteristics maturity (**robustness**), fault-tolerance, recoverability and compliance;

- **usability**, which is divided into the sub-characteristics understandability, learnability, operability, attractiveness and compliance;

- **efficiency**, which is divided into time behaviour (performance), resource utilization and compliance;

- **maintainability**, which consists of five sub-characteristics: analyzability, changeability, stability, testability and compliance;

- **portability**, which also consists of five sub-characteristics: adaptability, installability, co-existence, replaceability and compliance.

A common misconception is that non-functional testing occurs only during higher levels of testing such as system test, system integration test, and acceptance test. In fact, non-functional testing may be performed at all test levels; the higher the level of risk associated with each type of non-functional testing, the earlier in the lifecycle it should occur. Ideally, non-functional testing involves tests that quantifiably measure characteristics of the systems and software. For example, in performance testing we can measure transaction throughput, resource utilization, and response times. Generally, non-functional testing defines expected results in terms of the external behaviour of the software. This means that we typically use **black-box test design techniques**.

2.3.3 Testing of software structure/architecture (structural testing)

The third target of testing is the structure of the system or component. If we are talking about the structure of a system, we may call it the system architecture. Structural testing is often referred to as '**white-box**' or 'glass-box' because we are interested in what is happening 'inside the box'.

Structural testing is most often used as a way of measuring the thoroughness of testing through the coverage of a set of structural elements or coverage items. It can occur at any test level, although it is true to say that it tends to be mostly applied at component and integration and generally is less likely at higher test levels, except for business-process testing. At component integration level it may be based on the architecture of the system, such as a calling hierarchy. The test basis for system, system integration or acceptance testing could be a business model or menu structure.

At component level, and to a lesser extent at component integration testing, there is good tool support to measure **code coverage**. Coverage measurement tools assess the percentage of executable elements (e.g. statements or decision outcomes) that have been exercised (i.e. covered) by a test suite. If coverage is not 100%, then additional tests may need to be written and run to cover those parts that have not yet been exercised. This of course depends on the exit criteria. (Coverage techniques are covered in Chapter 4.)

The techniques used for structural testing are structure-based techniques, also referred to as **white-box test design techniques**. Control flow models are often used to support structural testing.

2.3.4 Testing related to changes (confirmation and regression testing)

The final target of testing is the testing of changes. This category is slightly different to the others because if you have made a change to the software, you will have changed the way it functions, the way it performs (or both) and its structure. However we are looking here at the specific types of tests relating to changes, even though they may include all of the other test types.

Confirmation testing (re-testing)

When a test fails and we determine that the cause of the failure is a software defect, the defect is reported, and we can expect a new version of the software that has had the defect fixed. In this case we will need to execute the test again to confirm that the defect has indeed been fixed. This is known as confirmation testing (also known as re-testing).

When doing confirmation testing, it is important to ensure that the test is executed in exactly the same way as it was the first time, using the same inputs, data and environment. If the test now passes does this mean that the software is now correct? Well, we now know that at least one part of the software is correct – where the defect was. But this is not enough. The fix may have introduced or uncovered a different defect elsewhere in the software. The way to detect these 'unexpected side-effects' of fixes is to do regression testing.

Regression testing

Like confirmation testing, regression testing involves executing test cases that have been executed before. The difference is that, for regression testing, the test cases probably passed the last time they were executed (compare this with the test cases executed in confirmation testing – they failed the last time).

Functionality The capability of the software product to provide functions which meet stated and implied needs when the software is used under specified conditions.

Reliability The ability of the software product to perform its required functions under stated conditions for a specified period of time, or for a specified number of operations.

Robustness The degree to which a component or system can function correctly in the presence of invalid inputs or stressful environmental conditions.

Usability The capability of the software to be understood, learned, used and attractive to the user when used under specified conditions.

Efficiency The capability of the software product to provide appropriate performance, relative to the amount of resources used under stated conditions.

Maintainability The ease with which a software product can be modified to correct defects, modified to meet new requirements, modified to make future maintenance easier, or adapted to a changed environment.

Portability The ease with which the software product can be transferred from one hardware or software environment to another.

Black-box (specification-based) test design technique Procedure to derive and/or select test cases based on an analysis of the specification, either functional or non-functional, of a component or system without reference to its internal structure.

White-box testing (structural testing, structure-based testing) Testing based on an analysis of the internal structure of the component or system.

Code coverage An analysis method that determines which parts of the software have been executed (covered) by the test suite and which parts have not been executed, e.g. statement coverage, decision coverage or condition coverage.

White-box (structural, structure-based) test design technique Procedure to derive and/or select test cases based on an analysis of the internal structure of a component or system.

The term 'regression testing' is something of a misnomer. It would be better if it were called 'anti-regression' testing because we are executing tests with the intent of checking that the system has not regressed (that is, it does not now have more defects in it as a result of some change). More specifically, the purpose of regression testing is to verify that modifications in the software or the environment have not caused unintended adverse side effects and that the system still meets its requirements.

It is common for organizations to have what is usually called a regression test suite or regression test pack. This is a set of test cases that is specifically used for regression testing. They are designed to collectively exercise most functions (certainly the most important ones) in a system but not test any one in detail. It is appropriate to have a regression test suite at every level of testing (component testing, integration testing, system testing, etc.). All of the test cases in a regression test suite would be executed every time a new version of software is produced and this makes them ideal candidates for automation. If the regression test suite is very large it may be more appropriate to select a subset for execution.

Regression tests are executed whenever the software changes, either as a result of fixes or new or changed functionality. It is also a good idea to execute them when some aspect of the environment changes, for example when a new version of a database management system is introduced or a new version of a source code compiler is used.

Maintenance of a regression test suite should be carried out so it evolves over time in line with the software. As new functionality is added to a system new regression tests should be added and as old functionality is changed or removed so too should regression tests be changed or removed. As new tests are added a regression test suite may become very large. If all the tests have to be executed manually it may not be possible to execute them all every time the regression suite is used. In this case a subset of the test cases has to be chosen. This selection should be made in light of the latest changes that have been made to the software. Sometimes a regression test suite of automated tests can become so large that it is not always possible to execute them all. It may be possible and desirable to eliminate some test cases from a large regression test suite for example if they are repetitive (tests which exercise the same conditions) or can be combined (if they are always run together). Another approach is to eliminate test cases that have not found a defect for a long time (though this approach should be used with some care!).

2.4 MAINTENANCE TESTING

Once deployed, a system is often in service for years or even decades. During this time the system and its operational environment is often corrected, changed or extended. Testing that is executed during this life cycle phase is called '**maintenance testing**'. Maintenance testing, along with the entire process of maintenance releases, must be carefully planned in advance. Not only must planned maintenance releases be considered, but the process for developing and testing hot fixes must be as well. Maintenance testing includes any type of testing of changes to an existing, operational system, whether the changes result from modifications, migration, or retirement of the software or system.

Modifications can result from planned enhancement changes such as those referred to as 'minor releases' that include new features and accumulated (non-emergency) bug fixes. Modifications can also result from corrective and more-urgent emergency changes. Modifications can also involve changes of environment, such as planned operating system or database upgrades, planned upgrade of Commercial-Off-The-Shelf software, or patches to correct newly exposed or discovered vulnerabilities of the operating system.

Migration involves moving from one platform to another. This can involve abandoning a platform no longer supported, or adding a new supported platform. Either way, testing must include operational tests of the new environment as well as of the changed software. Migration testing can also include conversion testing, where data from another application will be migrated into the system being maintained.

Note that maintenance testing is different from maintainability testing, which defines how easy it is to maintain the system). In this section, we'll discuss maintenance testing.

As we go through this section, watch for the Syllabus terms **impact analysis** and **maintenance testing**. You'll find these terms defined in the glossary.

The development and test process applicable to new developments does not change fundamentally for maintenance purposes. The same test process steps will apply and, depending on the size and risk of the changes made, several levels of testing are carried out: a component test, an integration test, a system test and an acceptance test. A maintenance test process usually begins with the receipt of an application for a change or a release plan. The test manager will use this as a basis for producing a test plan. On receipt of the new or changed specifications, corresponding test cases are specified or adapted. On receipt of the test object, the new and modified tests and the regression tests are executed. On completion of the testing, the testware is once again preserved.

Comparing maintenance testing to testing a new application is merely a matter of an approach from a different angle, which gives rise to a number of changes in emphasis. There are several areas where most differences occur, for example regarding the test basis. A 'catching-up' operation is frequently required when systems are maintained. Specifications are often 'missing', and a set of testware relating to the specifications simply does not exist. It may well be possible to carry out this catching-up operation along with testing a new maintenance release, which may reduce the cost. If it is impossible to compile any specifications from which test cases can be written, including expected results, an alternative test basis, e.g. a test oracle, should be sought by way of compromise. A search should be made for documentation which is closest to the specifications and which can be managed by developers as well as testers. In such cases it is advisable to draw the customer's attention to the lower test quality which may be achieved. Be aware of possible problems of 'daily production'. In the worst case nobody knows what is being tested, many test cases are executing

> **Maintenance testing** Testing the changes to an operational system or the impact of a changed environment to an operational system.

the same scenario and if an incident is found, it is often hard to trace it back to the actual defect since no traceability to test designs and/or requirements exists. Note that reproducibility of tests is also important for maintenance testing.

One aspect which, in many cases, differs somewhat from the development situation is the test organization. New development and their appropriate test activities are usually carried out as parts of a project, whereas maintenance tests are normally executed as an activity in the regular organization. As a result, there is often some lack of resources and flexibility, and the test process may experience more competition from other activities.

2.4.1 Impact analysis and regression testing

Usually maintenance testing will consist of two parts:

- testing the changes
- regression tests to show that the rest of the system has not been affected by the maintenance work.

> **Impact analysis** The assessment of change to the layers of development documentation, test documentation and components, in order to implement a given change to specified requirements.

In addition to testing what has been changed, maintenance testing includes extensive regression testing to parts of the system that have not been changed. A major and important activity within maintenance testing is **impact analysis**. During impact analysis, together with stakeholders, a decision is made on what parts of the system may be unintentionally affected and therefore need careful regression testing. Risk analysis will help to decide where to focus regression testing – it is unlikely that the team will have time to repeat all the existing tests.

If the test specifications from the original development of the system are kept, one may be able to reuse them for regression testing and to adapt them for changes to the system. This may be as simple as changing the expected results for your existing tests. Sometimes additional tests may need to be built. Extension or enhancement to the system may mean new areas have been specified and tests would be drawn up just as for the development. Don't forget that automated regression tests will also need to be updated in line with the changes; this can take significant effort, depending on the architecture of your automation.

2.4.2 Triggers for maintenance testing

As stated maintenance testing is done on an existing operational system. It is triggered by modifications, migration, or retirement of the system. Modifications include planned enhancement changes (e.g. release-based), corrective and emergency changes, and changes of environment, such as planned operating system or database upgrades, or patches to newly exposed or discovered vulnerabilities of the operating system. Maintenance testing for migration (e.g. from one platform to another) should include operational testing of the new environment, as well as the changed software. Maintenance testing for the retirement of a system may include the testing of data migration or archiving, if long data-retention periods are required.

Since modifications are most often the main part of maintenance testing for most organizations, this will be discussed in more detail. From the point of view of testing, there are two types of modifications. There are modifications in which testing may be planned, and there are ad-hoc corrective modifications, which cannot be planned at all. Ad-hoc corrective maintenance takes place when the search for solutions to defects cannot be delayed. Special test procedures are required at that time.

Planned modifications

The following types of planned modification may be identified:

- perfective modifications (adapting software to the user's wishes, for instance by supplying new functions or enhancing performance);
- adaptive modifications (adapting software to environmental changes such as new hardware, new systems software or new legislation);
- corrective planned modifications (deferrable correction of defects).

The standard structured test approach is almost fully applicable to planned modifications. On average, planned modification represents over 90% of all maintenance work on systems [Pol and van Veenendaal 1998].

Ad-hoc corrective modifications

Ad-hoc corrective modifications are concerned with defects requiring an immediate solution, e.g. a production run which fails late at night, a network that goes down with a few hundred users on line, a mailing with incorrect addresses. There are different rules and different procedures for solving problems of this kind. It will be impossible to take the steps required for a structured approach to testing. If, however, a number of activities are carried out prior to a possible malfunction, it may be possible to achieve a situation in which reliable tests can be executed in spite of 'panic stations' all round. To some extent this type of maintenance testing is often like first aid – patching up – and at a later stage the standard test process is then followed to establish a robust fix, test it and establish the appropriate level of documentation.

A risk analysis of the operational systems should be performed in order to establish which functions or programs constitute the greatest risk to the operational services in the event of disaster. It is then established – in respect of the functions at risk – which (test) actions should be performed if a particular malfunction occurs. Several types of malfunction may be identified and there are various ways of responding to them for each function at risk. A possible reaction might be that a relevant function at risk should always be tested, or that, under certain circumstances, testing might be carried out in retrospect (the next day, for instance). If it is decided that a particular function at risk should always be tested whenever relevant, a number of standard tests, which could be executed almost immediately, should be prepared for this purpose. The standard tests would obviously be prepared and maintained in accordance with the structured test approach.

Even in the event of ad-hoc modifications, it is therefore possible to bring about an improvement in quality by adopting a specific test approach. It is important to make a thorough risk analysis of the system and to specify a set of standard tests accordingly.

CHAPTER REVIEW

Let's review what you have learned in this chapter.

From Section 2.1, you should now understand the relationship between development and testing within a development life cycle, including the test activities and test (work) products. You should know that the development model to use should fit, or must be adapted to fit, the project and product characteristics. You should be able to recall the reasons for different levels of testing and characteristics of good testing in any life cycle model. You should know the glossary terms **agile manifesto, agile software development, Commercial Off-The-Shelf (COTS), incremental development model, integration, iterative development model, performance, requirement, test level, validation, verification,** and **V-model**.

From Section 2.2, you should know the typical levels of testing. You should be able to compare the different levels of testing with respect to their major objectives, typical objects of testing, typical targets of testing (e.g. functional or structural) and related work products. You should also know which persons perform the testing activities at the various test levels, the types of defects found and failures to be identified. You should know the glossary terms **acceptance testing, alpha testing, beta testing, component testing, driver, efficiency testing, field testing, functional requirement, integration testing, manitenance, non-functional requirement, robustness testing, stub, system testing, test driven development, test environment** and **user acceptance testing**.

From Section 2.3, you should know the four major types of test (functional, non-functional, structural and change-related) and should be able to provide some concrete examples for each of these. You should understand that functional and structural tests occur at any test level and be able to explain how they are applied in the various test levels. You should be able to identify and describe non-functional test types based on non-functional requirements and product quality characteristics. Finally you should be able to explain the purpose of confirmation testing (re-testing) and regression testing in the context of change-related testing. You should know the glossary terms **black box text design technique, black box testing, code coverage, efficiency, functional testing, functionality, functionality testing, interoperability testing, load testing, maintainability, maintainability testing, performance testing, portability, portability testing, reliability, reliability testing, robustness, security, security testing, specification based testing, stress testing, structural based testing, structural testing, test type, usability, usability testing, white-box test design techniques** and **white-box testing**.

From Section 2.4, you should be able to compare maintenance testing to testing of new applications. You should be able to identify triggers and reasons for maintenance testing, such as modifications, migration and retirement. Finally you should be able to describe the role of regression testing and impact analysis within maintenance testing. You should know the glossary terms **impact analysis** and **maintenance testing**.

SAMPLE EXAM QUESTIONS

Question 1 What are good practices for testing within the development life cycle?

a. Early test analysis and design.

b. Different test levels are defined with specific objectives.

c. Testers will start to get involved as soon as coding is done.

d. A and B above.

Question 2 Which option best describes objectives for test levels with a life cycle model?

a. Objectives should be generic for any test level.

b. Objectives are the same for each test level.

c. The objectives of a test level don't need to be defined in advance.

d. Each level has objectives specific to that level.

Question 3 Which of the following is a test type?

a. Component testing

b. Functional testing

c. System testing

d. Acceptance testing

Question 4 Which of the following is a non-functional quality characteristic?

a. Feasibility

b. Usability

c. Maintenance

d. Regression

Question 5 Which of these is a functional test?

a. Measuring response time on an on-line booking system.

b. Checking the effect of high volumes of traffic in a call-center system.

c. Checking the on-line bookings screen information and the database contents against the information on the letter to the customers.

d. Checking how easy the system is to use.

Question 6 Which of the following is a true statement regarding the process of fixing emergency changes?

a. There is no time to test the change before it goes live, so only the best developers should do this work and should not involve testers as they slow down the process.

b. Just run the retest of the defect actually fixed.

c. Always run a full regression test of the whole system in case other parts of the system have been adversely affected.

d. Retest the changed area and then use risk assessment to decide on a reasonable subset of the whole regression test to run in case other parts of the system have been adversely affected.

Question 7 A regression test:

a. Is only run once.

b. Will always be automated.

c. Will check unchanged areas of the software to see if they have been affected.

d. Will check changed areas of the software to see if they have been affected.

Question 8 Non-functional testing includes:

a. Testing to see where the system does not function correctly.

b. Testing the quality attributes of the system including reliability and usability.

c. Gaining user approval for the system.

d. Testing a system feature using only the software required for that function.

Question 9 Beta testing is:

a. Performed by customers at their own site.

b. Performed by customers at the software developer's site.

c. Performed by an independent test team.

d. Useful to test software developed for a specific customer or user.

CHAPTER THREE
Static techniques

Static test techniques provide a powerful way to improve the quality and productivity of software development. This chapter describes static test techniques, including reviews, and provides an overview of how they are conducted. The fundamental objective of static testing is to improve the quality of software work products by assisting engineers to recognize and fix their own defects early in the software development process. While static testing techniques will not solve all the problems, they are enormously effective. Static techniques can improve both quality and productivity by impressive factors. Static testing is not magic and it should not be considered a replacement for dynamic testing, but all software organizations should consider using reviews in all major aspects of their work including requirements, design, implementation, testing, and maintenance. Static analysis tools implement automated checks, e.g. on code.

3.1 STATIC TECHNIQUES AND THE TEST PROCESS

SYLLABUS LEARNING OBJECTIVES FOR 3.1 STATIC TECHNIQUES AND THE TEST PROCESS (K2)

LO-3.1.1   Recognize software work products that can be examined by the different static techniques. (K1)

LO-3.1.2   Describe the importance and value of considering static techniques for the assessment of software work products. (K2)

LO-3.1.3   Explain the difference between static and dynamic techniques, considering objectives, types of defects to be identified, and the role of these techniques within the software life cycle. (K2)

In this section, we consider how static testing techniques fit into the overall test process. Dynamic testing requires that we run the item or system under test, but static testing techniques allow us to find defects directly in work products, without the execution of the code and without the need to isolate the failure to locate the underlying defect. Static techniques include both reviews and static analysis, each of which we'll discuss in this chapter. Static techniques are efficient ways to find and remove defects, and can find certain defects that are hard to find with dynamic testing. As we go through this section, watch for the Syllabus terms **dynamic testing** and **static testing**. You'll find these terms defined in the glossary.

In Chapter 1, several testing terms were presented. Also testing itself was defined. The latter definition is repeated here as a means for explaining the two major types of testing.

The definition of testing outlines objectives that relate to evaluation, revealing defects and quality. As indicated in the definition two approaches can be used to achieve these objectives, **static testing** and **dynamic testing**.

With dynamic testing methods, software is executed using a set of input values and its output is then examined and compared to what is expected. During static testing, software work products are examined manually, or with a set of tools, but not executed. As a consequence, dynamic testing can only be applied to software code. Dynamic execution is applied as a technique to detect defects and to determine quality attributes of the code. This testing option is not applicable for the majority of the software work products. Among the questions that arise are: How can we evaluate or analyze a requirements document, a design document, a test plan, or a user manual? How can we effectively examine the source code before execution? One powerful technique that can be used is static testing, e.g. reviews. In principle all software work products can be tested using review techniques.

Dynamic testing and static testing are complementary methods, as they tend to find different types of defects effectively and efficiently. Types of defects that are easier to find during static testing are: deviations from standards, missing requirements, design defects, non-maintainable code and inconsistent interface specifications. Compared to dynamic testing, static testing finds defects rather than failures.

In addition to finding defects, the objectives of reviews are often also informational, communicational and educational, whereby participants learn about the content of software work products to help them understand the role of their own work and to plan for future stages of development. Reviews often represent project milestones, and support the establishment of a baseline for a software product. The type and quantity of defects found during reviews can also help testers focus their testing and select effective classes of tests. In some cases customers/users attend the review meeting and provide feedback to the development team, so reviews are also a means of customer/user communication.

Studies have shown that as a result of reviews, a significant increase in productivity and product quality can be achieved [Gilb and Graham 1993], [van Veenendaal 1999]. Reducing the number of defects early in the product life cycle also means that less time has to be spent on testing and maintenance. To summarize, the use of static testing, e.g. reviews, on software work products has various advantages:

- Since static testing can start early in the life cycle, early feedback on quality issues can be established, e.g. an early validation of user requirements and not just late in the life cycle during acceptance testing.

- By detecting defects at an early stage, rework costs are most often relatively low and thus a relatively cheap improvement of the quality of software products can be achieved.

- Since rework effort is substantially reduced, development productivity figures are likely to increase.

- The evaluation by a team has the additional advantage that there is an exchange of information between the participants.

- Static tests contribute to an increased awareness of quality issues.

In conclusion, static testing is a very suitable method for improving the quality of software work products. This applies primarily to the assessed products themselves,

Static testing Testing of a component or system at specification or implementation level without execution of that software, e.g. reviews or static analysis.

Dynamic testing Testing that involves the execution of the software of a component or system.

but it is also important that the quality improvement is not achieved once but has a more permanent nature. The feedback from the static testing process to the development process allows for process improvement, which supports the avoidance of similar errors being made in the future.

3.2 REVIEW PROCESS

SYLLABUS LEARNING OBJECTIVES FOR 3.2 REVIEW PROCESS (K2)

LO-3.2.1   Recall the activities, roles and responsibilities of a typical formal review. (K1)

LO-3.2.2   Explain the differences between different types of reviews: informal review, technical review, walkthrough and inspection. (K2)

LO-3.2.3   Explain the factors for successful performance of reviews. (K2)

In this section, we will focus on reviews as a distinct – and distinctly useful – form of static testing. We'll discuss the process for carrying out reviews. We'll talk about who does what in a review meeting and as part of the review process. We'll cover types of reviews that you can use, and success factors to enable the most effective and efficient reviews possible. As we go through this section, watch for the Syllabus terms **entry criteria, formal review, informal review, inspection, metric, moderator, peer review, reviewer, scribe, technical review,** and **walkthrough**. You'll find these terms defined in the glossary.

Informal review A review not based on a formal (documented) procedure.

Formal review A review characterized by documented procedures and requirements, e.g. inspection.

Reviews vary from very **informal** to **formal** (i.e. well structured and regulated). Although inspection is perhaps the most documented and formal review technique, it is certainly not the only one. The formality of a review process is related to factors such as the maturity of the development process, any legal or regulatory requirements or the need for an audit trail. In practice the informal review is perhaps the most common type of review. Informal reviews are applied at various times during the early stages in the life cycle of a document. A two-person team can conduct an informal review, as the author can ask a colleague to review a document or code. In later stages these reviews often involve more people and a meeting. This normally involves peers of the author, who try to find defects in the document under review and discuss these defects in a review meeting. The goal is to help the author and to improve the quality of the document. Informal reviews come in various shapes and forms, but all have one characteristic in common – they are not documented.

3.2.1 Phases of a formal review

In contrast to informal reviews, formal reviews follow a formal process. A typical formal review process consists of six main steps (*Please note – due to a formatting error, some versions of the ISTQB Foundation Syllabus version 2010 show a 12 step process, with obvious formatting problems. As of the time of writing, these problems*

*have been corrected in the ISTQB Foundation Syllabus version 2011, and the proper
version of the process is shown here*):

Typical formal review steps	
1 Planning	**4** Review meeting
2 Kick-off	**5** Rework
3 Preparation	**6** Follow-up

Planning

The Foundation Syllabus specifies the following elements of the planning step:

- Defining the review criteria.
- Selecting the personnel.
- Allocating roles.
- Defining the entry and exit criteria for more formal review types (e.g. inspections).
- Selecting which parts of documents to review.
- Checking entry criteria (for more formal review types).

Let's examine these in more detail.

The review process for a particular review begins with a 'request for review' by
the author to the **moderator** (or inspection leader). A moderator is often assigned to
take care of the scheduling (dates, time, place and invitation) of the review. On a
project level, the project planning needs to allow time for review and rework
activities, thus providing engineers with time to thoroughly participate in reviews.

For more formal reviews, e.g. inspections, the moderator always performs an entry
check and defines at this stage formal exit criteria. The entry check is carried out to
ensure that the reviewers' time is not wasted on a document that is not ready for review.
A document containing too many obvious mistakes is clearly not ready to enter a formal
review process and it could even be very harmful to the review process. It would possibly
de-motivate both reviewers and the author. Also, the review is most likely not effective
because the numerous obvious and minor defects will conceal the major defects.

Although more and other **entry criteria** can be applied, the following can be
regarded as the minimum set for performing the entry check:

- A short check of a product sample by the moderator (or expert) does not reveal a
large number of major defects. For example, after 30 minutes of checking, no
more than three major defects are found on a single page or fewer than ten major
defects in total in a set of five pages.
- The document to be reviewed is available with line numbers.
- The document has been cleaned up by running any automated checks that apply.
- References needed for the inspection are stable and available.
- The document author is prepared to join the review team and feels confident
with the quality of the document.

If the document passes the entry check, the moderator and author decide which
part of the document to review. Because the human mind can comprehend a limited
set of pages at one time, the number should not be too high. The maximum number
of pages depends, among other things, on the objective, review type and document
type and should be derived from practical experiences within the organization. For a

**Moderator (inspection
leader)** The leader and
main person responsible
for an inspection or other
review process.

Entry criteria The set of
generic and specific
conditions for permitting
a process to go forward
with a defined task, e.g.
test phase. The purpose
of entry criteria is to
prevent a task from
starting which would
entail more (wasted)
effort compared to the
effort needed to remove
the failed entry criteria.

review, the maximum size is usually between 10 and 20 pages. In formal inspection, only a page or two may be looked at in depth in order to find the most serious defects that are not obvious.

After the document size has been set and the pages to be checked have been selected, the moderator determines, in co-operation with the author, the composition of the review team. The team normally consists of four to six participants, including moderator and author. To improve the effectiveness of the review, different roles are assigned to each of the participants. These roles help the **reviewers** focus on particular types of defects during checking. This reduces the chance of different reviewers finding the same defects. The moderator assigns the roles to the reviewers.

Figure 3.1 shows the different roles within a review. The roles represent views of the document under review.

Within reviews the following focuses can be identified:

- focus on higher-level documents, e.g. does the design comply to the requirements;
- focus on standards, e.g. internal consistency, clarity, naming conventions, templates;
- focus on related documents at the same level, e.g. interfaces between software functions;
- focus on usage of the document, e.g. for testability or maintainability.

The author may raise additional specific roles and questions that have to be addressed. The moderator has the option to also fulfil a role, alongside the task of being a review leader. Checking the document improves the moderator's ability to lead the meeting, because it ensures better understanding. Furthermore, it improves the review efficiency because the moderator replaces an engineer that would otherwise have to check the document and attend the meeting. It is recommended that the moderator take the role of checking compliance to standards, since this tends to be a highly objective role, which leads to less discussion of the defects found.

Reviewer (inspector) The person involved in the review that identifies and describes anomalies in the product or project under review. Reviewers can be chosen to represent different viewpoints and roles in the review process.

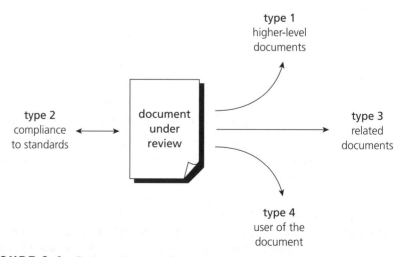

FIGURE 3.1   Basic review roles for a document under review

Kick-off

The Foundation Syllabus specifies the following elements of the optional kick-off step:

- Distributing documents.
- Explaining the objectives, process and documents to the participants.

Let's examine these in more detail.

The next step in a review process, which is optional, is a kick-off meeting. The goal of this meeting is to get everybody on the same wavelength regarding the document under review and to commit to the time that will be spent on checking. Also the result of the entry check and defined exit criteria are discussed in case of a more formal review. In general a kick-off is highly recommended since there is a strong positive effect of a kick-off meeting on the motivation of reviewers and thus the effectiveness of the review process. At customer sites, we have measured results of up to 70% more major defects found per page as a result of performing a kick-off [van Veenendaal and van der Zwan, 2000].

During the kick-off meeting the reviewers receive a short introduction to the objectives of the review and the documents. The relationships between the document under review and the other documents (sources) are explained, especially if the number of related documents is high.

Role assignments, checking rate, the pages to be checked, process changes and possible other questions are also discussed during this meeting. Of course the distribution of the document under review, source documents and other related documentation, can also be done during the kick-off.

Preparation

The Foundation Syllabus specifies the following elements of the preparation step:

- Preparing for the review meeting by reviewing the document(s).
- Noting potential defects, questions and comments.

Let's examine these in more detail.

In preparation, the participants work individually on the document under review using the related documents, procedures, rules and checklists provided. The individual participants identify defects, questions and comments, according to their understanding of the document and role. All issues are recorded, preferably using a logging form. Spelling mistakes are recorded on the document under review but not mentioned during the meeting. The annotated document will be given to the author at the end of the logging meeting. Using checklists during this phase can make reviews more effective and efficient, for example a specific checklist based on perspectives such as user, maintainer, tester or operations, or a checklist for typical coding problems.

A critical success factor for a thorough preparation is the number of pages checked per hour. This is called the checking rate. The optimum checking rate is the result of a mix of factors, including the type of document, its complexity, the number of related documents and the experience of the reviewer. Usually the checking rate is in the range of five to ten pages per hour, but may be much less for formal inspection, e.g. one page per hour. During preparation, participants should not exceed the checking rate they have been asked to use. By collecting data and measuring the review process, company-specific criteria for checking rate and document size (see planning phase) can be set, preferably specific to a document type.

Examination, evaluation, and recording of results (review meeting)

The Foundation Syllabus specifies the following elements of the review meeting step, which it refers to as examination, evaluation, and recording of results:

- Discussing or logging, with documented results or minutes (for more formal review types).
- Noting defects, making recommendations regarding handling the defects, making decisions about the defects.
- Examining, evaluating and recording issues during any physical meetings or tracking any group electronic communications.

Let's examine these in more detail.

The review meeting typically consists of the following elements (partly depending on the review type): logging phase, discussion phase and decision phase.

During the logging phase the issues, e.g. defects, that have been identified during the preparation are mentioned page by page, reviewer by reviewer and are logged either by the author or by a scribe. A separate person to do the logging (a scribe) is especially useful for formal review types such as an inspection. To ensure progress and efficiency, no real discussion is allowed during the logging phase. If an issue needs discussion, the item is noted as a discussion item and then handled in the discussion phase. A detailed discussion on whether or not an issue is a defect is not very meaningful, as it is much more efficient to simply log it and proceed to the next one. Furthermore, in spite of the opinion of the team, a discussed and discarded defect may well turn out to be a real one during rework.

Every defect and its severity should be logged. The participant who identifies the defect proposes the severity. Severity classes could be:

- *Critical:* defects will cause downstream damage; the scope and impact of the defect is beyond the document under inspection.
- *Major:* defects could cause a downstream effect (e.g. a fault in a design can result in an error in the implementation).
- *Minor:* defects are not likely to cause downstream damage (e.g. non-compliance with the standards and templates).

In order to keep the added value of reviews, spelling errors are not part of the defect classification. Spelling defects are noted, by the participants, in the document under review and given to the author at the end of the meeting or could be dealt with in a separate proofreading exercise.

During the logging phase the focus is on logging as many defects as possible within a certain timeframe. To ensure this, the moderator tries to keep a good logging rate (number of defects logged per minute). In a well-led and disciplined formal review meeting, the logging rate should be between one and two defects logged per minute.

For a more formal review, the issues classified as discussion items will be handled during this meeting phase. Informal reviews will often not have a separate logging phase and will start immediately with discussion. Participants can take part in the discussion by bringing forward their comments and reasoning. As chairman of the discussion meeting, the moderator takes care of people issues. For example, the moderator prevents discussions from getting too personal, rephrases remarks if necessary and calls for a break to cool down 'heated' discussions and/or participants.

Reviewers who do not need to be in the discussion may leave, or stay as a learning exercise. The moderator also paces this part of the meeting and ensures that all discussed items either have an outcome by the end of the meeting, or are defined as an action point if a discussion cannot be solved during the meeting. The outcome of discussions is documented for future reference.

At the end of the meeting, a decision on the document under review has to be made by the participants, sometimes based on formal exit criteria. The most important exit criterion is the average number of critical and/or major defects found per page (e.g. no more than three critical/major defects per page). If the number of defects found per page exceeds a certain level, the document must be reviewed again, after it has been reworked. If the document complies with the exit criteria, the document will be checked during follow-up by the moderator or one or more participants. Subsequently, the document can leave the review process.

If a project is under pressure, the moderator will sometimes be forced to skip re-reviews and exit with a defect-prone document. Setting (and agreeing to) quantified exit level criteria helps the moderator to make firm decisions at all times. Even if a limited sample of a document has been (formally) reviewed, an estimate of remaining defects per page can give an indication of likely problems later on.

In addition to the number of defects per page, other exit criteria are used that measure the thoroughness of the review process, such as ensuring that all pages have been checked at the right rate. The average number of defects per page is only a valid quality indicator if these process criteria are met.

Rework

The Foundation Syllabus specifies the following elements of the rework step:

- Fixing defects found (typically done by the author).
- Recording updated status of defects (in formal reviews).

Let's examine these in more detail.

During rework, the author will improve the document under review step by step based on the defects detected in the preparation and review meeting steps. Not every defect that is found leads to rework. It is often the author's responsibility to judge if a defect has to be fixed, though in some cases the review meeting attendees may make those decisions. If nothing is done about an issue for a certain reason, it should be reported to at least indicate that the author has considered the issue.

Changes that are made to the document should be easy to identify during follow-up. Therefore the author has to indicate where changes are made (e.g. using 'Track changes' in word-processing software).

Follow-up

The Foundation Syllabus specifies the following elements of the follow-up step:

- Checking that defects have been addressed.
- Gathering **metrics**.
- Checking exit criteria (for more formal review types)

Metric A measurement scale and the method used for measurement.

Let's examine these in more detail.

In the follow-up step, the moderator is responsible for ensuring that satisfactory actions have been taken on all (logged) defects, process improvement suggestions and change requests. Although the moderator checks to make sure that the author has taken action on all known defects, it is not necessary for the moderator to check all the corrections in detail. If it is decided that all participants will check the updated document, the moderator takes care of the distribution and collects the feedback. For more formal review types the moderator checks for compliance to the exit criteria.

In order to control and optimize the review process, a number of measurements are collected by the moderator at each step of the process. Examples of such measurements include number of defects found, number of defects found per page, time spent checking per page, total review effort, etc. It is the responsibility of the moderator to ensure that the information is correct and stored for future analysis.

3.2.2 Roles and responsibilities

The participants in any type of formal review should have adequate knowledge of the review process. The best, and most efficient, review situation occurs when the participants gain some kind of advantage for their own work during reviewing. In the case of an inspection or technical review, participants should have been properly trained as both types of review have proven to be far less successful without trained participants. This indeed is perceived as being a critical success factor.

The best formal reviews come from well-organized teams, guided by trained moderators (or review leaders). Within a review team, four types of participants can be distinguished: moderator, author, scribe and reviewer. In addition management needs to play a role in the review process.

The moderator

The moderator (or review leader) leads the review process. He or she determines, in co-operation with the author, the type of review, approach and the composition of the review team. The moderator performs the entry check and the follow-up on the rework, in order to control the quality of the input and output of the review process. The moderator also schedules the meeting, disseminates documents before the meeting, coaches other team members, paces the meeting, leads possible discussions and stores the data that is collected.

The author

As the writer of the document under review, the author's basic goal should be to learn as much as possible with regard to improving the quality of the document, but also to improve his or her ability to write future documents. The author's task is to illuminate unclear areas and to understand the defects found.

Scribe The person who records each defect mentioned and any suggestions for process improvement during a review meeting, on a logging form. The scribe should ensure that the logging form is readable and understandable.

The scribe

During the logging meeting, the **scribe** (or recorder) has to record each defect mentioned and any suggestions for process improvement. In practice it is often the author who plays this role, ensuring that the log is readable and understandable. If authors record their own defects, or at least make their own notes in their own words, it helps them to understand the log better during rework. However, having someone other than the author take the role of the scribe (e.g. the moderator) can have significant advantages, since the author is freed up to think about the document rather than being tied down with lots of writing.

The reviewers

The task of the reviewers (also called checkers or inspectors) is to check any material for defects, mostly prior to the meeting. The level of thoroughness required depends on the type of review. The level of domain knowledge or technical expertise needed by the reviewers also depends on the type of review. Reviewers should be chosen to represent different perspectives and roles in the review process. In addition to the document under review, the material reviewers receive includes source documents, standards, checklists, etc. In general, the fewer source and reference documents provided, the more domain expertise regarding the content of the document under review is needed.

The manager

The manager is involved in the reviews as he or she decides on the execution of reviews, allocates time in project schedules and determines whether review process objectives have been met. The manager will ensure that any review training requested by the participants takes place. Of course a manager can also be involved in the review itself depending on his or her background, playing the role of a reviewer if this would be helpful.

3.2.3 Types of review

A single document may be the subject of more than one review. If more than one type of review is used, the order may vary. For example, an informal review may be carried out before a technical review, or an inspection may be carried out on a requirements specification before a walkthrough with customers. It is apparent that none of the following types of review is the 'winner', but the different types serve different purposes at different stages in the life cycle of a document.

The main review types, their main characteristics and common objectives are described below.

Walkthrough

A **walkthrough** is characterized by the author of the document under review guiding the participants through the document and his or her thought processes, to achieve a common understanding and to gather feedback. This is especially useful if people from outside the software discipline are present, who are not used to, or cannot easily understand software development documents. The content of the document is explained step by step by the author, to reach consensus on changes or to gather information.

> **Walkthrough** A step-by-step presentation by the author of a document in order to gather information and to establish a common understanding of its content.

Within a walkthrough the author does most of the preparation. The participants, who are selected from different departments and backgrounds, are not required to do a detailed study of the documents in advance. Because of the way the meeting is structured, a large number of people can participate and this larger audience can bring a great number of diverse viewpoints regarding the contents of the document being reviewed as well as serving an educational purpose. If the audience represents a broad cross-section of skills and disciplines, it can give assurance that no major defects are 'missed' in the walk-through. A walkthrough is especially useful for higher-level documents, such as requirement specifications and architectural documents.

The specific goals of a walkthrough depend on its role in the creation of the document. In general the following goals can be applicable:

- to present the document to stakeholders both within and outside the software discipline, in order to gather information regarding the topic covered by the document:
- to explain (knowledge transfer) and evaluate the contents of the document;
- to establish a common understanding of the document;
- to examine and discuss the validity of proposed solutions and the viability of alternatives, establishing consensus.

Key characteristics of walkthroughs are:

- The meeting is led by the author or authors; often a separate scribe is present.
- Scenarios and dry runs may be used to validate the content.
- Separate pre-meeting preparation for reviewers is optional.

Technical review

Technical review A peer group discussion activity that focuses on achieving consensus on the technical approach to be taken.

A **technical review** is a discussion meeting that focuses on achieving consensus about the technical content of a document. Compared to inspections, technical reviews are less formal and there is little or no focus on defect identification on the basis of referenced documents, intended readership and rules. During technical reviews defects are found by experts, who focus on the content of the document. The experts that are needed for a technical review are, for example, architects, chief designers and key users. In practice, technical reviews vary from quite informal to very formal.

The goals of a technical review are to:

- assess the value of technical concepts and alternatives in the product and project environment;
- establish consistency in the use and representation of technical concepts;
- ensure, at an early stage, that technical concepts are used correctly;
- inform participants of the technical content of the document.

Key characteristics of a technical review are:

Peer review A review of a software work product by colleagues of the producer of the product for the purpose of identifying defects and improvements. Examples are inspection, technical review and walkthrough.

- It is a documented defect-detection process that involves peers and technical experts.
- It is often performed as a **peer review** without management participation.
- Ideally it is led by a trained moderator, but possibly also by a technical expert.
- A separate preparation is carried out during which the product is examined and the defects are found.
- More formal characteristics such as the use of checklists and a logging list or issue log are optional.

Inspection A type of peer review that relies on visual examination of documents to detect defects, e.g. violations of development standards and non-conformance to higher level documentation. The most formal review technique and therefore always based on a documented procedure.

Inspection

Inspection is the most formal review type. The document under inspection is prepared and checked thoroughly by the reviewers before the meeting, comparing the work product with its sources and other referenced documents, and using rules and checklists. In the inspection meeting the defects found are logged and any discussion is postponed until the discussion phase. This makes the inspection meeting a very efficient meeting.

The reason for carrying out inspections can be explained by using Weinberg's concept of egoless engineering [Weinberg 1971]. Weinberg refers to the human tendency to self-justify actions. Since we tend not to see evidence that conflicts with our strong beliefs, our ability to find errors in our own work is impaired. Because of this tendency, many engineering organizations have established independent test groups that specialize in finding defects. Similar principles have led to the introduction of inspections and reviews in general.

Depending on the organization and the objectives of a project, inspections can be balanced to serve a number of goals. For example, if the time to market is extremely important, the emphasis in inspections will be on efficiency. In a safety-critical market, the focus will be on effectiveness.

The generally accepted goals of inspection are to:

- help the author to improve the quality of the document under inspection;
- remove defects efficiently, as early as possible;
- improve product quality, by producing documents with a higher level of quality;
- create a common understanding by exchanging information among the inspection participants;
- train new employees in the organization's development process;
- learn from defects found and improve processes in order to prevent recurrence of similar defects;
- sample a few pages or sections from a larger document in order to measure the typical quality of the document, leading to improved work by individuals in the future, and to process improvements.

Key characteristics of an inspection are:

- It is usually led by a trained moderator (certainly not by the author).
- It uses defined roles during the process.
- It involves peers to examine the product.
- Rules and checklists are used during the preparation phase.
- A separate preparation is carried out during which the product is examined and the defects are found.
- The defects found are documented in a logging list or issue log.
- A formal follow-up is carried out by the moderator applying exit criteria.
- Optionally, a causal analysis step is introduced to address process improvement issues and learn from the defects found.
- Metrics are gathered and analyzed to optimize the process.

3.2.4 Success factors for reviews

Implementing (formal) reviews is not easy as there is no one way to success and there are numerous ways to fail. The next list contains a number of critical success factors that improve the chances of success when implementing reviews. It aims to answer the question, 'How do you start (formal) reviews?'

Find a 'champion'

A champion is needed, one who will lead the process on a project or organizational level. They need expertise, enthusiasm and a practical mindset in order to guide moderators and participants. The authority of this champion should be clear to the entire organization. Management support is also essential for success. They should, among other things, incorporate adequate time for review activities in project schedules.

Pick things that really count

Select the documents for review that are most important in a project. Reviewing highly critical, upstream documents like requirements and architecture will most certainly show the benefits of the review process to the project. These invested review hours will have a clear and high return on investment.

Pick the right techniques

In the previous subsection, we discussed a number of techniques, each of which has its strengths and weaknesses, advantageous scenarios of use and disadvantageous scenarios of use. You should be careful to select and use review techniques that will best enable the achievement of the objectives of the project and the review itself. Also, be sure to consider the type, importance, and risk level of the work product to be reviewed, and the reviewers who will participate.

In addition make sure each review has a clear objective and the correct type of review is selected that matches the defined objective. Don't try to review everything by inspection; fit the review to the risk associated with the document. Some documents may only warrant an informal review and others will repay using inspection. Of course it is also of utmost importance that the right people are involved.

Explicitly plan and track review activities

To ensure that reviews become part of the day-to-day activities, the hours to be spent should be made visible within each project plan. The engineers involved are prompted to schedule time for preparation and, very importantly, rework. Tracking these hours will improve planning of the next review. As stated earlier, management plays an important part in planning of review activities.

Train participants

It is important that training is provided in review techniques, especially the more formal techniques, such as inspection. Otherwise the process is likely to be impeded by those who don't understand the process and the reasoning behind it. Special training should be provided to the moderators to prepare them for their critical role in the review process.

Manage people issues

Reviews are about evaluating someone's document. Some reviews tend to get too personal when they are not well managed by the moderator. People issues and psychological aspects should be dealt with by the moderator and should be part of the review training, thus making the review a positive experience for the author. During the review, defects should be welcomed and expressed objectively. It is important that all participants create and operate in an atmosphere of trust. Managers especially must commit not to use metrics or other information from reviews for the evaluation of the author or the participants.

Follow the rules but keep it simple

Follow all the formal rules until you know why and how to modify them, but make the process only as formal as the project culture or maturity level allows. Do not become too theoretical or too detailed. Checklists and roles are recommended to increase the effectiveness of defect identification.

Continuously improve process and tools

Continuous improvement of process and supporting tools (e.g. checklists), based upon the ideas of participants, ensures the motivation of the engineers involved. Motivation is the key to a successful change process. There should also be an emphasis, in addition to defect finding, on learning and process improvement.

Report results

Report quantified results and benefits to all those involved as soon as possible, and discuss the consequences of defects if they had not been found this early. Costs should of course be tracked, but benefits, especially when problems don't occur in the future, should be made visible by quantifying the benefits as well as the costs.

Use testers

As discussed in Chapter 1, testers are professional pessimists. This focus on what could go wrong makes them good contributors to reviews, provided they observe the earlier points about keeping the review experience a positive one. In addition to providing valuable input to the review itself, testers who participate in reviews often learn about the product. This supports earlier testing, one of the principles discussed in Chapter 1.

Just do it!

The process is simple but not easy. Every step of the process is clear, but experience is needed to execute them correctly. So, try to get experienced people to observe and help where possible. But most importantly, start doing reviews and start learning from every review.

3.3 STATIC ANALYSIS BY TOOLS

> **SYLLABUS LEARNING OBJECTIVES FOR**
> **3.3 STATIC ANALYSIS BY TOOLS (K2)**
>
> LO-3.3.1 Recall typical defects and errors identified by static analysis and compare them to reviews and dynamic testing. (K1)
>
> LO-3.3.2 Describe, using examples, the typical benefits of static analysis. (K2)
>
> LO-3.3.3 List typical code and design defects that may be identified by static analysis tools. (K1)

In this section, we'll focus on static analysis as a form of static testing. We'll look at ways to use tools to find defects effectively, efficiently, and very quickly using such static analysis tools. We'll talk about the benefits and challenges of static analysis using tools. As we go through this section, watch for the Syllabus terms **compiler, complexity, control flow, cyclomatic complexity, data flow,** and **static analysis**. You'll find these terms defined in the glossary.

There is much to be done examining software work products without actually running the system. For example, we saw in the previous section that we can carefully review requirements, designs, code, test plans and more, to find defects and fix them before we deliver a product to a customer. In this section, we focus on a different kind of static testing, where we carefully examine requirements, designs and code, usually with automated assistance to ferret out additional defects before the code is actually run. Thus, what is called static analysis is just another form of testing.

Static analysis Analysis of software artifacts, e.g. requirements or code, carried out without execution of these software development artifacts. Static analysis is usually carried out by means of a supporting tool.

Static analysis is an examination of requirements, design and code that differs from more traditional dynamic testing in a number of important ways:

- Static analysis is performed on requirements, design or code without actually executing the software artefact being examined.
- Static analysis is ideally performed before the types of formal review discussed in Section 3.2.
- Static analysis is unrelated to dynamic properties of the requirements, design and code, such as test coverage.
- The goal of static analysis is to find defects, whether or not they may cause failures. As with reviews, static analysis finds defects rather than failures.

For static analysis there are many tools, and most of them focus on software code. Static analysis tools are typically used by developers before, and sometimes during, component and integration testing and by designers during software modelling. The tools can show not only structural attributes (code metrics), such as depth of nesting or cyclomatic complexity number and check against coding standards, but also graphic depictions of control flow, data relationships and the number of distinct paths from one line of code to another. Even the **compiler** can be considered a static analysis tool, since it builds a symbol table, points out incorrect usage and checks for non-compliance to coding language conventions (syntax). Additional static analysis features are often available in compilers by setting the appropriate values at compilation time.

Compiler A software tool that translates programs expressed in a high order language into their machine language equivalents.

One of the reasons for using static analysis (to check coding standards and the like) is related to the characteristics of the programming languages themselves. One may think that the languages are safe to use, because at least the standards committee knows where the problems are. But this would be wrong. Adding to the holes left by the standardization process, programmers continue to report features of the language, which though well-defined, lead to recognizable fault modes. By the end of the 1990s, approximately 700 of these additional problems had been identified in standard C. It is now clear that such fault modes exist. It can be demonstrated that they frequently escape the scrutiny of conventional dynamic testing, ending up in commercial products. These problems can be found by using static analysis tools to detect them. In fact, many of the 700 fault modes reported in C can be detected in this way! In a typical C program, there is an average of approximately eight such faults per 1000 lines of source code; they are embedded in the released code, just waiting to cause the code to fail [Hatton 1997]. Dynamic testing simply did not detect them. C is not the culprit here; this exercise can be carried out for other languages with broadly the same results. All programming languages have problems and programmers cannot assume that they are protected against them. And nothing in the current international process of standardizing languages will prevent this from happening in the future.

So, what kinds of defects can programmers find during static analysis of code? That depends on the tool, but some typical defects include:

- Referencing a variable with an undefined value (i.e. before the variable has been properly initialized).
- Inconsistent interfaces between modules and components, such as the improper use of an object, method, or function, including the wrong parameters.
- The improper declaration of variables, or the declaration of variables that are never used.
- Unreachable ('dead') code that can safely be removed.
- Certain types of missing or erroneous logic, such as potentially infinite loops.
- Highly complex functions or other constructs (as will be discussed below).
- Various types of programming standards violations, both violations that create the risk of actual failures and violations that create long-term testability, analyzability, and other code maintainability problems.
- Security vulnerabilities, such as security problems related to buffer overflows that are created by failing to check buffer length before copying into a buffer.
- Syntax violations of code and software models (though these are often caught by compilers).

When used to analyze code, static analysis tools are typically used by developers to check for the kinds of problems mentioned above. This checking can occur during the coding process, prior to code reviews, before and during component and integration testing, or when checking code into the source code repository in the configuration management system. In addition, system designers can use various kinds of model validation and other static analysis tools during software modelling. Finally, various kinds of static analysis and modelling tool are also available for requirements.

One thing to be aware of, when initiating the use of static code analysis, is that a very large number of violations may lie hidden in the existing code base. When first used, these static analysis tools can produce an enormous number of warning messages, many of which turn out to be related to very low-risk situations. Therefore, our clients that have succeeded with the introduction of these tools have employed careful management strategies to deal with the volume of information. One strategy which works well is to enforce the static analysis tools only for new and changed classes and/or functions. This leads to a gradual, manageable, incremental improvement in the quality of the code over the long-term without a spike in short-term code-clean-up tasks which can be risky in their own right.

The various features of static analysis tools are discussed below, with a special focus toward static code analysis tools since these are the most common in day-to-day practice. Note that static analysis tools analyze software code, as well as generated output such as HTML and XML.

3.3.1 Coding standards

Checking for adherence to coding standards is certainly the most well-known of all features. The first action to be taken is to define or adopt a coding standard. Usually a coding standard consists of a set of programming rules (e.g. 'Always check boundaries on an array when copying to that array'), naming conventions (e.g. 'Classes should start with capital C') and layout specifications (e.g. 'Indent 4 spaces'). It is recommended that existing standards are adopted. The main advantage of this is that it saves a lot of effort. An extra reason for adopting this approach is that if you take a well-known coding standard there will probably be checking tools available that support this standard. It can even be put the other way around: purchase a static code analyzer and declare (a selection of) the rules in it as your coding standard. Without such tools, the enforcement of a coding standard in an organization is likely to fail. There are three main causes for this: the number of rules in a coding standard is usually so large that nobody can remember them all; some context-sensitive rules that demand reviews of several files are very hard to check by human beings; and if people spend time checking coding standards in reviews, that will distract them from other defects they might otherwise find, making the review process less effective.

3.3.2 Code metrics

As stated, when performing static code analysis, usually information is calculated about structural attributes of the code, such as comment frequency, depth of nesting, cyclomatic complexity number and number of lines of code. This information can be computed not only as the design and code are being created but also as changes are made to a system, to see if the design or code is becoming bigger, more complex and more difficult to understand and maintain. The measurements also help us to decide among several design alternatives, especially when redesigning portions of existing code.

There are many different kinds of structural measures, each of which tells us something about the effort required to write the code in the first place, to understand the code when making a change, or to test the code using particular tools or techniques.

Experienced programmers know that 20% of the code will cause 80% of the problems, and complexity analysis helps to find that all-important 20%, which relate back to the principle of defect clustering as explained in Chapter 1. **Complexity** metrics identify high risk, complex areas.

The **cyclomatic complexity** metric is based on the number of decisions in a program. It is important to testers because it provides an indication of the amount of testing (including reviews) necessary to detect a sufficient number of defects and to have adequate confidence in the system. In other words, areas of code identified as more complex are candidates for reviews and additional dynamic tests. While there are many ways to calculate cyclomatic complexity, the easiest way is to sum the number of binary decision statements (e.g. if, while, for, etc.) and add 1 to it. A more formal definition regarding the calculation rules is provided in the glossary.

Below is a simple program as an example:

```
IF A = 354
THEN IF B > C
   THEN A = B
   ELSE A = C
   ENDIF
ENDIF
Print A
```

The **control flow** generated from the program would look like Figure 3.2.

Complexity The degree to which a component or system has a design and/or internal structure that is difficult to understand, maintain and verify.

Cyclomatic complexity The number of independent paths through a program. Cyclomatic complexity is defined as:
L – N + 2P, where
- L = the number of edges/links in a graph
- N = the number of nodes in a graph
- P = the number of disconnected parts of the graph (e.g. a called graph or subroutine).

Control flow A sequence of events (paths) in the execution through a component or system.

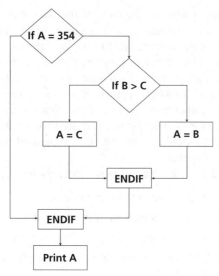

FIGURE 3.2   Control flow of a simple program

The control flow shows seven nodes (shapes) and eight edges (lines), thus using the formal formula the cyclomatic complexity is $8 - 7 + 2 = 3$. In this case there is no called graph or subroutine. Alternatively one may calculate the cyclomatic complexity using the decision points rule. Since there are two decision points, the cyclomatic complexity is $2 + 1 = 3$.

3.3.3 Code structure

There are many different kinds of structural measures, each of which tells us something about the effort required to write the code in the first place, to understand the code when making a change, or to test the code using particular tools or techniques. It is often assumed that a large module takes longer to specify, design, code and test than a smaller one. But in fact the code's structure plays a big part.

There are several aspects of code structure to consider:

- control flow structure;
- **data flow** structure;
- data structure.

The control flow structure addresses the sequence in which the instructions are executed. This aspect of structure reflects the iterations and loops in a program's design. If only the size of a program is measured, no information is provided on how often an instruction is executed as it is run. Control flow analysis can also be used to identify unreachable (dead) code. In fact many of the code metrics relate to the control flow structure, e.g. number of nested levels or cyclomatic complexity.

Data flow structure follows the trail of a data item as it is accessed and modified by the code. Many times, the transactions applied to data are more complex than the instructions that implement them. Thus, using data flow measures it is shown how the data act as they are transformed by the program. Defects can be found such as referencing a variable with an undefined value and variables that are never used.

Data flow An abstract representation of the sequence and possible changes of the state of data objects, where the state of an object is any of: creation, usage, or destruction.

Data structure refers to the organization of the data itself, independent of the program. When data are arranged as a list, queue, stack, or other well-defined structure, the algorithms for creating, modifying or deleting them are more likely to be well-defined, too. Thus, the data structure provides a lot of information about the difficulty in writing programs to handle the data and in designing test cases to show program correctness. That is, sometimes a program is complex because it has a complex data structure, rather than because of complex control or data flow.

The important thing for the tester is to be aware that the above mentioned static analysis measures can be used as early warning signals of how good the code is likely to be when it is finished.

In summary the value of static analysis is especially for:

- early detection of defects prior to test execution;
- early warning about suspicious aspects of the code, design or requirements;
- identification of defects not easily found in dynamic testing;
- improved maintainability of code and design since engineers work according to documented standards and rules;
- prevention of defects, provided that engineers are willing to learn from their errors and continuous improvement is practised.

CHAPTER REVIEW

Let's review what you have learned in this chapter.

From Section 3.1, you should be able to explain the importance and advantages of static testing. You should know the difference between static testing and dynamic testing, and also understand the concept of reviews. You should be able to recognize the software work products that can be examined by static testing. You should know the glossary terms **dynamic testing** and **static testing**.

From Section 3.2, you should understand the difference between formal and informal reviews. You should be able to recall the main phases of a typical formal review. The main roles within reviews and their responsibilities should be clear to you. You should know the differences between the various types of formal review: technical review, walkthrough and inspection. Finally you should be able to explain the factors for successful performance of reviews. You should know the glossary terms **entry criteria, formal review, informal review, inspection, metric, moderator, peer review, reviewer, scribe, technical review,** and **walkthrough**.

From Section 3.3, you should understand the objective of static analysis and be able to compare it to static and dynamic testing. You should be able to describe the main features of static analysis and recall typical defects that can be found using static analysis. Finally, you should be able to recall the benefits of using static analysis. You should know the glossary terms **compiler, complexity, control flow, cyclomatic complexity, data flow,** and **static analysis**.

SAMPLE EXAM QUESTIONS

Question 1 Which of the following artefacts can be examined by using review techniques?

a. Software code

b. Requirements specification

c. Test designs

d. All of the above

Question 2 Which statement about the function of a static analysis tool is true?

a. Gives quality information about the code without executing it.

b. Checks expected results against actual results.

c. Can detect memory leaks.

d. Gives information about what code has and has not been exercised.

Question 3 Which is not a type of review?

a. Walkthrough

b. Inspection

c. Informal review

d. Management approval

Question 4 What statement about reviews is true?

a. Inspections are led by a trained moderator, whereas technical reviews are not necessarily.

b. Technical reviews are led by a trained leader, inspections are not.

c. In a walkthrough, the author does not attend.

d. Participants for a walkthrough always need to be thoroughly trained.

Question 5 What is the main difference between a walkthrough and an inspection?

a. An inspection is led by the authors, while a walkthrough is led by a trained moderator.

b. An inspection has a trained leader, while a walkthrough has no leader.

c. Authors are not present during inspections, while they are during walkthroughs.

d. A walkthrough is led by the author, while an inspection is led by a trained moderator.

Question 6 Which of the following characteristics and types of review processes belong together?

1 Led by the author

2 Undocumented

3 No management participation

4 Led by a trained moderator or leader

5 Uses entry and exit criteria

s. Inspection

t. Technical review

u. Informal review

v. Walkthrough

a. s = 4, t = 3, u = 2 and 5, v = 1

b. s = 4 and 5, t = 3, u = 2, v = 1

c. s = 1 and 5, t = 3, u = 2, v = 4

d. s = 5, t = 4, u = 3, v = 1 and 2

Question 7 What statement about static analysis is true?

a. With static analysis, defects can be found that are difficult to find with dynamic testing.

b. Compiling is not a form of static analysis.

c. When properly performed, static analysis makes functional testing redundant.

d. Static analysis finds all faults.

Question 8 Which of the following statements about early test design are true and which are false?

1 Defects found during early test design are more expensive to fix.

2 Early test design can find defects.

3 Early test design can cause changes to the requirements.

4 Early test design takes more effort.

a. 1 and 3 are true. 2 and 4 are false.

b. 2 is true. 1, 3 and 4 are false.

c. 2 and 3 are true. 1 and 4 are false.

d. 2, 3 and 4 are true. 1 is false.

Question 9 Static code analysis typically identifies all but one of the following problems. Which is it?

a. Unreachable code

b. Undeclared variables

c. Faults in the requirements

d. Too few comments

CHAPTER FOUR

Test design techniques

Chapter 3 covered static testing, looking at documents and code, but not running the code we are interested in. This chapter looks at dynamic testing, where the software we are interested in is run by executing tests on the running code.

4.1 THE TEST DEVELOPMENT PROCESS

SYLLABUS LEARNING OBJECTIVES FOR 4.1 THE TEST DEVELOPMENT PROCESS (K3)

LO-4.1.1   Differentiate between a test design specification, test case specification and test procedure specification. (K2)

LO-4.1.2   Compare the terms test condition, test case and test procedure. (K2)

LO-4.1.3   Evaluate the quality of test cases in terms of clear traceability to the requirements and expected results. (K2)

LO-4.1.4   Translate test cases into a well-structured test procedure specification at a level of detail relevant to the knowledge of the testers. (K3)

Before we can actually execute a test, we need to know what we are trying to test, the inputs, the results that should be produced by those inputs, and how we actually get ready for and run the tests.

In this section we are looking at three things: test conditions, test cases and test procedures (or scripts) – they are described in the sections below. Each is specified in its own document, according to the Test Documentation Standard [IEEE 829].

Test conditions are documented in a Test Design Specification. We will look at how to choose test conditions and prioritize them.

Test cases are documented in a **test case specification**. We will look at how to write a good test case, showing clear traceability to the test basis (e.g. the requirement specification) as well as to test conditions.

Test procedures are documented (as you may expect) in a Test Procedure Specification (also known as a test script or a manual test script). We will look at how to translate test cases into test procedures relevant to the knowledge of the tester who will be executing the test, and we will look at how to produce a test execution schedule, using prioritization and technical and logical dependencies.

> **Test case specification** A document specifying a set of test cases (objective, inputs, test actions, expected results, and execution preconditions) for a test item.

In this section, look for the definitions of the glossary terms **horizontal trace-ability, test case specification, test design technique, test execution schedule, test script, traceability** and **vertical traceability**.

4.1.1 Formality of test documentation

Testing may be performed with varying degrees of formality. Very formal testing would have extensive documentation which is well controlled, and would expect the documented detail of the tests to include the exact and specific input and expected outcome of the test. Very informal testing may have no documentation at all, or only notes kept by individual testers, but we'd still expect the testers to have in their minds and notes some idea of what they intended to test and what they expected the outcome to be. Most people are probably somewhere in between! The right level of formality for you depends on your context: a commercial safety-critical application has very different needs than a one-off application to be used by only a few people for a short time.

The level of formality is also influenced by your organization – its culture, the people working there, how mature the development process is, how mature the testing process is, etc. The thoroughness of your test documentation may also depend on your time constraints; under excessive deadline pressure, keeping good documentation may be compromised.

In this chapter we will describe a fairly formal documentation style. If this is not appropriate for you, you might adopt a less formal approach, but you will be aware of how to increase formality if you need to.

4.1.2 Test analysis: identifying test conditions

Test analysis is the process of looking at something that can be used to derive test information. This basis for the tests is called the 'test basis'. It could be a system requirement, a technical specification, the code itself (for structural testing), or a business process. Sometimes tests can be based on an experienced user's knowledge of the system, which may not be documented. The test basis includes whatever the tests are based on. This was also discussed in Chapter 1.

From a testing perspective, we look at the test basis in order to see what could be tested – these are the test conditions. A test condition is simply something that we could test. If we are looking to measure coverage of code decisions (branches), then the test basis would be the code itself, and the list of test conditions would be the decision outcomes (True and False). If we have a requirements specification, the table of contents can be our initial list of test conditions.

A good way to understand requirements better is to try to define tests to meet those requirements, as pointed out by [Hetzel 1988].

For example, if we are testing a customer management and marketing system for a mobile phone company, we might have test conditions that are related to a marketing campaign, such as age of customer (pre-teen, teenager, young adult, mature), gender, postcode or zip code, and purchasing preference (pay-as-you-go or contract). A particular advertising campaign could be aimed at male teenaged customers in the mid-west of the USA on pay-as-you-go, for example.

Testing experts use different names to represent the basic idea of 'a list of things that we could test'. For example, Marick refers to 'test requirements' as things that should be tested. Although it is not intended to imply that everything must be tested, it is too easily interpreted in that way [Marick 1994]. In contrast, Hutcheson talks about the 'test inventory' as a list of things that could be tested [Hutcheson 2003]; Craig talks about 'test objectives' as broad categories of things to test and 'test inventories' as the actual list of things that need to be tested [Craig 2002]. These authors are all referring to what the ISTQB glossary calls a test condition.

When identifying test conditions, we want to 'throw the net wide' to identify as many as we can, and then we will start being selective about which ones to take forward to develop in more detail and combine into test cases. We could call them 'test possibilities'.

In Chapter 1 we explained that testing everything is known as exhaustive testing (defined as exercising every combination of inputs and preconditions) and we demonstrated that this is an impractical goal. Therefore, as we cannot test everything, we have to select a subset of all possible tests. In practice the subset we select may be a very small subset and yet it has to have a high probability of finding most of the defects in a system. We need some intelligent thought processes to guide our selection; **test techniques** (i.e. **test design techniques**) are such thought processes.

> **Test design technique** Procedure used to derive and/or select test cases.

A testing technique helps us select a good set of tests from the total number of all possible tests for a given system. Different techniques offer different ways of looking at the software under test, possibly challenging assumptions made about it. Each technique provides a set of rules or guidelines for the tester to follow in identifying test conditions and test cases. Techniques are described in detail later in this chapter.

The test conditions that are chosen will depend on the test strategy or detailed test approach. For example, they might be based on risk, models of the system, likely failures, compliance requirements, expert advice or heuristics. The word 'heuristic' comes from the same Greek root as *eureka*, which means 'I find'. A heuristic is a way of directing your attention, a common sense rule useful in solving a problem.

> **Traceability** The ability to identify related items in documentation and software, such as requirements with associated tests. See also horizontal traceability, vertical traceability.

Test conditions should be able to be linked back to their sources in the test basis – this is called **traceability**.

Traceability can be either **horizontal** through all the test documentation for a given test level (e.g. system testing, from test conditions through test cases to test scripts) or **vertical** through the layers of development documentation (e.g. from requirements to components).

Why is traceability important? Consider these examples:

> **Horizontal traceability** The tracing of requirements for a test level through the layers of test documentation (e.g. test plan, test design specification, test case specification and test procedure specification or test script).

- The requirements for a given function or feature have changed. Some of the fields now have different ranges that can be entered. Which tests were looking at those boundaries? They now need to be changed. How many tests will actually be affected by this change in the requirements? These questions can be answered easily if the requirements can easily be traced to the tests.

- A set of tests that has run OK in the past has started to have serious problems. What functionality do these tests actually exercise? Traceability between the tests and the requirement being tested enables the functions or features affected to be identified more easily.

> **Vertical traceability** The tracing of requirements through the layers of development documentation to components.

- Before delivering a new release, we want to know whether or not we have tested all of the specified requirements in the requirements specification. We have the list of the tests that have passed – was every requirement tested?

Having identified a list of test conditions, it is important to prioritize them, so that the most important test conditions are identified (before a lot of time is spent in designing test cases based on them). It is a good idea to try and think of twice as many test conditions as you need – then you can throw away the less important ones, and you will have a much better set of test conditions!

Note that spending some extra time now, while identifying test conditions, doesn't take very long, as we are only listing things that we could test. This is a good investment of our time – we don't want to spend time implementing poor tests!

Test conditions can be identified for test data as well as for test inputs and test outcomes, for example, different types of record, different distribution of types of record within a file or database, different sizes of records or fields in a record. The test data should be designed to represent the most important types of data, i.e. the most important data conditions.

Test conditions are documented in the IEEE 829 document called a Test Design Specification, shown below. (This document could have been called a Test Condition Specification, as the contents referred to in the standard are actually test conditions.)

IEEE 829 STANDARD: TEST DESIGN SPECIFICATION TEMPLATE

Test design specification identifier

Features to be tested

Approach refinements

Test identification

Feature pass/fail criteria

4.1.3 Test design: specifying test cases

Test conditions can be rather vague, covering quite a large range of possibilities as we saw with our mobile phone company example (e.g. a teenager in the mid-west), or a test condition may be more specific (e.g. a particular male customer on pay-as-you-go with less than $10 credit). However when we come to make a test case, we are required to be very specific; in fact we now need exact and detailed specific inputs, not general descriptions (e.g. Jim Green, age 17, living in Grand Rapids, Michigan, with credit of $8.64, expected result: add to Q4 marketing campaign). Note that one test case covers a number of conditions (teenager, male, mid-west area, pay-as-you-go, and credit of less than $10).

For a test condition of 'an existing customer', the test case input needs to be 'Jim Green' where Jim Green already exists on the customer database, or part of this test would be to set up a database record for Jim Green.

A test case needs to have input values, of course, but just having some values to input to the system is not a test! If you don't know what the system is supposed to do with the inputs, you can't tell whether your test has passed or failed.

Should these detailed test cases be written down? They can be formally documented, as we will describe below. However, it is possible to test without documenting at the test-case level. If you give an experienced user acceptance tester with a strong business background a list of high-level test conditions, they could probably do a good job of testing. But if you gave the same list to a new starter who didn't know the system at all, they would probably be lost, so they would benefit from having more detailed test cases.

Test cases can be documented as described in the IEEE 829 Standard for Test Documentation. Note that the contents described in the standard don't all have to be separate physical documents. But the standard's list of what needs to be kept track of is a good starting point, even if the test conditions and test cases for a given functionality or feature are all kept in one physical document.

One of the most important aspects of a test is that it assesses that the system does what it is supposed to do. Copeland says 'At its core, testing is the process of comparing "what is" with "what ought to be" ' [Copeland 2003]. If we simply put in some inputs and think 'that was fun, I guess the system is probably OK because it didn't crash', then are we actually testing it? We don't think so. You have observed that the system does what the system does – this is not a test. Boris Beizer refers to this as 'kiddie testing' [Beizer 1990]. We may not know what the right answer is in detail every time, and we can still get some benefit from this approach at times, but it isn't really testing.

In order to know what the system *should* do, we need to have a source of information about the correct behaviour of the system – this is called an 'oracle' or a test oracle. This has nothing to do with databases or companies that make them. It comes from the ancient Greek Oracle at Delphi, who supposedly could predict the future with unerring accuracy. Actually her answers were so vague that people interpreted them in whatever way they wanted – perhaps a bit like requirements specifications!

Once a given input value has been chosen, the tester needs to determine what the expected result of entering that input would be and document it as part of the test case.

Expected results include information displayed on a screen in response to an input, but they also include changes to data and/or states, and any other consequences of the test (e.g. a letter to be printed overnight).

What if we don't decide on the expected results before we run a test? We can still look at what the system produces and would probably notice if something was wildly wrong. However, we would probably not notice small differences in calculations, or results that seemed to look OK (i.e. are plausible). So we would conclude that the test had passed, when in fact the software has not given the correct result. Small differences in one calculation can add up to something very major later on, for example if results are multiplied by a large factor.

Ideally expected results should be predicted before the test is run – then your assessment of whether or not the software did the right thing will be more objective.

For a few applications it may not be possible to predict or know exactly what an expected result should be; we can only do a 'reasonableness check'. In this case we have a 'partial oracle' – we know when something is very wrong, but would probably have to accept something that looked reasonable. An example is when a system has been written to calculate something where it may not be possible to manually produce expected results in a reasonable timescale because the calculations are so complex.

In addition to the expected results, the test case also specifies the environment and other things that must be in place before the test can be run (the preconditions) and any things that should apply after the test completes (the postconditions).

IEEE 829 STANDARD: TEST CASE SPECIFICATION TEMPLATE

Test case specification identifier   Environmental needs

Test items   Special procedural requirements

Input specifications   Intercase dependencies

Output specifications

The test case should also say why it exists – i.e. the objective of the test it is part of or the test conditions that it is exercising (traceability). Test cases can now be prioritized so that the most important test cases are executed first, and low priority test cases are executed later, or even not executed at all. This may reflect the priorities already established for test conditions or the priority may be determined by other factors related to the specific test cases, such as a specific input value that has proved troublesome in the past, the risk associated with the test, or the most sensible sequence of running the tests. Chapter 5 gives more detail of risk-based testing.

Test cases need to be detailed so that we can accurately check the results and know that we have exactly the right response from the system. If tests are to be automated, the testing tool needs to know exactly what to compare the system output to.

4.1.4 Test implementation: specifying test procedures or scripts

The next step is to group the test cases in a sensible way for executing them and to specify the sequential steps that need to be done to run the test. For example, a set of simple tests that cover the breadth of the system may form a regression suite, or all of the tests that explore the working of a given functionality or feature in depth may be grouped to be run together.

Some test cases may need to be run in a particular sequence. For example, a test may create a new customer record, amend that newly created record and then delete it. These tests need to be run in the correct order, or they won't test what they are meant to test.

Test script Commonly used to refer to a test procedure specification, especially an automated one.

The document that describes the steps to be taken in running a set of tests (and specifies the executable order of the tests) is called a test procedure in IEEE 829, and is often also referred to as a **test script**. It could be called a manual test script for tests that are intended to be run manually rather than using a test execution tool. Test script is also used to describe the instructions to a test execution tool. An automation script is written in a programming language that the tool can interpret. (This is an automated test procedure.) See Chapter 6 for more information on this and other types of testing tools.

Test execution schedule A scheme for the execution of test procedures. The test procedures are included in the test execution schedule in their context and in the order in which they are to be executed.

The test procedures, or test scripts, are then formed into a **test execution schedule** that specifies which procedures are to be run first – a kind of superscript. The test schedule would say when a given script should be run and by whom. The schedule could vary depending on newly perceived risks affecting the priority of a script that addresses that risk, for example. The logical and technical dependencies between the scripts would also be taken into account when scheduling the scripts. For example, a regression script may always be the first to be run when a new release of the software arrives, as a smoke test or sanity check.

Returning to our example of the mobile phone company's marketing campaign, we may have some tests to set up customers of different types on the database. It may be sensible to run all of the setup for a group of tests first. So our first test procedure would entail setting up a number of customers, including Jim Green, on the database.

> Test procedure DB15: Set up customers for marketing campaign Y.
>
> Step 1: Open database with write privilege
>
> Step 2: Set up customer Bob Flounders male, 62, Hudsonville, contract
>
> Step 3: Set up customer Jim Green male, 17, Grand Rapids, pay-as-you-go, $8.64
>
> Step 4: ...

We may then have another test procedure to do with the marketing campaign:

> Test procedure MC03: Special offers for low-credit teenagers
>
> Step 1: Get details for Jim Green from database
>
> Step 2: Send text message offering double credit
>
> Step 3: Jim Green requests $20 credit, $40 credited

Writing the test procedure is another opportunity to prioritize the tests, to ensure that the best testing is done in the time available. A good rule of thumb is 'Find the scary stuff first'. However the definition of what is 'scary' depends on the business, system or project. For example, is it worse to raise Bob Founders' credit limit when he is not a good credit risk (he may not pay for the credit he asked for) or to refuse to raise his credit limit when he is a good credit risk (he may go elsewhere for his phone service and we lose the opportunity of lots of income from him).

IEEE 829 STANDARD: TEST PROCEDURE SPECIFICATION TEMPLATE

Test procedure specification identifier

Purpose

Special requirements

Procedure steps

4.2 CATEGORIES OF TEST DESIGN TECHNIQUES

SYLLABUS LEARNING OBJECTIVES FOR 4.2 CATEGORIES OF TEST DESIGN TECHNIQUES (K2)

LO-4.2.1   Recall reasons that both specification-based (black-box) and structure-based (white-box) test design techniques are useful and list the common techniques for each. (K1)

LO-4.2.2   Explain the characteristics, commonalities, and differences between specification-based testing, structure-based testing and experience-based testing. (K2)

In this section we will look at the different types of test design technique, how they are used and how they differ. The three types or categories are distinguished by their primary source: a specification, the structure of the system or component, or a person's experience. All categories are useful and the three are complementary.

Reflecting back on the fundamental test process introduced earlier, it's worth mentioning that there is a fuzzy distinction between test analysis and test design, which is reflected in the Foundation syllabus itself. In section 4.2, the Foundation syllabus says, 'The purpose of a test design technique is to identify test conditions, test cases, and test data'. While identifying test conditions during test design is certainly a common practice, in well-defined test processes, it is more accurate to say, as the Foundation syllabus says in section 4.1, 'During test analysis, the test basis documentation is analyzed in order to determine what to test, i.e. to identify the test conditions'.

In our opinion, the ideal case is that test conditions are identified during analysis, and then used to define test cases and test data during test design. For example, in risk based testing strategies, we identify risk items (which are the test conditions) when performing an analysis of the risks to product quality. Those risk items, along with their corresponding levels of risk, are subsequently used to design the test cases and implement the test data. Risk based testing will be discussed in Chapter 5.

In this section, look for the definitions of the glossary terms **experience-based test design technique,** and **structure-based test design technique**.

4.2.1 Introduction

There are many different types of software testing technique, each with its own strengths and weaknesses. Each individual technique is good at finding particular types of defect and relatively poor at finding other types. For example, a technique that explores the upper and lower limits of a single input range is more likely to find boundary value defects than defects associated with combinations of inputs. Similarly, testing performed at different stages in the software development life cycle will find different types of defects; component testing is more likely to find coding logic defects than system design defects.

Each testing technique falls into one of a number of different categories. Broadly speaking there are two main categories, static and dynamic. Static techniques were discussed in Chapter 3. Dynamic techniques are subdivided into three more categories: specification-based (black-box, also known as behavioural techniques), structure-based (white-box or structural techniques) and experience-based. Specification-based techniques include both functional and non-functional techniques (i.e. quality characteristics). The techniques covered in the syllabus are summarized in Figure 4.1.

4.2.2 Static testing techniques

As we saw in Chapter 3, static testing techniques do not execute the code being examined and are generally used before any tests are executed on the software. They could be called non-execution techniques. Most static testing techniques can be used to 'test' any form of document including source code, design documents and models, functional specifications and requirement specifications. However, 'static analysis' is a tool-supported type of static testing that concentrates on testing formal languages and so is most often used to statically test source code.

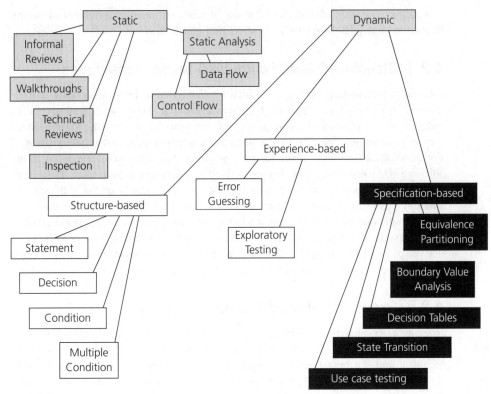

FIGURE 4.1   Testing techniques

4.2.3 Specification-based (black-box) testing techniques

The first of the dynamic testing techniques we will look at are the specification-based testing techniques. These are also known as 'black-box' or input/output-driven testing techniques because they view the software as a black-box with inputs and outputs, but they have no knowledge of how the system or component is structured inside the box. In essence, the tester is concentrating on what the software does, not how it does it.

All specification-based techniques have the common characteristic that they are based on a model (formal or informal) of some aspect of the specification, which enables test cases to be derived from them in a systematic way.

Notice that the definition mentions both functional and non-functional testing. Functional testing is concerned with what the system does, its features or functions. Non-functional testing is concerned with examining how well the system does something, rather than what it does. Non-functional aspects (also known as quality characteristics or quality attributes) include performance, usability, portability, maintainability, etc. Techniques to test these non-functional aspects are less procedural and less formalized than those of other categories as the actual tests are more dependent on the type of system, what it does and the resources available for the tests.

Non-functional testing is part of the Syllabus and is also covered in Chapter 2. There are techniques for deriving non-functional tests [Gilb 1988], [Testing Standards], but they are not covered at the Foundation level.

Categorizing tests into black and white-box is mentioned in a number of testing books, including [Beizer 1990], [Black 2007] and [Copeland 2003].

4.2.4 Structure-based (white-box) testing techniques

Structure-based testing techniques (which are also dynamic rather than static) use the internal structure of the software to derive test cases. They are commonly called 'white-box' or 'glass-box' techniques (implying you can see into the system) since they require knowledge of how the software is implemented, that is, how it works. For example, a structural technique may be concerned with exercising loops in the software. Different test cases may be derived to exercise the loop once, twice, and many times. This may be done regardless of the functionality of the software. All structure-based techniques have the common characteristic that they are based on how the software under test is constructed or designed. This structural information is used to assess which parts of the software have been exercised by a set of tests (often derived by other techniques). Additional test cases can then be derived in a systematic way to cover the parts of the structure that have not been touched by any test before.

4.2.5 Experience-based testing techniques

Experience-based test design technique
Procedure to derive and/ or select test cases based on the tester's experience, knowledge and intuition.

In **experience-based techniques**, people's knowledge, skills and background are a prime contributor to the test conditions and test cases. The experience of both technical and business people is important, as they bring different perspectives to the test analysis and design process. Due to previous experience with similar systems, they may have insights into what could go wrong, which is very useful for testing. While previous versions of the Foundation syllabus classified experience-based techniques as black-box types of test design, the Foundation syllabus now implicitly acknowledges the common practice of using both structural and behavioural insights to design experience-based tests.

All experience-based techniques have the common characteristic that they are based on human knowledge and experience, both of the system itself (including the knowledge of users and stakeholders) and of likely defects. Test cases are therefore derived in a less systematic way, but may be more effective.

4.2.6 Where to apply the different categories of techniques

Specification-based techniques are appropriate at all levels of testing (component testing through to acceptance testing) where a specification exists. When performing system or acceptance testing, the requirements specification or functional specification may form the basis of the tests. When performing component or integration testing, a design document or low-level specification forms the basis of the tests.

Structure-based techniques can also be used at all levels of testing. Developers use structure-based techniques in component testing and component integration testing, especially where there is good tool support for code coverage. Structure-based techniques are also used in system and acceptance testing, but the structures are different. For example, the coverage of menu options or major business transactions could be the structural element in system or acceptance testing.

Experience-based techniques are used to complement specification-based and structure-based techniques, and are also used when there is no specification, or if the specification is inadequate or out of date. This may be the only type of technique used for low-risk systems, but this approach may be particularly useful under extreme time pressure – in fact this is one of the factors leading to exploratory testing.

4.3 SPECIFICATION-BASED OR BLACK-BOX TECHNIQUES

> **SYLLABUS LEARNING OBJECTIVES FOR 4.3 SPECIFICATION-BASED OR BLACK-BOX TECHNIQUES (K3)**
>
> **LO-4.3.1**   Write test cases from given software models using equivalence partitioning, boundary value analysis, decision tables and state transition diagrams/tables. (K3)
>
> **LO-4.3.2**   Explain the main purpose of each of the four testing techniques, what level and type of testing could use the technique, and how coverage may be measured. (K2)
>
> **LO-4.3.3**   Explain the concept of use case testing and its benefits. (K2)

In this section we will look in detail at four specification-based or black-box techniques. These four techniques are K3 in the Syllabus – this means that you need to be able to use these techniques to design test cases. We will also cover briefly (not at K3 level) the specification-based technique of use case testing. In Section 4.4, we will look at the K3 structure-based techniques.

In this section, look for the definitions of the glossary terms **boundary value, boundary value analysis, decision table, decision table testing, equivalence partition, equivalence partitioning, state diagram, state table, state transition testing,** and **use case testing**.

The four specification-based techniques we will cover in detail are:

- equivalence partitioning;
- boundary value analysis;
- decision tables;
- state transition testing.

Note that we will discuss the first two together, because they are closely related.

4.3.1 Equivalence partitioning and boundary value analysis

Equivalence partitioning

Equivalence partitioning (EP) is a good all-round specification-based black-box technique. It can be applied at any level of testing and is often a good technique to use first. It is a common sense approach to testing, so much so that most testers practise it informally even though they may not realize it. However, while it is better to use the technique informally than not at all, it is much better to use the technique in a formal way to attain the full benefits that it can deliver. This technique will be found in most testing books, including [Myers 1979] and [Copeland 2003].

The idea behind the technique is to divide (i.e. to partition) a set of test conditions into groups or sets that can be considered the same (i.e. the system should handle

> **Equivalence partitioning** A black box test design technique in which test cases are designed to execute representatives from equivalence partitions. In principle test cases are designed to cover each partition at least once.

them equivalently), hence 'equivalence partitioning'. **Equivalence partitions** are also known as equivalence classes – the two terms mean exactly the same thing.

The equivalence-partitioning technique then requires that we need test only one condition from each partition. This is because we are assuming that all the conditions in one partition will be treated in the same way by the software. If one condition in a partition works, we assume all of the conditions in that partition will work, and so there is little point in testing any of these others. Conversely, if one of the conditions in a partition does not work, then we assume that none of the conditions in that partition will work so again there is little point in testing any more in that partition. Of course these are simplifying assumptions that may not always be right but if we write them down, at least it gives other people the chance to challenge the assumptions we have made and hopefully help to identify better partitions. If you have time, you may want to try more than one value from a partition, especially if you want to confirm a selection of typical user inputs.

For example, a savings account in a bank earns a different rate of interest depending on the balance in the account. In order to test the software that calculates the interest due, we can identify the ranges of balance values that earn the different rates of interest. For example, if a balance in the range $0 up to $100 has a 3% interest rate, a balance over $100 and up to $1000 has a 5% interest rate, and balances of $1000 and over have a 7% interest rate, we would initially identify three valid equivalence partitions and one invalid partition as shown below.

Invalid partition	Valid (for 3% interest)	Valid (for 5%)	Valid (for 7%)
–$0.01	$0.00 $100.00	$100.01 $999.99	$1000.00

Notice that we have identified four partitions here, even though the specification only mentions three. This illustrates a very important task of the tester – not only do we test what is in our specification, but we also think about things that haven't been specified. In this case we have thought of the situation where the balance is less than zero. We haven't (yet) identified an invalid partition on the right, but this would also be a good thing to consider. In order to identify where the 7% partition ends, we would need to know what the maximum balance is for this account (which may not be easy to find out). In our example we have left this open for the time being. Note that non-numeric input is also an invalid partition (e.g. the letter 'a') but we discuss only the numeric partitions for now.

We have made an assumption here about what the smallest difference is between two values. We have assumed two decimal places, i.e. $100.00, but we could have assumed zero decimal places (i.e. $100) or more than two decimal places (e.g. $100.0000) In any case it is a good idea to state your assumptions – then other people can see them and let you know if they are correct or not.

We have also made an assumption about exactly which amount starts the new interest rate: a penny over to go into the 5% interest rate, but exactly on the $1000.00 to go into the 5% rate. By making our assumptions explicit, by documenting them in this technique, we may highlight any differences in understanding what the specification means.

When designing the test cases for this software we would ensure that the three valid equivalence partitions are each covered once, and we would also test the invalid partition at least once. So for example, we might choose to calculate the interest on balances of –$10.00, $50.00, $260.00 and $1348.00. If we hadn't specifically identified these partitions, it is possible that at least one of them could have been missed at the expense of testing another one several times over. Note that we could also apply equivalence partitioning to outputs as well. In this case we have three interest rates: 3%, 5% and 7%, plus the error message for the invalid partition (or partitions). In this example, the output partitions line up exactly with the input partitions.

How would someone test this without thinking about the partitions? A naïve tester (let's call him Robbie) might have thought that a good set of tests would be to test every $50. That would give the following tests: $50.00, $100.00, $150.00, $200.00, $250.00, ... say up to $800.00 (then Robbie would have got tired of it and thought that enough tests had been carried out). But look at what Robbie has tested: only two out of four partitions! So if the system does not correctly handle a negative balance or a balance of $1000 or more, he would not have found these defects – so the naïve approach is less effective than equivalence partitioning. At the same time, Robbie has four times more tests (16 tests versus our four tests using equivalence partitions), so he is also much less efficient! This is why we say that using techniques such as this makes testing both more effective and more efficient.

Note that when we say a partition is 'invalid', it doesn't mean that it represents a value that cannot be entered by a user or a value that the user isn't supposed to enter. It just means that it is not one of the expected inputs for this particular field. The software should correctly handle values from the invalid partition, by replying with an error message such as 'Balance must be at least $0.00'.

Note also that the invalid partition may be invalid only in the context of crediting interest payments. An account that is overdrawn will require some different action.

Boundary value analysis

Boundary value analysis (BVA) is based on testing at the boundaries between partitions. It is essentially an enhancement or extension of equivalence partitioning, and can also be used to extend other black-box (and white-box) test design techniques. If you have ever done 'range checking', you were probably using the boundary value analysis technique, even if you weren't aware of it. Note that we have both valid boundaries (in the valid partitions) and invalid boundaries (in the invalid partitions).

Boundary value analysis A black box test design technique in which test cases are designed based on boundary values.

As an example, consider a printer that has an input option of the number of copies to be made, from 1 to 99.

Invalid	Valid	Invalid
0 | 1		99 | 100

To apply boundary value analysis, we will take the minimum and maximum **(boundary) values** from the valid partition (1 and 99 in this case) together with the first or last value respectively in each of the invalid partitions adjacent to the valid partition (0 and 100 in this case). In this example we would have three equivalence partitioning tests (one from each of the three partitions) and four boundary value tests.

Consider the bank system described in the section about equivalence partitioning.

Boundary value An input value or output value which is on the edge of an equivalence partition or at the smallest incremental distance on either side of an edge, for example the minimum or maximum value of a range.

Invalid partition	Valid (for 3% interest)	Valid (for 5%)	Valid (for 7%)
–$0.01 | $0.00	$100.00 | $100.01	$999.99 | $1000.00	

Because the boundary values are defined as those values on the edge of a partition, we have identified the following boundary values: –$0.01 (an invalid boundary value because it is at the edge of an invalid partition), $0.00, $100.00, $100.01, $999.99 and $1000.00, all valid boundary values.

So by applying boundary value analysis we will have six tests for boundary values. Compare what our naïve tester Robbie had done: he did actually hit one of the boundary values ($100) though it was more by accident than design. So in addition to testing only half of the partitions, Robbie has only tested one-sixth of the boundaries (so he will be less effective at finding any boundary defects). If we consider all of our tests for both equivalence partitioning and boundary value analysis, the techniques give us a total of nine tests, compared to the 16 that Robbie had, so we are still considerably more efficient as well as being over three times more effective (testing four partitions and six boundaries, so 10 conditions in total compared to three).

Note that in the bank interest example, we have valid partitions next to other valid partitions. If we were to consider an invalid boundary for the 3% interest rate, we have –$0.01, but what about the value just above $100.00? The value of $100.01 is not an *invalid* boundary; it is actually a *valid* boundary because it falls into a valid partition. So the partition for 5%, for example, has no invalid boundary values associated with partitions next to it.

A good way to represent the valid and invalid partitions and boundaries is in a table such as Table 4.1:

TABLE 4.1 Equivalence partitions and boundaries

Test conditions	Valid partitions	Invalid partitions	Valid boundaries	Invalid boundaries
Balance in account	$0.00 – $100.00	< $0.00	$0.00	– $0.01
	$100.01 – $999.99	> $Max	$100.00	$Max+ 0.01
	$1000.00 – $Max	non-integer (if balance is an input field)	$100.01	
			$999.99	
			$1000.00	
			$Max	
Interest rates	3%	Any other value	Not applicable	Not applicable
	5%	Non-integer		
	7%	No interest calculated		

By showing the values in the table, we can see that no maximum has been specified for the 7% interest rate. We would now want to know what the maximum value is for an account balance, so that we can test that boundary. This is called an 'open boundary', because one of the sides of the partition is left open, i.e. not defined. But that doesn't mean we can ignore it – we should still try to test it, but how? We have called it '$Max' to remind ourselves to investigate this.

Open boundaries are more difficult to test, but there are ways to approach them. Actually the best solution to the problem is to find out what the boundary should be specified as! One approach is to go back to the specification to see if a maximum has been stated somewhere else for a balance amount. If so, then we know what our boundary value is. Another approach might be to investigate other related areas of the system. For example, the field that holds the account balance figure may be only six figures plus two decimal figures. This would give a maximum account balance of $999 999.99 so we could use that as our maximum boundary value. If we really cannot find anything about what this boundary should be, then we probably need to use an intuitive or experience-based approach to probe various large values trying to make it fail.

We could also try to find out about the lower open boundary – what is the lowest negative balance? Although we have omitted this from our example, setting it out in the table shows that we have omitted it, so helps us be more thorough if we wanted to be.

Representing the partitions and boundaries in a table such as this also makes it easier to see whether or not you have tested each one (if that is your objective).

Extending equivalence partitioning and boundary value analysis

So far, by using EP and BVA we have identified conditions that could be tested, i.e. partitions and boundary values. The techniques are used to identify test conditions, which could be at a fairly high level (e.g. 'low-interest account') or at a detailed level (e.g. 'value of $100.00'). We have been looking at applying these techniques to ranges of numbers. However, we can also apply the techniques to other things.

For example, if you are booking a flight, you have a choice of Economy/Coach, Premium Economy, Business or First Class tickets. Each of these is an equivalence partition in its own right and should be tested, but it doesn't make sense to talk about boundaries for this type of partition, which is a collection of valid things. The invalid partition would be an attempt to type in any other type of flight class (e.g. 'Staff'). If this field is implemented using a drop-down list, then it should not be possible to type anything else in, but it is still a good test to try at least once in some drop-down field. When you are analyzing the test basis (e.g. a requirements specification), equivalence partitioning can help to identify where a drop-down list would be appropriate.

When trying to identify a defect, you might try several values in a partition. If this results in different behaviour where you expected it to be the same, then there may be two (or more) partitions where you initially thought there was only one.

We can apply equivalence partitioning and boundary value analysis to all levels of testing. The examples here were at a fairly detailed level probably most appropriate in component testing or in the detailed testing of a single screen.

At a system level, for example, we may have three basic configurations which our users can choose from when setting up their systems, with a number of options for each configuration. The basic configurations could be system administrator, manager and customer liaison. These represent three equivalence partitions that could be tested. We could have serious problems if we forget to test the configuration for the system administrator, for example.

We can also apply equivalence partitioning and boundary value analysis more than once to the same specification item. For example, if an internal telephone system for a company with 200 telephones has 3-digit extension numbers from 100 to 699, we can identify the following partitions and boundaries:

- digits (characters 0 to 9) with the invalid partition containing non-digits;

- number of digits, 3 (so invalid boundary values of 2 digits and 4 digits);

- range of extension numbers, 100 to 699 (so invalid boundary values of 099 and 700);

- extensions that are in use and those that are not (two valid partitions, no boundaries);

- the lowest and highest extension numbers that are in use could also be used as boundary values.

One test case could test more than one of these partitions/boundaries. For example, Extension 409 which is in use would test four valid partitions: digits, the number of digits, the valid range, and the 'in use' partition. It also tests the boundary values for digits, 0 and 9.

How many test cases would we need to test all of these partitions and boundaries, both valid and invalid? We would need a non-digit, a 2-digit and 4-digit number, the values of 99, 100, 699 and 700, one extension that is not in use, and possibly the lowest and highest extensions in use. This is 10 or 11 test cases – the exact number would depend on what we could combine in one test case.

Using equivalence partitioning and boundary value analysis helps us to identify tests that are most likely to find defects, and to use fewer test cases to find them. This is because the contents of a partition are representative of all of the possible values. Rather than test all 10 individual digits, we test one in the middle (e.g. 4) and the two edges (0 and 9). Instead of testing every possible non-digit character, one can represent all of them.

As we mentioned earlier, we can also apply these techniques to output partitions. Consider the following extension to our bank interest rate example. Suppose that a customer with more than one account can have an extra 1% interest on this account if they have at least $1000 in it. Now we have two possible output values (7% interest and 8% interest) for the same account balance, so we have identified another test condition (8% interest rate). (We may also have identified that same output condition by looking at customers with more than one account, which is a partition of types of customer.)

Equivalence partitioning can be applied to different types of input as well. Our examples have concentrated on inputs that would be typed in by a (human) user when using the system. However, systems receive input data from other sources as well, such as from other systems via some interface – this is also a good place to look for partitions (and boundaries). For example, the value of an interface parameter may fall into valid and invalid equivalence partitions. This type of defect is often difficult to find in testing once the interfaces have been joined together, so is particularly useful to apply in integration testing (either component integration or system integration).

Boundary value analysis can be applied to the whole of a string of characters (e.g. a name or address). The number of characters in the string is a partition, e.g. between 1 and 30 characters is the valid partition with valid boundaries of 1 and 30. The invalid boundaries would be 0 characters (null, just hit the Return key) and 31 characters. Both of these should produce an error message.

Partitions can also be identified when setting up test data. If there are different types of record, your testing will be more representative if you include a data record of each type. The size of a record is also a partition with boundaries, so we could include maximum and minimum size records in the test database.

If you have some inside knowledge about how the data is physically organized, you may be able to identify some hidden boundaries. For example, if an overflow storage block is used when more than 255 characters are entered into a field, the boundary value tests would include 255 and 256 characters in that field. This may be verging on white-box testing, since we have some knowledge of how the data is structured, but it doesn't matter how we classify things as long as our testing is effective at finding defects. Don't get hung up on a fine distinction – just do whatever testing makes sense, based on what you know. An old Chinese proverb says, 'It doesn't matter whether the cat is white or black; all that matters is that the cat catches mice'.

With boundary value analysis, we think of the boundary as a dividing line between two things. Hence we have a value on each side of the boundary (but the boundary itself is not a value).

Invalid	Valid	Invalid
0	1 99	100

Looking at the values for our printer example, 0 is in an invalid partition, 1 and 99 are in the valid partition and 100 is in the other invalid partition. So the boundary is between the values of 0 and 1, and between the values of 99 and 100. There is a school of thought that regards an actual value as a boundary value. By tradition, these are the values in the valid partition (i.e. the values specified). This approach then requires three values for every boundary, so you would have 0, 1 and 2 for the left boundary, and 98, 99 and 100 for the right boundary in this example. The boundary values are said to be 'on and either side of the boundary' and the value that is 'on' the boundary is generally taken to be in the valid partition.

Note that Beizer talks about domain testing, a generalization of equivalence partitioning, with three-value boundaries. He makes a distinction between open and closed boundaries, where a closed boundary is one where the point is included in the domain. So the convention is for the valid partition to have closed boundaries. You may be pleased to know that you don't have to know this for the exam! British Standard 7925–2 Standard for Software Component Testing also defines a three-value approach to boundary value analysis.

So which approach is best? If you use the two-value approach together with equivalence partitioning, you are equally effective and slightly more efficient than the three-value approach. (We won't go into the details here but this can be demonstrated.) In this book we will use the two-value approach. In the exam, you may have a question based on either the two-value or the three-value approach, but it should be clear what the correct choice is in either case.

Designing test cases

Having identified the conditions that you wish to test, in this case by using equivalence partitioning and boundary value analysis, the next step is to design the test cases. The more test conditions that can be covered in a single test case, the fewer test cases will be needed in order to cover all the conditions. This is usually the best approach to take for positive tests and for tests that you are reasonably confident will pass. However if a test fails, then we need to find out why it failed – which test condition was handled incorrectly? We need to get a good balance between covering too many and too few test conditions in our tests.

Let's look at how one test case can cover one or more test conditions. Using the bank balance example, our first test could be of a new customer with a balance of $500. This would cover a balance in the partition from $100.01 to $999.99 and an output partition of a 5% interest rate. We would also be covering other partitions that we haven't discussed yet, for example a valid customer, a new customer, a customer with only one account, etc. All of the partitions covered in this test are valid partitions.

When we come to test invalid partitions, the safest option is probably to try to cover only one invalid test condition per test case. This is because programs may stop processing input as soon as they encounter the first problem. So if you have an invalid customer name, invalid address, and invalid balance, you may get an error message saying 'invalid input' and you don't know whether the test has detected only one invalid input or all of them. (This is also why specific error messages are much better than general ones!)

However, if it is known that the software under test is required to process all input regardless of its validity, then it is sensible to continue as before and design test cases that cover as many invalid conditions in one go as possible. For example, if every invalid field in a form has some red text above or below the field saying that this field is invalid and why, then you know that each field has been checked, so you have tested all of the error processing in one test case. In either case, there should be separate test cases covering valid and invalid conditions.

To cover the boundary test cases, it may be possible to combine all of the minimum valid boundaries for a group of fields into one test case and also the maximum boundary values. The invalid boundaries could be tested together if the validation is done on every field; otherwise they should be tested separately, as with the invalid partitions.

Why do both equivalence partitioning and boundary value analysis?

Technically, because every boundary is in some partition, if you did only boundary value analysis you would also have tested every equivalence partition. However, this approach may cause problems if that value fails – was it only the boundary value that failed or did the whole partition fail? Also by testing only boundaries we would probably not give the users much confidence as we are using extreme values rather than normal values. The boundaries may be more difficult (and therefore more costly) to set up as well.

For example, in the printer copies example described earlier we identified the following boundary values:

Invalid	Valid	Invalid
0	1 99	100

Suppose we test only the valid boundary values 1 and 99 and nothing in between. If both tests pass, this seems to indicate that all the values in between should also work. However, suppose that one page prints correctly, but 99 pages do not. Now we don't know whether any set of more than one page works, so the first thing we would do would be to test for say 10 pages, i.e. a value from the equivalence partition.

We recommend that you test the partitions separately from boundaries – this means choosing partition values that are NOT boundary values.

However, if you use the three-value boundary value approach, then you would have valid boundary values of 1, 2, 98 and 99, so having a separate equivalence value in addition to the extra two boundary values would not give much additional benefit. But notice that one equivalence value, e.g. 10, replaces both of the extra two boundary values (2 and 98). This is why equivalence partitioning with two-value boundary value analysis is more efficient than three-value boundary value analysis.

Which partitions and boundaries you decide to exercise (you don't need to test them all), and which ones you decide to test first, depends on your test objectives. If your goal is the most thorough approach, then follow the procedure of testing valid partitions first, then invalid partitions, then valid boundaries and finally invalid boundaries. However if you are under time pressure and cannot test everything (and who isn't?), then your test objectives will help you decide what to test. If you are after user confidence of typical transactions with a minimum number of tests, you may do valid partitions only. If you want to find as many defects as possible as quickly as possible, you may start with boundary values, both valid and invalid. If you want confidence that the system will handle bad inputs correctly, you may do mainly invalid partitions and boundaries. Your previous experience of types of defects found can help you find similar defects; for example if there are typically a number of boundary defects, then you would start by testing boundaries.

Equivalence partitioning and boundary value analysis are described in most testing books, including [Myers 1979] and [Copeland 2003]. Examples of types of equivalence classes to look out for are given in [Kaner *et al.* 1993] Equivalence partitioning and boundary value analysis are described in [BS7925-2], including designing tests and measuring coverage.

4.3.2 Decision table testing

Why use decision tables?

The techniques of equivalence partitioning and boundary value analysis are often applied to specific situations or inputs. However, if different combinations of inputs result in different actions being taken, this can be more difficult to show using equivalence partitioning and boundary value analysis, which tend to be more focused on the user interface. The other two specification-based techniques, **decision table testing** and state transition testing are more focused on business logic or business rules.

A **decision table** is a good way to deal with combinations of things (e.g. inputs). This technique is sometimes also referred to as a 'cause–effect' table. The reason for this is that there is an associated logic diagramming technique called 'cause–effect graphing' which was sometimes used to help derive the decision table (Myers describes this as a combinatorial logic network [Myers 1979]). However, most people find it more useful just to use the table described in [Copeland 2003].

If you begin using decision tables to explore what the business rules are that should be tested, you may find that the analysts and developers find the tables very helpful and want to begin using them too. Do encourage this, as it will make your job easier in the future. Decision tables provide a systematic way of stating

Decision table testing A black box test design technique in which test cases are designed to execute the combinations of inputs and/or stimuli (causes) shown in a decision table.

Decision table A table showing combinations of inputs and/or stimuli (causes) with their associated outputs and/or actions (effects), which can be used to design test cases.

complex business rules, which is useful for developers as well as for testers. Decision tables can be used in test design whether or not they are used in specifications, as they help testers explore the effects of combinations of different inputs and other software states that must correctly implement business rules. Helping the developers do a better job can also lead to better relationships with them.

Testing combinations can be a challenge, as the number of combinations can often be huge. Testing all combinations may be impractical if not impossible. We have to be satisfied with testing just a small subset of combinations but making the choice of which combinations to test and which to leave out is not trivial. If you do not have a systematic way of selecting combinations, an arbitrary subset will be used and this may well result in an ineffective test effort.

Decision tables aid the systematic selection of effective test cases and can have the beneficial side-effect of finding problems and ambiguities in the specification. It is a technique that works well in conjunction with equivalence partitioning. The combination of conditions explored may be combinations of equivalence partitions.

In addition to decision tables, there are other techniques that deal with testing combinations of things: pairwise testing and orthogonal arrays. These are described in [Copeland 2003]. Other sources of techniques are [Pol *et al.* 2001, Black 2007]. Decision tables and cause-effect graphing are described in [BS7925-2], including designing tests and measuring coverage.

Using decision tables for test design

The first task is to identify a suitable function or subsystem that has a behaviour which reacts according to a combination of inputs or events. The behaviour of interest must not be too extensive (i.e. should not contain too many inputs) otherwise the number of combinations will become cumbersome and difficult to manage. It is better to deal with large numbers of conditions by dividing them into subsets and dealing with the subsets one at a time.

Once you have identified the aspects that need to be combined, then you put them into a table listing all the combinations of True and False for each of the aspects. Take an example of a loan application, where you can enter the amount of the monthly repayment or the number of years you want to take to pay it back (the term of the loan). If you enter both, the system will make a compromise between the two if they conflict. The two conditions are the loan amount and the term, so we put them in a table (see Table 4.2).

TABLE 4.2 Empty decision table

Conditions	Rule 1	Rule 2	Rule 3	Rule 4
Repayment amount has been entered				
Term of loan has been entered				

TABLE 4.3 Decision table with input combinations

Conditions	Rule 1	Rule 2	Rule 3	Rule 4
Repayment amount has been entered	T	T	F	F
Term of loan has been entered	T	F	T	F

Next we will identify all of the combinations of True and False (see Table 4.3). With two conditions, each of which can be True or False, we will have four combinations (two to the power of the number of things to be combined). Note that if we have three things to combine, we will have eight combinations, with four things, there are 16, etc. This is why it is good to tackle small sets of combinations at a time. In order to keep track of which combinations we have, we will alternate True and False on the bottom row, put two Trues and then two Falses on the row above the bottom row, etc., so the top row will have all Trues and then all Falses (and this principle applies to all such tables).

The next step (at least for this example) is to identify the correct outcome for each combination (see Table 4.4). In this example, we can enter one or both of the two fields. Each combination is sometimes referred to as a rule.

At this point, we may realize that we hadn't thought about what happens if the customer doesn't enter anything in either of the two fields. The table has highlighted a combination that was not mentioned in the specification for this example. We could assume that this combination should result in an error message, so we need to add another action (see Table 4.5). This highlights the strength of this technique to discover omissions and ambiguities in specifications. It is not unusual for some combinations to be omitted from specifications; therefore this is also a valuable technique to use when reviewing the test basis.

TABLE 4.4 Decision table with combinations and outcomes

Conditions	Rule 1	Rule 2	Rule 3	Rule 4
Repayment amount has been entered	T	T	F	F
Term of loan has been entered	T	F	T	F
Actions/Outcomes				
Process loan amount	Y	Y		
Process term	Y		Y	

TABLE 4.5 Decision table with additional outcomes

Conditions	Rule 1	Rule 2	Rule 3	Rule 4
Repayment amount has been entered	T	T	F	F
Term of loan has been entered	T	F	T	F
Actions/Outcomes				
Process loan amount	Y	Y		
Process term	Y		Y	
Error message				Y

Suppose we change our example slightly, so that the customer is not allowed to enter both repayment and term. Now our table will change, because there should also be an error message if both are entered, so it will look like Table 4.6.

You might notice now that there is only one 'Yes' in each column, i.e. our actions are mutually exclusive – only one action occurs for each combination of conditions. We could represent this in a different way by listing the actions in the cell of one row, as shown in Table 4.7. Note that if more than one action results from any of the combinations, then it would be better to show them as separate rows rather than combining them into one row.

The final step of this technique is to write test cases to exercise each of the four rules in our table.

TABLE 4.6 Decision table with changed outcomes

Conditions	Rule 1	Rule 2	Rule 3	Rule 4
Repayment amount has been entered	T	T	F	F
Term of loan has been entered	T	F	T	F
Actions/Outcomes				
Process loan amount		Y		
Process term			Y	
Error message	Y			Y

TABLE 4.7 Decision table with outcomes in one row

Conditions	Rule 1	Rule 2	Rule 3	Rule 4
Repayment amount has been entered	T	T	F	F
Term of loan has been entered	T	F	T	F
Actions/Outcomes				
Result	Error message	Process loan amount	Process term	Error message
			Y	
	Y			Y

In this example we started by identifying the input conditions and then identifying the outcomes. However in practice it might work the other way around – we can see that there are a number of different outcomes, and have to work back to understand what combination of input conditions actually drive those outcomes. The technique works just as well doing it in this way, and may well be an iterative approach as you discover more about the rules that drive the system.

Credit card worked example

Let's look at another example. If you are a new customer opening a credit card account, you will get a 15% discount on all your purchases today. If you are an existing customer and you hold a loyalty card, you get a 10% discount. If you have a coupon, you can get 20% off today (but it can't be used with the 'new customer' discount). Discount amounts are added, if applicable. This is shown in Table 4.8.

TABLE 4.8 Decision table for credit card example

Conditions	Rule 1	Rule 2	Rule 3	Rule 4	Rule 5	Rule 6	Rule 7	Rule 8
New customer (15%)	T	T	T	T	F	F	F	F
Loyalty card (10%)	T	T	F	F	T	T	F	F
Coupon (20%)	T	F	T	F	T	F	T	F
Actions								
Discount (%)	X	X	20	15	30	10	20	0

In Table 4.8, the conditions and actions are listed in the left hand column. All the other columns in the decision table each represent a separate rule, one for each combination of conditions. We may choose to test each rule/combination and if there are only a few this will usually be the case. However, if the number of rules/ combinations is large we are more likely to sample them by selecting a rich subset for testing.

Note that we have put X for the discount for two of the columns (Rules 1 and 2) – this means that this combination should not occur. You cannot be both a new customer and already hold a loyalty card! There should be an error message stating this, but even if we don't know what that message should be, it will still make a good test.

We have made an assumption in Rule 3. Since the coupon has a greater discount than the new customer discount, we assume that the customer will choose 20% rather than 15%. We cannot add them, since the coupon cannot be used with the 'new customer' discount. The 20% action is an assumption on our part, and we should check that this assumption (and any other assumptions that we make) is correct, by asking the person who wrote the specification or the users.

For Rule 5, however, we can add the discounts, since both the coupon and the loyalty card discount should apply (at least that's our assumption).

Rules 4, 6 and 7 have only one type of discount and Rule 8 has no discount, so 0%.

If we are applying this technique thoroughly, we would have one test for each column or rule of our decision table. The advantage of doing this is that we may test a combination of things that otherwise we might not have tested and that could find a defect.

However, if we have a lot of combinations, it may not be possible or sensible to test every combination. If we are time-constrained, we may not have time to test all combinations. Don't just assume that all combinations need to be tested; it is better to prioritize and test the most important combinations. Having the full table enables us to see which combinations we decided to test and which not to test this time.

There may also be many different actions as a result of the combinations of conditions. In the example above we just had one: the discount to be applied. The decision table shows which actions apply to each combination of conditions.

In the example above all the conditions are binary, i.e. they have only two possible values: True or False (or, if you prefer Yes or No). Often it is the case that conditions are more complex, having potentially many possible values. Where this is the case the number of combinations is likely to be very large, so the combinations may only be sampled rather than exercising all of them.

4.3.3 State transition testing

State transition testing is used where some aspect of the system can be described in what is called a 'finite state machine'. This simply means that the system can be in a (finite) number of different states, and the transitions from one state to another are determined by the rules of the 'machine'. This is the model on which the system and the tests are based. Any system where you get a different output for the same input, depending on what has happened before, is a finite state system. A finite state system is often shown as a **state diagram** (see Figure 4.2).

For example, if you request to withdraw $100 from a bank ATM, you may be given cash. Later you may make exactly the same request but be refused the money (because your balance is insufficient). This later refusal is because the state of your bank account has changed from having sufficient funds to cover the withdrawal to

State transition testing A black box test design technique in which test cases are designed to execute valid and invalid state transitions.

State diagram A diagram that depicts the states that a component or system can assume, and shows the events or circumstances that cause and/or result from a change from one state to another.

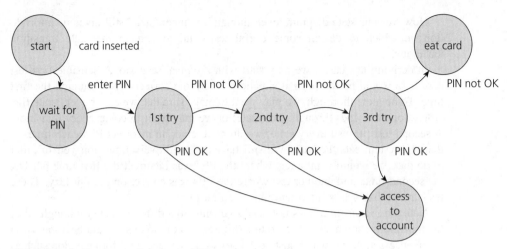

FIGURE 4.2 State diagram for PIN entry

having insufficient funds. The transaction that caused your account to change its state was probably the earlier withdrawal. A state diagram can represent a model from the point of view of the system, the account or the customer.

Another example is a word processor. If a document is open, you are able to close it. If no document is open, then 'Close' is not available. After you choose 'Close' once, you cannot choose it again for the same document unless you open that document. A document thus has two states: open and closed.

A state transition model has four basic parts:

- the states that the software may occupy (open/closed or funded/insufficient funds);
- the transitions from one state to another (not all transitions are allowed);
- the events that cause a transition (closing a file or withdrawing money);
- the actions that result from a transition (an error message or being given your cash).

Note that in any given state, one event can cause only one action, but that the same event – from a different state – may cause a different action and a different end state.

We will look first at test cases that execute valid state transitions.

Figure 4.2 shows an example of entering a Personal Identity Number (PIN) to a bank account. The states are shown as circles, the transitions as lines with arrows and the events as the text near the transitions. (We have not shown the actions explicitly on this diagram, but they would be a message to the customer saying things such as 'Please enter your PIN'.)

The state diagram shows seven states but only four possible events (Card inserted, Enter PIN, PIN OK and PIN not OK). We have not specified all of the possible transitions here – there would also be a time-out from 'wait for PIN' and from the three tries which would go back to the start state after the time had elapsed and would probably eject the card. There would also be a transition from the 'eat card' state back to the start state. We have not specified all the possible events either – there would be a 'cancel' option from 'wait for PIN' and from the three tries, which would also go back to the start state and eject the card. The 'access account' state would be the beginning of another state diagram showing the valid transactions that could now be performed on the account.

However this state diagram, even though it is incomplete, still gives us information on which to design some useful tests and to explain the state transition technique.

In deriving test cases, we may start with a typical scenario. A sensible first test case here would be the normal situation, where the correct PIN is entered the first time. To be more thorough, we may want to make sure that we cover every state (i.e. at least one test goes through each state) or we may want to cover every transition. A second test (to visit every state) would be to enter an incorrect PIN each time, so that the system eats the card. We still haven't tested every transition yet. In order to do that, we would want a test where the PIN was incorrect the first time but OK the second time, and another test where the PIN was correct on the third try. These tests are probably less important than the first two.

Note that a transition does not need to change to a different state (although all of the transitions shown above do go to a different state). So there could be a transition from 'access account' which just goes back to 'access account' for an action such as 'request balance'.

Test conditions can be derived from the state graph in various ways. Each state can be noted as a test condition, as can each transition. In the Syllabus, we need to be able to identify the coverage of a set of tests in terms of transitions.

Going beyond the level expected in the Syllabus, we can also consider transition pairs and triples and so on. Coverage of all individual transitions is also known as 0-switch coverage, coverage of transition pairs is 1-switch coverage, coverage of transition triples is 2-switch coverage, etc. Deriving test cases from the state transition model is a black-box approach. Measuring how much you have tested (covered) is getting close to a white-box perspective. However, state transition testing is regarded as a black-box technique.

One of the advantages of the state transition technique is that the model can be as detailed or as abstract as you need it to be. Where a part of the system is more important (that is, requires more testing) a greater depth of detail can be modelled. Where the system is less important (requires less testing), the model can use a single state to signify what would otherwise be a series of different states.

Testing for invalid transitions

Deriving tests only from a state graph (also known as a state chart) is very good for seeing the valid transitions, but we may not easily see the negative tests, where we try to generate invalid transitions. In order to see the total number of combinations of states and transitions, both valid and invalid, a **state table** is useful.

State table A grid showing the resulting transitions for each state combined with each possible event, showing both valid and invalid transitions.

The state table lists all the states down one side of the table and all the events that cause transitions along the top (or vice versa). Each cell then represents a state–event pair. The content of each cell indicates which state the system will move to, when the corresponding event occurs while in the associated state. This will include possible erroneous events – events that are not expected to happen in certain states. These are negative test conditions.

Table 4.9 lists the states in the first column and the possible inputs across the top row. So, for example, if the system is in State 1, inserting a card will take it to State 2. If we are in State 2, and a valid PIN is entered, we go to State 6 to access the account. In State 2 if we enter an invalid PIN, we go to State 3. We have put a

TABLE 4.9   State table for the PIN example

	Insert card	Valid PIN	Invalid PIN
S1) Start state	S2	–	–
S2) Wait for PIN	–	S6	S3
S3) 1st try invalid	–	S6	S4
S4) 2nd try invalid	–	S6	S5
S5) 3rd try invalid	–	–	S7
S6) Access account	–	?	?
S7) Eat card	S1 (for new card)	–	–

dash in the cells that should be impossible, i.e. they represent invalid transitions from that state.

We have put a question mark for two cells, where we enter either a valid or invalid PIN when we are accessing the account. Perhaps the system will take our PIN number as the amount of cash to withdraw? It might be a good test! Most of the other invalid cells would be physically impossible in this example. Invalid (negative) tests will attempt to generate invalid transitions, transitions that shouldn't be possible (but often make good tests when it turns out they are possible).

A more extensive description of state machines is found in [Marick 1994]. State transition testing is also described in [Craig 2002], [Copeland 2003], [Beizer 1990], [Broekman 2003], and [Black 2007]. State transition testing is described in [BS7925-2], including designing tests and coverage measures.

4.3.4 Use case testing

Use case testing is a technique that helps us identify test cases that exercise the whole system on a transaction by transaction basis from start to finish. They are described by Ivar Jacobson in his book *Object-Oriented Software Engineering: A Use Case Driven Approach* [Jacobson 1992].

A use case is a description of a particular use of the system by an actor (a user of the system). Each use case describes the interactions the actor has with the system in order to achieve a specific task (or, at least, produce something of value to the user). Actors are generally people but they may also be other systems. Use cases are a sequence of steps that describe the interactions between the actor and the system.

Use cases are defined in terms of the actor, not the system, describing what the actor does and what the actor sees rather than what inputs the system expects and what the system outputs. They often use the language and terms of the business rather than technical terms, especially when the actor is a business user. They serve as the foundation for developing test cases mostly at the system and acceptance testing levels.

Use case testing A black box test design technique in which test cases are designed to execute scenarios of use cases.

Use cases can uncover integration defects, that is, defects caused by the incorrect interaction between different components. Used in this way, the actor may be something that the system interfaces to such as a communication link or sub-system.

Use cases describe the process flows through a system based on its most likely use. This makes the test cases derived from use cases particularly good for finding defects in the real-world use of the system (i.e. the defects that the users are most likely to come across when first using the system). Each use case usually has a mainstream (or most likely) scenario and sometimes additional alternative branches (covering, for example, special cases or exceptional conditions). Each use case must specify any preconditions that need to be met for the use case to work. Use cases must also specify postconditions that are observable results and a description of the final state of the system after the use case has been executed successfully.

The PIN example that we used for state transition testing could also be defined in terms of use cases, as shown in Figure 4.3. We show a success scenario and the extensions (which represent the ways in which the scenario could fail to be a success).

For use case testing, we would have a test of the success scenario and one test for each extension. In this example, we may give extension 4b a higher priority than 4a from a security point of view.

System requirements can also be specified as a set of use cases. This approach can make it easier to involve the users in the requirements gathering and definition process.

	Step	Description
Main Success Scenario **A: Actor** **S: System**	1	A: Inserts card
	2	S: Validates card and asks for PIN
	3	A: Enters PIN
	4	S: Validates PIN
	5	S: Allows access to account
Extensions	2a	Card not valid S: Display message and reject card
	4a	PIN not valid S: Display message and ask for re-try (twice)
	4b	PIN invalid 3 times S: Eat card and exit

FIGURE 4.3 Partial use case for PIN entry

4.4 STRUCTURE-BASED OR WHITE-BOX TECHNIQUES

SYLLABUS LEARNING OBJECTIVES FOR 4.4 STRUCTURE-BASED OR WHITE-BOX TECHNIQUES (K4)

LO-4.4.1   Describe the concept and value of code coverage. (K2)

LO-4.4.2   Explain the concepts of statement and decision coverage, and give reasons why these concepts can also be used at test levels other than component testing (e.g. on business procedures at system level). (K2)

LO-4.4.3   Write test cases from given control flows using statement and decision test design techniques. (K3)

LO-4.4.4   Assess statement and decision coverage for completeness with respect to defined exit criteria. (K4)

In this section we will look in detail at the concept of coverage and how it can be used to measure some aspects of the thoroughness of testing. In order to see how coverage actually works, we will use some code-level examples (although coverage also applies to other levels such as business procedures). In particular, we will show how to measure coverage of statements and decisions, and how to write test cases to extend coverage if it is not 100%.

As mentioned, we will illustrate white-box techniques that would typically apply at the component level of testing. At this level, white-box techniques focus on the structure of a software component, such as statements, decisions, branches or even distinct paths. These techniques can also be applied at the integration level. At this level, white-box techniques can examine structures such as a call tree, which is a diagram that shows how modules call other modules. These techniques can also be applied at the system level. At this level, white-box techniques can examine structures such as a menu structure, business process or web page structure.

In this section, look for the definitions of the glossary terms **branch coverage, coverage, decision coverage, statement coverage,** and **test coverage**.

4.4.1 Using structure-based techniques to measure coverage and design tests

Structure-based techniques serve two purposes: test coverage measurement and structural test case design. They are often used first to assess the amount of testing performed by tests derived from specification-based techniques, i.e. to assess coverage. They are then used to design additional tests with the aim of increasing the **test coverage**.

Structure-based test design techniques are a good way of generating additional test cases that are different from existing tests. They can help ensure more breadth of testing, in the sense that test cases that achieve 100% **coverage** in any measure will be exercising all parts of the software from the point of view of the items being covered.

Coverage (test coverage) The degree, expressed as a percentage, to which a specified coverage item has been exercised by a test suite.

What is test coverage?

Test coverage measures in some specific way the amount of testing performed by a set of tests (derived in some other way, e.g. using specification-based techniques). Wherever we can count things and can tell whether or not each of those things has been tested by some test, then we can measure coverage. The basic coverage measure is

$$\text{Coverage} = \frac{\text{Number of coverage items exercised}}{\text{Total number of coverage items}} \times 100\%$$

where the 'coverage item' is whatever we have been able to count and see whether a test has exercised or used this item.

There is danger in using a coverage measure; 100% coverage does *not* mean 100% tested! Coverage techniques measure only one dimension of a multi-dimensional concept. Two different test cases may achieve exactly the same coverage but the input data of one may find an error that the input data of the other doesn't.

One drawback of code coverage measurement is that it measures coverage of what *has* been written, i.e. the code itself; it cannot say anything about the software that has *not* been written. If a specified function has not been implemented, specification-based testing techniques will reveal this. If a function was omitted from the specification, then experience-based techniques may find it. But structure-based techniques can only look at a structure which is already there.

Types of coverage

Test coverage can be measured based on a number of different structural elements in a system or component. Coverage can be measured at component-testing level, integration-testing level or at system- or acceptance-testing levels. For example, at system or acceptance level, the coverage items may be requirements, menu options, screens, or typical business transactions. Other coverage measures include things such as database structural elements (records, fields and sub-fields) and files. It is worth checking for any new tools, as the test tool market develops quite rapidly.

At integration level, we could measure coverage of interfaces or specific inter-actions that have been tested. The call coverage of module, object or procedure calls can also be measured (and is supported by tools to some extent).

We can measure coverage for each of the specification-based techniques as well:

- EP: percentage of equivalence partitions exercised (we could measure valid and invalid partition coverage separately if this makes sense).
- BVA: percentage of boundaries exercised (we could also separate valid and invalid boundaries if we wished).
- Decision tables: percentage of business rules or decision table columns tested.
- State transition testing: there are a number of possible coverage measures:
  - Percentage of states visited
  - Percentage of (valid) transitions exercised (this is known as Chow's 0-switch coverage)
  - Percentage of pairs of valid transitions exercised ('transition pairs' or Chow's 1-switch coverage) – and longer series of transitions, such as transition triples, quadruples, etc.
  - Percentage of invalid transitions exercised (from the state table).

The coverage measures for specification-based techniques would apply at whichever test level the technique has been used (e.g. system or component level).

When coverage is discussed by business analysts, system testers or users, it most likely refers to the percentage of requirements that have been tested by a set of tests. This may be measured by a tool such as a requirements management tool or a test management tool.

However, when coverage is discussed by programmers, it most likely refers to the coverage of code, where the structural elements can be identified using a tool, since there is good tool support for measuring code coverage. We will cover statement and decision coverage shortly. However, at this point, note that the word 'coverage' is often misused to mean, 'How many or what percentage of tests have been run'. This is not what the term 'coverage' refers to. Coverage is the coverage **of** something else **by** the tests. The percentage of tests run should be called 'test completeness' or something similar.

Statements and decision outcomes are both structures that can be measured in code and there is good tool support for these coverage measures. Code coverage is normally done in component and component integration testing – if it is done at all. If someone claims to have achieved code coverage, it is important to establish exactly what elements of the code have been covered, as statement coverage (often what is meant) is significantly weaker than decision coverage or some of the other code-coverage measures.

How to measure coverage

For most practical purposes, coverage measurement is something that requires tool support. However, knowledge of the steps typically taken to measure coverage is useful in understanding the relative merits of each technique. Our example assumes an intrusive coverage measurement tool that alters the code by inserting instrumentation:

1 Decide on the structural element to be used, i.e. the coverage items to be counted.

2 Count the structural elements or items.

3 Instrument the code.

4 Run the tests for which coverage measurement is required.

5 Using the output from the instrumentation, determine the percentage of elements or items exercised.

Instrumenting the code (step 3) implies inserting code alongside each structural element in order to record when that structural element has been exercised. Determining the actual coverage measure (step 5) is then a matter of analyzing the recorded information.

Coverage measurement of code is best done using tools (as described in Chapter 6) and there are a number of such tools on the market. These tools can help to increase quality and productivity of testing. They increase quality by ensuring that more structural aspects are tested, so defects on those structural paths can be found. They increase productivity and efficiency by highlighting tests that may be redundant, i.e. testing the same structure as other tests (although this is not necessarily a bad thing, since we may find a defect testing the same structure with different data).

In common with all structure-based testing techniques, code coverage techniques are best used on areas of software code where more thorough testing is required. Safety-critical code, code that is vital to the correct operation of a system, and complex pieces of code are all examples of where structure-based techniques are particularly worth applying. For example, DO178-B [RTCA] requires structural coverage for certain types of system to be used by the military. Structural coverage techniques should always be used in addition to specification-based and experience-based testing techniques rather than as an alternative to them.

Structure-based test case design

If you are aiming for a given level of coverage (say 95%) but you have not reached your target (e.g. you only have 87% so far), then additional test cases can be designed with the aim of exercising some or all of the structural elements not yet reached. This is structure-based test design. These new tests are then run through the instrumented code and a new coverage measure is calculated. This is repeated until the required coverage measure is achieved (or until you decide that your goal was too ambitious!). Ideally all the tests ought to be run again on the un-instrumented code.

We will look at some examples of structure-based coverage and test design for statement and decision testing below.

4.4.2 Statement coverage and statement testing

Statement coverage The percentage of executable statements that have been exercised by a test suite.

Statement coverage is calculated by:

$$\text{Statement coverage} = \frac{\text{Number of statements exercised}}{\text{Total number of statements}} \times 100\%$$

Studies and experience in the industry have indicated that what is considered reasonably thorough black-box testing may actually achieve only 60% to 75% statement coverage. Typical ad hoc testing is likely to be around 30% – this leaves 70% of the statements untested.

Different coverage tools may work in slightly different ways, so they may give different coverage figures for the same set of tests on the same code, although at 100% coverage they should be the same.

We will illustrate the principles of coverage on code. In order to simplify our examples, we will use a basic pseudo-code – this is not any specific programming language, but should be readable and understandable to you, even if you have not done any programming yourself.

For example, consider code sample 4.1.

```
READ A
READ B
IF A > B THEN C = 0
ENDIF
```

Code sample 4.1

To achieve 100% statement coverage of this code segment just one test case is required, one which ensures that variable A contains a value that is greater than the value of variable B, for example, A = 12 and B = 10. Note that here we are doing structural test *design* first, since we are choosing our input values in order ensure to statement coverage.

Let's look at an example where we measure coverage first. In order to simplify the example, we will regard each line as a statement. (Different tools and methods may count different things as statements, but the basic principle is the same however they are counted.) A statement may be on a single line, or it may be spread over several lines. One line may contain more than one statement, just one statement, or only part of a statement. Some statements can contain other statements inside them. In code sample 4.2, we have two read statements, one assignment statement, and then one IF statement on three lines, but the IF statement contains another statement (print) as part of it.

```
1 READ A
2 READ B
3 C = A + 2*B
4 IF C > 50 THEN
5       PRINT 'Large C'
6 ENDIF
```

Code sample 4.2

Although it isn't completely correct, we have numbered each line and will regard each line as a statement. (Some tools may group statements that would always be executed together in a basic block which is regarded as a single statement.) However, we will just use numbered lines to illustrate the principle of coverage of statements (lines). Let's analyze the coverage of a set of tests on our six-statement program:

TEST SET 1

Test 1_1: A = 2, B = 3
Test 1_2: A = 0, B = 25
Test 1_3: A = 47, B = 1

Which statements have we covered?

- In Test 1_1, the value of C will be 8, so we will cover the statements on lines 1 to 4 and line 6.
- In Test 1_2, the value of C will be 50, so we will cover exactly the same statements as Test 1_1.
- In Test 1_3, the value of C will be 49, so again we will cover the same statements.

Since we have covered five out of six statements, we have 83% statement coverage (with three tests). What test would we need in order to cover statement 5, the one statement that we haven't exercised yet? How about this one:

Test 1_4: A = 20, B = 25

This time the value of C is 70, so we will print 'Large C' and we will have exercised all six of the statements, so now statement coverage = 100%. Notice that we measured coverage first, and then designed a test to cover the statement that we had not yet covered.

Note that Test 1_4 on its own is more effective (towards our goal of achieving 100% statement coverage) than the first three tests together. Just taking Test 1_4 on its own is also more efficient than the set of four tests, since it has used only one test instead of four. Being more effective and more efficient is the mark of a good test technique.

4.4.3 Decision coverage and decision testing

A decision is an IF statement, a loop control statement (e.g. DO–WHILE or REPEAT–UNTIL), or a CASE statement, where there are two or more possible exits or outcomes from the statement. With an IF statement, the exit can either be TRUE or FALSE, depending on the value of the logical condition that comes after IF. With a loop control statement, the outcome is either to perform the code within the loop or not – again a True or False exit. **Decision coverage** is calculated by:

> **Decision coverage** The percentage of decision outcomes that have been exercised by a test suite. 100% decision coverage implies both 100% branch coverage and 100% statement coverage.

$$\text{Decision coverage} = \frac{\text{Number of decision outcomes exercised}}{\text{Total number of decision outcomes}} \times 100\%$$

What feels like reasonably thorough functional testing may achieve only 40% to 60% decision coverage. Typical ad hoc testing may cover only 20% of the decisions, leaving 80% of the possible outcomes untested. Even if your testing seems reasonably thorough from a functional or specification-based perspective, you may have only covered two-thirds or three-quarters of the decisions. Decision coverage is stronger than statement coverage. It 'subsumes' statement coverage – this means that 100% decision coverage always guarantees 100% statement coverage. Any stronger coverage measure may require more test cases to achieve 100% coverage. For example, consider code sample 4.1 again.

We saw earlier that just one test case was required to achieve 100% statement coverage. However, decision coverage requires each decision to have had both a True and False outcome. Therefore, to achieve 100% decision coverage, a second test case is necessary where A is less than or equal to B. This will ensure that the decision statement 'IF A > B' has a False outcome. So one test is sufficient for 100% statement coverage, but two tests are needed for 100% decision coverage. Note that 100% decision coverage guarantees 100% statement coverage, but *not* the other way around!

```
1 READ A
2 READ B
3 C = A - 2*B
4 IF C < 0 THEN
5      PRINT 'C negative'
6 ENDIF
```

Code sample 4.3

Let's suppose that we already have the following test, which gives us 100% statement coverage for code sample 4.3.

TEST SET 2

Test 2_1: A = 20, B = 15

Which decision outcomes have we exercised with our test? The value of C is −10, so the condition 'C < 0' is True, so we will print 'C negative' and we have exercised the True outcome from that decision statement. But we have not exercised the decision outcome of False. What other test would we need to exercise the False outcome and to achieve 100% decision coverage?

Before we answer that question, let's have a look at another way to represent this code. Sometimes the decision structure is easier to see in a control flow diagram (see Figure 4.4).

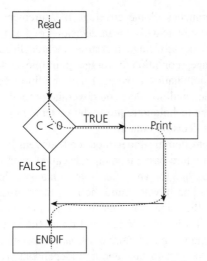

FIGURE 4.4   Control flow diagram for code sample 4.3

The dotted line shows where Test 2_1 has gone and clearly shows that we haven't yet had a test that takes the False exit from the IF statement.

Let's modify our existing test set by adding another test:

TEST SET 2

$$\text{Test } 2\_1\text{: } A = 20, \ B = 15$$
$$\text{Test } 2\_2\text{: } A = 10, \ B = 2$$

This now covers both of the decision outcomes, True (with Test 2_1) and False (with Test 2_2). If we were to draw the path taken by Test 2_2, it would be a straight line from the read statement down the False exit and through the ENDIF. Note that we could have chosen other numbers to achieve either the True or False outcomes.

As a final note on decision testing, let us point out that two slightly different terms are used in both the ISTQB Syllabus and Glossary. One term is 'decision testing' and the other is 'branch testing'. Some people distinguish between the terms, saying that branches originate from decision points in the code and show the transfer of control to different locations in the code. Therefore, some would say that branch testing focuses on the execution of the branches, the distinct segments of code, while decision testing focuses on the outcome of the decisions. Since the outcome of the decisions determines the branches taken, this strikes us as a distinction without a practical difference.

4.4.4 Other structure-based techniques

There are other structure-based techniques that can be used to achieve testing to different degrees of thoroughness. Some techniques are stronger (require more tests to achieve 100% coverage and therefore, have a greater chance of detecting defects) and others are weaker.

For example, **branch coverage** is closely related to decision coverage and at 100% coverage they give exactly the same results. Decision coverage measures the coverage of conditional branches; branch coverage measures the coverage of both conditional and unconditional branches. The Syllabus uses decision coverage, as it

Branch coverage The percentage of branches that have been exercised by a test suite. 100% branch coverage implies both 100% decision coverage and 100% statement coverage.

is the source of the branches. Some coverage measurement tools may talk about branch coverage when they actually mean decision coverage, or vice versa.

Other control-flow code-coverage measures include linear code sequence and jump (LCSAJ) coverage, condition coverage, multiple condition coverage (also known as condition combination coverage) and condition determination coverage (also known as multiple condition decision coverage or modified condition decision coverage, MCDC). This technique requires the coverage of all conditions that can affect or determine the decision outcome.

Another popular, but often misunderstood, code-coverage measure is path coverage. Sometimes any structure-based technique is called 'path testing' [Patton 2001]. However, strictly speaking, for any code that contains a loop, path coverage is impossible since a path that travels round the loop three times is different from the path that travels round the same loop four times. This is true even if the rest of the paths are identical. So if it is possible to travel round the loop an unlimited number of times then there are an unlimited number of paths through that piece of code. For this reason it is more correct to talk about 'independent path segment coverage' though the shorter term 'path coverage' is frequently used.

The idea of coverage, the number of things that have been tested compared to the total number of things, can be applied not just to code structure, but also at integration and system level, although the things being counted would be different. For example an integration test may measure the coverage of modules called, components integrated or classes exercised. Tool support is generally better for component coverage than integration or system coverage.

Structure-based measures and related test design techniques are described in [BS7925-2]. Structure-based techniques are also discussed in [Copeland 2003] and [Myers 1979]. A good description of the graph theory behind structural testing can be found in [Jorgensen 1995] and [Hetzel 1988] also shows a structural approach. [Pol *et al.* 2001] describes a structure-based approach called an algorithm test.

4.5 EXPERIENCE-BASED TECHNIQUES

> **SYLLABUS LEARNING OBJECTIVES FOR 4.5**
> **EXPERIENCE-BASED TECHNIQUES (K2)**
>
> **LO-4.5.1** Recall reasons for writing test cases based on intuition, experience and knowledge about common defects. (K1)
>
> **LO-4.5.2** Compare experience-based techniques with specification-based testing techniques. (K2)

In this section we will look at two experience-based techniques, why and when they are useful, and how they fit with specification-based techniques.

Although it is true that testing should be rigorous, thorough and systematic, this is not all there is to testing. There is a definite role for non-systematic techniques, i.e. tests based on a person's knowledge, experience, imagination and intuition. The reason is that some defects are hard to find using more systematic approaches, so a good 'bug hunter' can be very creative at finding those elusive defects.

In this section, look for the definitions of the glossary terms **attack, exploratory testing** and **fault attack**.

4.5.1 Error guessing and fault attacks

Error guessing is a technique that should always be used as a complement to other more formal techniques. The success of error guessing is very much dependent on the skill of the tester, as good testers know where the defects are most likely to lurk. Some people seem to be naturally good at testing and others are good testers because they have a lot of experience either as a tester or working with a particular system and so are able to pin-point its weaknesses. This is why an error-guessing approach, used after more formal techniques have been applied to some extent, can be very effective. In using more formal techniques, the tester is likely to gain a better understanding of the system, what it does and how it works. With this better understanding, he or she is likely to be better at guessing ways in which the system may not work properly.

There are no rules for error guessing. The tester is encouraged to think of situations in which the software may not be able to cope. Typical conditions to try include division by zero, blank (or no) input, empty files and the wrong kind of data (e.g. alphabetic characters where numeric are required). If anyone ever says of a system or the environment in which it is to operate 'That could never happen', it might be a good idea to test that condition, as such assumptions about what will and will not happen in the live environment are often the cause of failures. A structured approach to the error-guessing technique is to list possible defects or failures and to design tests that attempt to produce them. These defect and failure lists can be built based on the tester's own experience or that of other people, available defect and failure data, and from common knowledge about why software fails. This way of trying to force specific types of fault to occur is called an '**attack**' or '**fault attack**'. See [Whittaker 2003].

> **Fault attack**
> **(attack)** Directed and focused attempt to evaluate the quality, especially reliability, of a test object by attempting to force specific failures to occur.

4.5.2 Exploratory testing

Exploratory testing is a hands-on approach in which testers are involved in minimum planning and maximum test execution. The planning involves the creation of a test charter, a short declaration of the scope of a short (1 to 2 hour) time-boxed test effort, the objectives and possible approaches to be used.

> **Exploratory testing** An informal test design technique where the tester actively controls the design of the tests as those tests are performed and uses information gained while testing to design new and better tests.

The test design and test execution activities are performed in parallel typically without formally documenting the test conditions, test cases or test scripts. This does not mean that other, more formal testing techniques will not be used. For example, the tester may decide to use boundary value analysis but will think through and test the most important boundary values without necessarily writing them down. Some notes will be written during the exploratory-testing session, so that a report can be produced afterwards.

Test logging is undertaken as test execution is performed, documenting the key aspects of what is tested, any defects found and any thoughts about possible further testing. A key aspect of exploratory testing is learning: learning by the tester about the software, its use, its strengths and its weaknesses. As its name implies, exploratory testing is about exploring, finding out about the software, what it does, what it doesn't do, what works and what doesn't work. The tester is constantly making decisions about what to test next and where to spend the (limited) time.

This is an approach that is most useful when there are no or poor specifications and when time is severely limited. It can also serve to complement other, more formal testing, helping to establish greater confidence in the software. In this way, exploratory testing can be used as a check on the formal test process by helping to ensure that the most serious defects have been found.

Exploratory testing is described in [Kaner 2002] and [Copeland 2003]. Other ways of testing in an exploratory way ('attacks') are described by [Whittaker 2003].

4.6 CHOOSING TEST TECHNIQUES

> **SYLLABUS LEARNING OBJECTIVES FOR 4.6 CHOOSING TEST TECHNIQUES (K2)**
>
> **LO-4.6.1** **Classify test design techniques according to their fitness to a given context, for the test basis, respective models and software characteristics. (K2)**

In this final section we will look at the factors that go into the decision about which techniques to use when. There are no Syllabus terms for this section.

Which technique is best? This is the wrong question! Each technique is good for certain things, and not as good for other things. For example, one of the benefits of structure-based techniques is that they can find things in the code that aren't supposed to be there, such as 'Trojan horses' or other malicious code. However, if there are parts of the specification that are missing from the code, specification-based techniques can find that – structure-based techniques can only test what is there. If there are things missing from the specification and from the code, then only experience-based techniques would find them. Each individual technique is aimed at particular types of defect as well. For example, state transition testing is unlikely to find boundary defects.

The choice of which test techniques to use depends on a number of factors, including the type of system, regulatory standards, customer or contractual requirements, level of risk, type of risk, test objective, documentation available, knowledge of the testers, time and budget, development life cycle, use case models and previous experience of types of defects found.

Some techniques are more applicable to certain situations and test levels; others are applicable to all test levels.

This chapter has covered the most popular and commonly used software testing techniques. There are many others that fall outside the scope of the Syllabus that this book is based on. With so many testing techniques to choose from how are testers to decide which ones to use?

Perhaps the single most important thing to understand is that the best testing technique is no single testing technique. Because each testing technique is good at finding one specific class of defect, using just one technique will help ensure that many (perhaps most but not all) defects of that particular class are found. Unfortunately, it may also help to ensure that many defects of other classes are missed! Using a variety of techniques will therefore help ensure that a variety of defects are found, resulting in more effective testing.

So how can we choose the most appropriate testing techniques to use? The decision will be based on a number of factors, both internal and external.

The internal factors that influence the decision about which technique to use are:

- *Models used* – Since testing techniques are based on models, the models available (i.e. developed and used during the specification, design and implementation of the system) will to some extent govern which testing techniques can be used. For example, if the specification contains a state transition diagram, state transition testing would be a good technique to use.

- *Tester knowledge/experience* – How much testers know about the system and about testing techniques will clearly influence their choice of testing techniques. This knowledge will in itself be influenced by their experience of testing and of the system under test.

- *Likely defects* – Knowledge of the likely defects will be very helpful in choosing testing techniques (since each technique is good at finding a particular type of defect). This knowledge could be gained through experience of testing a previous version of the system and previous levels of testing on the current version.

- *Test objective* – If the test objective is simply to gain confidence that the software will cope with typical operational tasks then use cases would be a sensible approach. If the objective is for very thorough testing then more rigorous and detailed techniques (including structure-based techniques) should be chosen.

- *Documentation* – Whether or not documentation (e.g. a requirements specification) exists and whether or not it is up to date will affect the choice of testing techniques. The content and style of the documentation will also influence the choice of techniques (for example, if decision tables or state graphs have been used then the associated test techniques should be used).

- *Life cycle model* – A sequential life cycle model will lend itself to the use of more formal techniques whereas an iterative life cycle model may be better suited to using an exploratory testing approach.

The external factors that influence the decision about which technique to use are:

- *Risk* – The greater the risk (e.g. safety-critical systems), the greater the need for more thorough and more formal testing. Commercial risk may be influenced by quality issues (so more thorough testing would be appropriate) or by time-to-market issues (so exploratory testing would be a more appropriate choice).

- *Customer/contractual requirements* – Sometimes contracts specify particular testing techniques to use (most commonly statement or branch coverage).

- *Type of system* – The type of system (e.g. embedded, graphical, financial, etc.) will influence the choice of techniques. For example, a financial application involving many calculations would benefit from boundary value analysis.

- *Regulatory requirements* – Some industries have regulatory standards or guidelines that govern the testing techniques used. For example, the aircraft industry requires the use of equivalence partitioning, boundary value analysis and state transition testing for high integrity systems together with statement, decision or modified condition decision coverage depending on the level of software integrity required.

- *Time and budget* – Ultimately how much time there is available will always affect the choice of testing techniques. When more time is available we can afford to select more techniques and when time is severely limited we will be limited to those that we know have a good chance of helping us find just the most important defects.

It's important to remember that intelligent, experienced testers see test design techniques – and indeed test strategies, which we'll discuss in Chapter 5 – as tools to be employed wherever needed and useful. You should use whatever techniques and strategies, in whatever combinations, make sense to ensure adequate coverage of the system under test, and achievement of the objectives of testing. Feel free to combine the test design techniques discussed in this chapter with whatever inspiration you have, along with process, rule and data-driven techniques. Use your brain, and do what makes sense.

CHAPTER REVIEW

Let's review what you have learned in this chapter.

From Section 4.1, you should now be able to differentiate between a test condition, a test case and a test procedure, and know that they are documented in a test design specification, a test case specification and a test procedure specification respectively. You should be able to write test cases that include expected results and that show clear traceability to the test basis (e.g. requirements). You should be able to translate test cases into a test procedure specification at the appropriate level of detail for testers and you should be able to write a test execution schedule for a given set of test cases that takes into account priorities as well as technical and logical dependencies. You should know the glossary terms **horizontal traceability, test case specification, test design specification, test design technique, test execution schedule, test script, traceability** and **vertical traceability**.

From Section 4.2 (categories of test design techniques), you should be able to give reasons why both specification-based (black-box), structure-based (white-box), and experience-based approaches are useful, and list the common techniques for each of these approaches. You should be able to explain the characteristics and differences between specification-based, structure-based and experience-based techniques. You should know the glossary terms **experience-based test design technique, specification-based test design technique, structure-based** and **test design technique**.

From Section 4.3, you should be able to write test cases from given software models using equivalence partitioning, boundary value analysis, decision tables and state transition diagrams. You should understand the main purpose of each of these four techniques, what level and type of testing could use each technique and how coverage can be measured for each of them. You should also understand the concept and benefits of use case testing. You should know the glossary terms **boundary value, boundary value analysis, decision table, decision table testing, equivalence partition, equivalence partitioning, state diagram, state table, state transition testing**, and **use case testing**.

From Section 4.4, you should be able to describe the concept and importance of code coverage. You should be able to explain the concepts of statement and decision coverage and understand that these concepts can also be used at test levels other than component testing (such as business procedures at system test level). You should be able to write test cases from given control flows using statement testing and decision testing, and you should be able to assess statement and decision coverage for completeness. You should know the glossary terms **branch coverage, code coverage, coverage, decision coverage, statement coverage,** and **test coverage**.

From Section 4.5, you should be able to remember the reasons for writing test cases based on intuition, experience and knowledge about common defects and you should be able to compare experience-based techniques with specification-based techniques. You should know the glossary terms **attack**, **exploratory testing** and **fault attack**.

From Section 4.6, you should be able to list the factors that influence the selection of the appropriate test design technique for a particular type of problem, such as the type of system, risk, customer requirements, models for use case modelling, requirements models or testing knowledge. There are no glossary terms for this section.

SAMPLE EXAM QUESTIONS

Question 1 In which document described in IEEE 829 would you find instructions for the steps to be taken for a test including set-up, logging, environment and measurement?

a. Test plan

b. Test design specification

c. Test case specification

d. Test procedure specification

Question 2 With a highly experienced tester with a good business background, which approach to defining test procedures would be effective and most efficient for a project under severe time pressure?

a. A high-level outline of the test conditions and general steps to take.

b. Every step in the test spelled out in detail.

c. A high-level outline of the test conditions with the steps to take discussed in detail with another experienced tester.

d. Detailed documentation of all test cases and careful records of each step taken in the testing.

Question 3 Put the test cases that implement the following test conditions into the best order for the test execution schedule, for a test that is checking modifications of customers on a database.

1 Print modified customer record.

2 Change customer address: house number and street name.

3 Capture and print the on-screen error message.

4 Change customer address: postal code.

5 Confirm existing customer is on the database by opening that record.

6 Close the customer record and close the database.

7 Try to add a new customer with no details at all.

a. 5, 4, 2, 1, 3, 7, 6

b. 4, 2, 5, 1, 6, 7, 3

c. 5, 4, 2, 1, 7, 3, 6

d. 5, 1, 2, 3, 4, 7, 6

Question 4 Why are both specification-based and structure-based testing techniques useful?

a. They find different types of defect.

b. Using more techniques is always better.

c. Both find the same types of defect.

d. Because specifications tend to be unstructured.

Question 5 What is a key characteristic of structure-based testing techniques?

a. They are mainly used to assess the structure of a specification.

b. They are used both to measure coverage and to design tests to increase coverage.

c. They are based on the skills and experience of the tester.

d. They use a formal or informal model of the software or component.

Question 6 Which of the following would be an example of decision-table testing for a financial application applied at the system-test level?

a. A table containing rules for combinations of inputs to two fields on a screen.

b. A table containing rules for interfaces between components.

c. A table containing rules for mortgage applications.

d. A table containing rules for chess.

Question 7 Which of the following could be a coverage measure for state transition testing?

V All states have been reached.

W The response time for each transaction is adequate.

X Every transition has been exercised.

Y All boundaries have been exercised.

Z Specific sequences of transitions have been exercised.

a. X, Y and Z

b. V, X, Y and Z

c. W, X and Y

d. V, X and Z

Question 8 Postal rates for 'light letters' are 25p up to 10g, 35p up to 50g plus an extra 10p for each additional 25g up to 100g.

Which test inputs (in grams) would be selected using equivalence partitioning?

a. 8, 42, 82, 102

b. 4, 15, 65, 92, 159

c. 10, 50, 75, 100

d. 5, 20, 40, 60, 80

Question 9 Which of the following could be used to assess the coverage achieved for specification-based (black-box) test techniques?

V Decision outcomes exercised

W Partitions exercised

X Boundaries exercised

Y State transitions exercised

Z Statements exercised

a. V, W, Y or Z

b. W, X or Y

c. V, X or Z

d. W, X, Y or Z

Question 10 Which of the following would structure-based test design techniques be most likely to be applied to?

1 Boundaries between mortgage interest rate bands.

2 An invalid transition between two different arrears statuses.

3 The business process flow for mortgage approval.

4 Control flow of the program to calculate repayments.

a. 2, 3 and 4

b. 2 and 4

c. 3 and 4

d. 1, 2 and 3

Question 11 Use case testing is useful for which of the following?

P Designing acceptance tests with users or customers.

Q Making sure that the mainstream business processes are tested.

R Finding defects in the interaction between components.

S Identifying the maximum and minimum values for every input field.

T Identifying the percentage of statements exercised by a sets of tests.

a. P, Q and R

b. Q, S and T

c. P, Q and S

d. R, S and T

Question 12 Which of the following statements about the relationship between statement coverage and decision coverage is correct?

a. 100% decision coverage is achieved if statement coverage is greater than 90%.

b. 100% statement coverage is achieved if decision coverage is greater than 90%.

c. 100% decision coverage always means 100% statement coverage.

d. 100% statement coverage always means 100% decision coverage.

Question 13 If you are flying with an economy ticket, there is a possibility that you may get upgraded to business class, especially if you hold a gold card in the airline's frequent flier program. If you don't hold a gold card, there is a possibility that you will get 'bumped' off the flight if it is full and you check in late. This is shown in Figure 4.5. Note that each box (i.e. statement) has been numbered.

Three tests have been run:

Test 1: Gold card holder who gets upgraded to business class.

Test 2: Non-gold card holder who stays in economy.

Test 3: A person who is bumped from the flight. What is the statement coverage of these three tests?

a. 60%

b. 70%

c. 80%

d. 90%

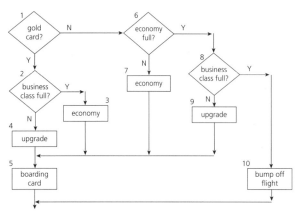

FIGURE 4.5   Control flow diagram for flight check-in

Question 14   Why are error guessing and exploratory testing good to do?

a. They can find defects missed by specification-based and structure-based techniques.

b. They don't require any training to be as effective as formal techniques.

c. They can be used most effectively when there are good specifications.

d. They will ensure that all of the code or system is tested.

Question 15   How do experience-based techniques differ from specification-based techniques?

a. They depend on the tester's understanding of the way the system is structured rather than on a documented record of what the system should do.

b. They depend on having older testers rather than younger testers.

c. They depend on a documented record of what the system should do rather than on an individual's personal view.

d. They depend on an individual's personal view rather than on a documented record of what the system should do.

Question 16   When choosing which technique to use in a given situation, which factors should be taken into account?

U Previous experience of types of defects found in this or similar systems.

V The existing knowledge of the testers.

W Regulatory standards that apply.

X The type of test execution tool that will be used.

Y The documentation available.

Z Previous experience in the development language.

a. V, W, Y and Z

b. U, V, W and Y

c. U, X and Y

d. V, W and Y

Question 17   Given the state diagram in Figure 4.6, which test case is the minimum series of valid transitions to cover every state?

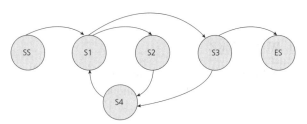

FIGURE 4.6   State diagram for PIN entry

a. SS – S1 – S2 – S4 – S1 – S3 – ES

b. SS – S1 – S2 – S3 – S4 – ES

c. SS – S1 – S2 – S4 – S1 – S3 – S4 – S1 – S3 – ES

d. SS – S1 – S4 – S2 – S1 – S3 – ES

EXERCISES: TEST DESIGN TECHNIQUES

Exercises based on the techniques covered in this chapter are given in this section. Worked solutions are given in the next section.

Equivalence Partitioning/Boundary Value Analysis exercise

Scenario: If you take the train before 9:30 am or in the afternoon after 4:00 pm until 7:30 pm ('the rush hour'), you must pay full fare. A saver ticket is available for trains between 9:30 am and 4:00 pm, and after 7:30 pm.

What are the partitions and boundary values to test the train times for ticket types? Which are valid partitions and which are invalid partitions? What are the boundary values? (A table may be helpful to organize your partitions and boundaries.) Derive test cases for the partitions and boundaries.

Are there any questions you have about this 'requirement'? Is anything unclear?

Decision table exercise

Scenario: If you hold an 'over 60s' rail card, you get a 34% discount on whatever ticket you buy. If you are travelling with a child (under 16), you can get a 50% discount on any ticket if you hold a family rail card, otherwise you get a 10% discount. You can only hold one type of rail card.

Produce a decision table showing all the combinations of fare types and resulting discounts and derive test cases from the decision table.

State transition exercise

Scenario: A website shopping basket starts out as empty. As purchases are selected, they are added to the shopping basket. Items can also be removed from the shopping basket. When the customer decides to check out, a summary of the items in the basket and the total cost are shown, for the customer to say whether this is OK or not. If the contents and price are OK, then you leave the summary display and go to the payment system. Otherwise you go back to shopping (so you can remove items if you want).

a. Produce a state diagram showing the different states and transitions. Define a test, in terms of the sequence of states, to cover all transitions.

b. Produce a state table. Give an example test for an invalid transition.

Statement and decision testing exercise

Scenario: A vending machine dispenses either hot or cold drinks. If you choose a hot drink (e.g. tea or coffee), it asks if you want milk (and adds milk if required), then it asks if you want sugar (and adds sugar if required), then your drink is dispensed.

a. Draw a control flow diagram for this example. (Hint: regard the selection of the type of drink as one statement.)

b. Given the following tests, what is the statement coverage achieved? What is the decision coverage achieved?

Test 1: Cold drink
Test 2: Hot drink with milk and sugar

c. What additional tests would be needed to achieve 100% statement coverage? What additional tests would be needed to achieve 100% decision coverage?

EXERCISE SOLUTIONS

EP/BVA exercise

The first thing to do is to establish exactly what the boundaries are between the full fare and saver fare. Let's put these in a table to organize our thoughts:

Scheduled departure time	≦ 9:29 am	9:30 am – 4:00 pm	4:01 pm – 7:30 pm	≧ 7:31 pm
Ticket type	full	saver	full	saver

We have assumed that the boundary values are: 9:29 am, 9:30 am, 4:00 pm, 4:01 pm, 7:30 pm and 7:31 pm. By setting out exactly what we think is meant by the specification, we may highlight some ambiguities or, at least, raise some questions – this is one of the benefits of using the technique! For example:

'When does the morning rush hour start? At midnight? At 11:30 pm the previous day? At the time of the first train of the day? If so, when is the first train? 5:00 am?'

This is a rather important omission from the specification. We could make an assumption about when it starts, but it would be better to find out what is correct.

- If a train is due to leave at exactly 4:00 pm, is a saver ticket still valid?
- What if a train is due to leave before 4:00 pm but is delayed until after 4:00 pm? Is a saver ticket still valid? (i.e. if the actual departure time is different to the scheduled departure time.)

Our table above has helped us to see where the partitions are. All of the partitions in the table above are valid partitions. It may be that an invalid partition would be a time that no train was running, e.g. before 5:00 am, but our specification didn't mention that! However it would be good to show this possibility also. We could be a bit more formal by listing all valid and invalid partitions and boundaries in a table, as we described in Section 4.3.1, but in this case it doesn't actually add a lot, since all partitions are valid.

Here are the test cases we can derive for this example:

Test case reference	Input	Expected outcome
1	Depart 4:30 am	Pay full fare
2	Depart 9:29 am	Pay full fare
3	Depart 9:30 am	Buy saver ticket
4	Depart 11:37 am	Buy saver ticket
5	Depart 4:00 pm	Buy saver ticket
6	Depart 4:01 pm	Pay full fare
7	Depart 5:55 pm	Pay full fare
8	Depart 7:30 pm	Pay full fare
9	Depart 7:31 pm	Buy saver ticket
10	Depart 10:05 pm	Buy saver ticket

Note that test cases 1, 4, 7 and 10 are based on equivalence partition values; test cases 2, 3, 5, 6, 8 and 9 are based on boundary values. There may also be other information about the test cases, such as preconditions, that we have not shown here.

Decision table exercise

The fare types mentioned include an 'over 60s' rail card, a family rail card, and whether you are travelling with a child or not. With three conditions or causes, we have eight columns in our decision table below.

Causes (inputs)	R1	R2	R3	R4	R5	R6	R7	R8
over 60s rail card?	Y	Y	Y	Y	N	N	N	N
family rail card?	Y	Y	N	N	Y	Y	N	N
child also travelling?	Y	N	Y	N	Y	N	Y	N
Effects (outputs)								
Discount (%)	X/?/50%	X/?/34%	34%	34%	50%	0%	10%	0%

When we come to fill in the effects, we may find this a bit more difficult. For the first two rules, for example, what should the output be? Is it an X because holding more than one rail card should not be possible? The specification doesn't actually say what happens if someone does hold more than one card, i.e. it has not specified the output, so perhaps we should put a question mark in this column. Of course, if someone does hold two rail cards, they probably wouldn't admit this, and perhaps they would claim the 50% discount with their family rail card if they are travelling with a child, so perhaps we should put 50% for Rule 1 and 34% for Rule 2 in this column. Our notation shows that we don't know what the expected outcome should be for these rules!

This highlights the fact that our natural language (English) specification is not very clear as to what the effects should actually be. A strength of this technique is that it forces greater clarity. If the answers are spelled out in a decision table, then it is clear what the effect should be. When different people come up with different answers for the outputs, then you have an unclear specification!

The word 'otherwise' in the specification is ambiguous. Does 'otherwise' mean that you always get at least a 10% discount or does it mean that if you travel with a child and an over 60s card but not a family card you get 10% and 34%? Depending on what assumption you make for the meaning of 'otherwise', you will get a different last row in your decision table.

Note that the effect or output is the same (34%) for both Rules 3 and 4. This means that our third cause (whether or not a child is also travelling) actually has no influence on the output. These columns could therefore be combined with 'don't care' as the entry for the third cause. This 'rationalizing' of the table means we will have fewer columns and therefore fewer test cases. The reduction in test cases is based on the assumption we are making about the factor having no effect on the outcome, so a more thorough approach would be to include each column in the table.

Here is a rationalized table, where we have shown our assumptions about the first two outcomes and we have also combined Rules 6 and 8 above, since having a family rail card has no effect if you are not travelling with a child.

Causes (inputs)	R1	R2	R3	R5	R6	R7
over 60s rail card?	Y	Y	Y	N	N	N
family rail card?	Y	Y	N	Y	–	N
child also travelling?	Y	N	–	Y	N	Y
Effects (outputs)						
Discount (%)	50%	34%	34%	50%	0%	10%

Here are the test cases that we derive from this table. (If you didn't rationalize the table, then you will have eight test cases rather than six.) Note that you wouldn't necessarily test each column, but the table enables you to make a decision about which combinations to test and which not to test this time.

Test case reference	Input	Expected outcome
1	S. Wilkes, with over 60s rail card and family rail card, travelling with grandson Josh (age 11)	50% discount for both tickets
2	Mrs. M. Davis, with over 60s rail card and family rail card, travelling alone	34% discount
3	J. Rogers, with over 60s rail card, travelling with his wife	34% discount (for J. Rogers only, not the wife)
4	S. Gray, with family rail card, travelling with her daughter Betsy	50% discount for both tickets
5	Miss Congeniality, no rail card, travelling alone	No discount
6	Joe Bloggs with no rail card, travelling with his 5-year-old niece	10% discount for both tickets

Note that we may have raised some additional issues when we designed the test cases. For example, does the discount for a rail card apply only to the traveller or to someone travelling with them? Here we have assumed that it applies to all travellers for the family rail card, but to the individual passenger only for the over 60s rail card.

State transition exercise

The state diagram is shown in Figure 4.7. The initial state (S1) is when the shopping basket is empty. When an item is added to the basket, it goes to state (S2), where there are potential purchases. Any additional items added to the basket do not change the state (just the total number of things to purchase). Items can be removed, which does not change the state unless the total items ordered goes from 1 to 0. In this case, we go back to the empty basket (S1). When we want to check out, we go to the summary state (S3) for approval. If the list and prices are

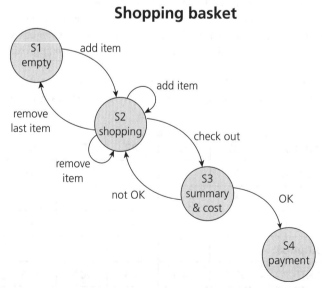

FIGURE 4.7 State diagram for shopping basket

approved, we go to payment (S4); if not, we go back to the shopping state (possibly to remove some items to reduce the total price we have to pay). There are four states and seven transitions.

Note that S1 is our Start State for this example and S4 is the End State – this means that we are not concerned with any event that happens once we get to State S4.

Here is a test to cover all transitions. Note that the end state from one step or event is the start state for the next event, so these steps must be done in this sequence.

State	Event (action)
S1	Add item
S2	Remove (last) item
S1	Add item
S2	Add item
S2	Remove item
S2	Check out
S3	Not OK
S2	Check out
S3	OK
S4	

Although our example is not interested in what happens from State 4, there would be other events and actions once we enter the payment process that could be shown by another state diagram (e.g. check validity of the credit card, deduct the amount, email a receipt, etc.).

The corresponding state table is:

State or event	Add item	Remove item	Remove last item	Check out	Not OK	OK
S1 Empty	S2	–	–	–	–	–
S2 Shopping	S2	S2	S1	S3	–	–
S3 Summary	–	–	–	–	S2	S4
S4 Payment	–	–	–	–	–	–

All of the boxes that contain – are invalid transitions in this example. Example negative tests would include:

- attempt to add an item from the summary and cost state (S3)
- try to remove an item from the empty shopping basket (S1)
- try to enter 'OK' while in the Shopping state (S2).

Statement and decision testing exercise

The control flow diagram is shown in Figure 4.8. Note that drawing a control diagram here illustrates that structural testing can also be applied to the structure of general processes, not just to computer algorithms. Flowcharts are generally easier to understand than text when you are trying to describe the results of decisions taken on later events.

On Figure 4.9, we can see the route that Tests 1 and 2 have taken through our control flow graph. Test 1 has gone straight down the left-hand side to select a cold drink. Test 2 has gone to the right at each opportunity, adding both milk and sugar to a hot drink.

Every statement (represented by a box on the diagram) has been covered by our two tests, so we have 100% statement coverage.

We have not taken the No Exit from either the 'milk?' or 'sugar?' decisions, so there are two decision outcomes that we have not tested yet. We did test both of the outcomes from the 'hot or cold?' decision, so we have covered four out of six decision outcomes. Decision coverage is 4/6 or 67% with the two tests.

No additional tests are needed to achieve statement coverage, as we already have 100% coverage of the statements.

One additional test is needed to achieve 100% decision coverage:

Test 3: Hot drink, no milk, no sugar

This test will cover both of the 'No' decision outcomes from the milk and sugar decisions, so we will now have 100% decision coverage.

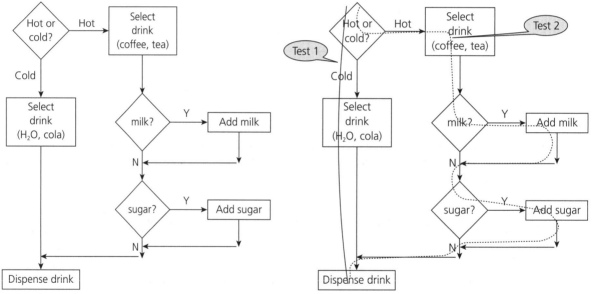

FIGURE 4.8   Control flow diagram for drinks dispenser

FIGURE 4.9   Control flow diagram showing coverage of tests

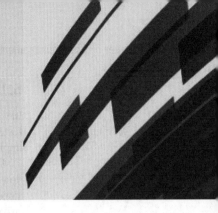

CHAPTER FIVE

Test management

Testing is a complex activity. Testing is often a distinct sub-project within the larger software development, maintenance, or integration project. Testing usually accounts for a substantial proportion of the overall project budget. Therefore, we must understand how we should manage the testing we do.

In this chapter, we cover essential topics for **test management** in six sections. The first relates to how to organize the testers and the testing. The second concerns the estimation, planning and strategizing of the test effort. The third addresses test progress monitoring, test reporting and test control. The fourth explains configuration management and its relationship to testing. The fifth covers the central topic of risk and how testing affects and is affected by product and project risks. The sixth and final section discusses the management of incidents, both product defects and other events that require further investigation.

> **Test management** The planning, estimating, monitoring and control of test activities, typically carried out by a test manager.

5.1 TEST ORGANIZATION

SYLLABUS LEARNING OBJECTIVES FOR 5.1 TEST ORGANIZATION (K2)

LO-5.1.1   Recognize the importance of independent testing. (K1)

LO-5.1.2   Explain the benefits and drawbacks of independent testing within an organization. (K2)

LO-5.1.3   Recognize the different team members to be considered for the creation of a test team. (K1)

LO-5.1.4   Recall the tasks of typical test leader and tester. (K1)

In this section, let's talk about organizing a test effort within a project. We'll look at the value of independent testing, and discuss the potential benefits and risks associated with independent testing. We will examine the various types of different test team members we might want on a test team. And we'll familiarize ourselves with the typical tasks performed by test leaders and testers.

As we go through this section, keep your eyes open for the glossary terms **tester, test leader, test manager** and **test management**.

5.1.1 Independent and integrated testing

In Chapter 1 we talked about independent testing from the perspective of individual **tester** psychology. In this chapter, we'll look at the organizational and managerial implications of independence.

The approaches to organizing a test team vary, as do the places in the organization structure where the test team fits. Since testing is an assessment of quality, and since that assessment may not always be perceived as positive, many organizations strive to create an organizational climate where testers can deliver an independent, objective assessment of quality.

When thinking about how independent the test team is, recognize that independence is not an either/or condition, but a continuum. At one end of the continuum lies the absence of independence, where the programmer performs testing within the programming team.

Moving toward independence, you find an integrated tester or group of testers working alongside the programmers, but still within and reporting to the development manager. You might find a team of testers who are independent and outside the development team, but reporting to project management.

Near the other end of the continuum lies complete independence. You might see a separate test team reporting into the organization at a point equal to the development or project team. You might find specialists in the business domain (such as users of the system), specialists in technology (such as database experts), and specialists in testing (such as security testers, certification testers, or test automation experts) in a separate test team, as part of a larger independent test team, or as part of a contract, outsourced test team. Let's examine the potential benefits and risks of independence, starting with the benefits.

An independent tester can often see more, other, and different defects than a tester working within a programming team – or a tester who is by profession a programmer. While business analysts, marketing staff, designers, and programmers bring their own assumptions to the specification and implementation of the item under test, an independent tester brings a different set of assumptions to testing and to reviews, which often helps expose hidden defects and problems related to the group's way of thinking, as we discussed in Chapter 3. An independent tester brings a sceptical attitude of professional pessimism, a sense that, if there's any doubt about the observed behaviour, they should ask: Is this a defect?

At the team level, an independent test team reporting to a senior or executive manager may enjoy (once they earn it) more credibility in the organization than a **test leader** or tester who is part of the programming team. An independent tester who reports to senior management may be able to report his results honestly and without concern for reprisals that might result from pointing out problems in co-workers' or, worse yet, the manager's work. An independent test team often has a separate budget, which helps ensure the proper level of money is spent on tester training, testing tools, test equipment, and so forth. In addition, in some organizations, testers in an independent test team may find it easier to have a career path that leads up into more senior roles in testing.

Independent test teams are not risk-free. It's possible for the testers and the test team to become isolated. This can take the form of interpersonal isolation from the programmers, the designers, and the project team itself, or it can take the form of isolation from the broader view of quality and the business objectives (e.g. obsessive focus on defects, often accompanied by a refusal to accept business prioritization of

tester A skilled professional who is involved in the testing of a component or system.

Test manager (test leader) The person responsible for project management of testing activities and resources, and evaluation of a test object. The individual who directs, controls, administers, plans and regulates the evaluation of a test object.

defects). This leads to communication problems, feelings of alienation and antipathy, a lack of identification with and support for the project goals, spontaneous blame festivals and political backstabbing.

Even well-integrated test teams can suffer problems. Other project stake-holders might come to see the independent test team – rightly or wrongly – as a bottleneck and a source of delay. Some programmers abdicate their responsibility for quality, saying, 'Well, we have this test team now, so why do I need to unit test my code?'

Due to a desire for the benefits of an independent test team, companies sometimes establish them, only to break them up again later. Why does that happen? A common cause is the failure of the test manager to effectively manage the risks of independence listed above. Some test teams succumb to the temptation to adopt a 'no can do' attitude, coming up with reasons why the project should bend to their needs rather than each side being flexible so as to enable project success. Testers take to acting as enforcers of process or as auditors without a proper management mandate and support. Resentments and pressures build, until at last the organization decides that the independent test team causes more problems than it solves. It's especially important for testers and test managers to understand the mission they serve and the reasons why the organization wants an independent test team. Often, the entire test team must realize that, whether they are part of the project team or independent, they exist to provide a service to the project team.

There is no one right approach to organizing testing. For each project, you must consider whether to use an independent test team, based on the project, the application domain, and the levels of risk, among other factors. As the size, complexity, and criticality of the project increases, it is important to have independence in later levels of testing (like integration test, system test and acceptance test), though some testing is often best done by other people such as project managers, quality managers, developers, business and domain experts or infrastructure or IT operations experts.

5.1.2 Working as a test leader

We have seen that the location of a test team within a project organization can vary widely. Similarly there is wide variation in the roles that people within the test team play. Some of these roles occur frequently, some infrequently. Two roles that are found within many test teams are those of the test leader and the tester, though the same people may play both roles at various points during the project. Let's take a look at the work done in these roles, starting with the test leader.

Test leaders tend to be involved in the planning, monitoring, and control of the testing activities and tasks discussed in Section 1.5 on the fundamental test process. At the outset of the project, test leaders, in collaboration with the other stakeholders, devise the test objectives, organizational test policies (if not already in place), test strategies and test plans. They estimate the testing to be done and negotiate with management to acquire the necessary resources. They recognize when test automation is appropriate and, if it is, they plan the effort, select the tools, and ensure training of the team. They may consult with other groups – e.g. programmers – to help them with their testing. They lead, guide and monitor the analysis, design, implementation and execution of the test cases, test procedures and test suites. They ensure proper configuration management of the testware produced and traceability of the tests to the test basis.

As test execution comes near, they make sure the test environment is put into place before test execution and managed during test execution. They schedule the tests for execution and then they monitor, measure, control and report on the test progress, the product quality status and the test results, adapting the test plan and compensating as needed to adjust to evolving conditions. During test execution and as the project winds down, they write summary reports on test status.

Sometimes test leaders wear different titles, such as test manager or test coordinator. Alternatively, the test leader role may wind up assigned to a project manager, a development manager or a quality assurance manager. (Regarding the first two people on this list, warning bells about independence should be ringing in your head now, in addition to thoughts about how we can ensure that such non-testers gain the knowledge and outlook needed to manage testing.) Whoever is playing the role, expect them to plan, monitor and control the testing work.

5.1.3 Working as a tester

As with test leaders, projects should include testers at the outset, though more testers may be required at later stages of testing. In the planning and preparation phases of the testing, testers should review and contribute to test plans, as well as analyzing, reviewing and assessing requirements and design specifications. They may be involved in or even be the primary people identifying test conditions and creating test designs, test cases, test procedure specifications and test data, and may automate or help to automate the tests. They often set up the test environments or assist system administration and network management staff in doing so.

As test execution begins, the number of testers often increases, starting with the work required to implement tests in the test environment. (They may play such a role on all test levels, even those not under the direct control of the test group; e.g. they might implement unit tests which were designed by programmers.) Testers execute and log the tests, evaluate the results and document problems found. They monitor the testing and the test environment, often using tools for this task, and often gather performance metrics. Throughout the testing life cycle, they review each other's work, including test specifications, defect reports and test results.

5.1.4 Defining the skills test staff need

Doing testing properly requires more than defining the right positions and number of people for those positions. Good test teams have the right mix of skills based on the tasks and activities they need to carry out, and people outside the test team who are in charge of test tasks need the right skills, too.

People involved in testing need basic professional and social qualifications such as literacy, the ability to prepare and deliver written and verbal reports, the ability to communicate effectively, and so on. Going beyond that, when we think of the skills that testers need, three main areas come to mind:

- Application or business domain: A tester must understand the intended behaviour, the problem the system will solve, the process it will automate and so forth, in order to spot improper behaviour while testing and recognize the 'must work' functions and features.

- Technology: A tester must be aware of issues, limitations and capabilities of the chosen implementation technology, in order to effectively and efficiently locate problems and recognize the 'likely to fail' functions and features.

- Testing: A tester must know the testing topics discussed in this book – and often more advanced testing topics – in order to effectively and efficiently carry out the test tasks assigned.

The specific skills in each area and the level of skill required vary by project, organization, application, and the risks involved.

The set of testing tasks and activities are many and varied, and so too are the skills required, so we often see specialization of skills and separation of roles. For example, due to the special knowledge required in the areas of testing, technology and business domain, respectively, test automation experts may handle automating the regression tests, programmers may perform component and integration tests and users and operators may be involved in acceptance tests.

We have long advocated pervasive testing, the involvement of people throughout the project team in carrying out testing tasks. Let us close this section, though, on a cautionary note. Software and system companies (e.g. producers of shrink-wrapped software and consumer products) typically overestimate the technology knowledge required to be an effective tester. Businesses that use information technology (e.g. banks and insurance companies) typically overestimate the business domain knowledge needed.

All types of projects tend to underestimate the testing knowledge required. We have seen a project fail in part because people without proper testing skills tested critical components, leading to the disastrous discovery of fundamental architectural problems later. Most projects can benefit from the participation of professional testers, as amateur testing alone will usually not suffice.

5.2 TEST PLANNING AND ESTIMATION

SYLLABUS LEARNING OBJECTIVES FOR 5.2 TEST PLANNING AND ESTIMATION (K2)

LO-5.2.1 Recognize the different levels and objectives of test planning. (K1)

LO-5.2.2 Summarize the purpose and content of the test plan, test design specification and test procedure documents according to the 'Standard for Software Test Documentation' (IEEE Std 829-1998). (K2)

LO-5.2.3 Differentiate between conceptually different test approaches, such as analytical, model-based, methodical, process/standard compliant, dynamic/heuristic, consultative and regression-averse. (K2)

LO-5.2.4 Differentiate between the subject of test planning for a system and scheduling test execution. (K2)

LO-5.2.5 Write a test execution schedule for a given set of test cases, considering prioritization, and technical and logical dependencies. (K3)

LO-5.2.6 List test preparation and execution activities that should be considered during test planning. (K1)

> **LO-5.2.7**   **Recall typical factors that influence the effort related to testing. (K1)**
>
> **LO-5.2.8**   **Differentiate between two conceptually different estimation approaches: the metrics-based approach and the expert-based approach. (K2)**
>
> **LO-5.2.9**   **Recognize/justify adequate entry and exit criteria for specific test levels and groups of test cases (e.g. for integration testing, acceptance testing or test cases for usability testing). (K2)**

In this section, let's talk about a complicated trio of test topics: plans, estimates and strategies. Plans, estimates and strategies depend on a number of factors, including the level, targets and objectives of the testing we're setting out to do. Writing a plan, preparing an estimate and selecting test strategies tend to happen concurrently and ideally during the planning period for the overall project, though we must ready to revise them as the project proceeds and we gain more information.

Let's look closely at how to prepare a test plan, examining issues related to planning for a project, for a test level or phase, for a specific test type and for test execution. We'll examine typical factors that influence the effort related to testing, and see two different estimation approaches: metrics-based and expert-based. We'll discuss selecting test strategies and ways to establish adequate exit criteria for testing. In addition, we'll look at various tasks related to test preparation and execution that need planning.

There are no extra glossary terms in this section.

5.2.1 The purpose and substance of test plans

While people tend to have different definitions of what goes in a test plan, for us a test plan is the project plan for the testing work to be done. It is not a test design specification, a collection of test cases or a set of test procedures; in fact, most of our test plans do not address that level of detail.

Why do we write test plans? We have three main reasons.

First, writing a test plan guides our thinking. We find that if we can explain something in words, we understand it. If not, there's a good chance we don't. Writing a test plan forces us to confront the challenges that await us and focus our thinking on important topics. In Chapter 2 of Fred Brooks' brilliant and essential book on software engineering management, *The Mythical Man-Month*, he explains the importance of careful estimation and planning for testing as follows:

> *Failure to allow enough time for system test, in particular, is peculiarly disastrous. Since the delay comes at the end of the schedule, no one is aware of schedule trouble until almost the delivery date [and] delay at this point has unusually severe ... financial repercussions. The project is fully staffed, and cost-per-day is maximum [as are the associated opportunity costs]. It is therefore very important to allow enough system test time in the original schedule.*

[Brooks 1995]

We find that using a template when writing test plans helps us remember the important challenges. You can use the IEEE 829 test plan template shown in this chapter, use someone else's template, or create your own template over time.

The test planning process and the plan itself serve as vehicles for communicating with other members of the project team, testers, peers, managers, and other stakeholders. This communication allows the test plan to influence the project team and the project team to influence the test plan, especially in the areas of organization-wide testing policies and motivations; test scope, objectives, and critical areas to test; project and product risks, resource considerations and constraints; and the testability of the item under test.

You can accomplish this communication through circulation of one or two test plan drafts and through review meetings. Such a draft may include many notes such as the following examples:

> *[To Be Determined: Jennifer: Please tell me what the plan is for releasing the test items into the test lab for each cycle of system test execution?]*
>
> *[Dave – please let me know which version of the test tool will be used for the regression tests of the previous increments.]*

As you document the answers to these kinds of questions, the test plan becomes a record of previous discussions and agreements between the testers and the rest of the project team.

The test plan also helps us manage change. During early phases of the project, as we gather more information, we revise our plans. As the project evolves and situations change, we adapt our plans. Written test plans give us a baseline against which to measure such revisions and changes. Furthermore, updating the plan at major milestones helps keep testing aligned with project needs. As we run the tests, we make final adjustments to our plans based on the results. You might not have the time – or the energy – to update your test plans every time a variance occurs, as some projects can be quite dynamic. In Chapter 6 [Black 2009], we describe a simple approach for documenting variances from the test plan that you can implement using a database or spreadsheet. You can include these change records in a periodic test plan update, as part of a test status report, or as part as an end-of-project test summary.

We've found that it's better to write multiple test plans in some situations. For example, when we manage both integration and system test levels, those two test execution periods occur at different points in time and have different objectives. For some systems projects, a hardware test plan and a software test plan will address different techniques and tools as well as different audiences. However, since there might be overlap between these test plans, a master test plan that addresses the common elements can reduce the amount of redundant documentation.

5.2.2 What to do with your brain while planning tests

Writing a good test plan is easier than writing a novel, but both tasks require an organized approach and careful thought. In fact, since a good test plan is kept short and focused, unlike some novels, some might argue that it's harder to write a good test plan. Let's look at some of the planning tasks you need to carry out.

At a high level, you need to consider the purpose served by the testing work. In terms of the overall organizational needs, this purpose is referred to variously as the test team's mission or the organization's testing policy. In terms of the specific

IEEE 829 STANDARD TEST PLAN TEMPLATE

Test plan identifier   Test deliverables
Introduction   Test tasks
Test items   Environmental needs
Features to be tested   Responsibilities
Features not to be tested   Staffing and training needs
Approach   Schedule
Item pass/fail criteria   Risks and contingencies
Suspension and resumption criteria   Approvals

project, understanding the purpose of testing means knowing the answers to questions such as:

● What is in scope and what is out of scope for this testing effort?

● What are the test objectives?

● What are the important project and product risks? (More on risks in Section 5.5.)

● What constraints affect testing (e.g. budget limitations, hard deadlines, etc.)?

● What is most critical for this product and project?

● Which aspects of the product are more (or less) testable?

● What should be the overall test execution schedule and how should we decide the order in which to run specific tests? (Product and planning risks, discussed later in this chapter, will influence the answers to these questions.)

You should then select strategies which are appropriate to the purpose of testing (more on the topic of selecting strategies in a few pages).

In addition, you need to decide how to split the testing work into various levels, as discussed in Chapter 2 (e.g. component, integration, system and acceptance). If that decision has already been made, you need to decide how to best fit your testing work in the level you are responsible for with the testing work done in those other test levels. During the analysis and design of tests, you'll want to reduce gaps and overlap between levels and, during test execution, you'll want to coordinate between the levels. Such details dealing with inter-level coordination are often addressed in the master test plan.

In addition to integrating and coordinating between test levels, you should also plan to integrate and coordinate all the testing work to be done with the rest of the project. For example, what items must be acquired for the testing? Are there on-going supply issues, such as with imitation bills (i.e. simulated banknotes) for a financial application such as an ATM? When will the programmers complete work on the system under test? What operations support is required for the test environment? What kind of information must be delivered to the maintenance team at the end of testing?

Moving down into the details, what makes a plan a plan – rather than a statement of principles, a laundry list of good ideas or a collection of suggestions – is that the author specifies in it who will do what when and (at least in a general way) how.

Resources are required to carry out the work. These are often hard decisions that require careful consideration and building a consensus across the team, including with the project manager.

The entire testing process – from planning through to closure – produces information, some of which you will need to document. How precisely should testers write the test designs, cases and procedures? How much should they leave to the judgment of the tester during test execution, and what are the reproducibility issues associated with this decision? What kinds of templates can testers use for the various documents they'll produce? How do those documents relate to one another? If you intend to use tools for tasks such as test design and execution, as discussed in Chapter 6, you'll need to understand how the models or automated tests will integrate with manual testing and plan and who will be responsible for automation design, implementation and support. There may be a separate Test Automation Plan, but this needs to be coordinated with other Test Plans.

Some information you'll need to gather in the form of raw data and then distil. What metrics to do you intend to use to monitor, control and manage the testing? Which of those metrics – and perhaps other metrics – will you use to report your results? We'll look more closely at possible answers to those questions in Section 5.3, but a good test plan provides answers early in the project.

Finally, moving back up to a higher level, think about what would be true about the project when the project was ready to start executing tests. What would be true about the project when the project was ready to declare test execution done? At what point can you safely start a particular test level or phase, test suite or test target? When can you finish it? The factors to consider in such decisions are often called 'entry criteria' and 'exit criteria.'

Typical factors for entry criteria are:

- Acquisition and supply: the availability of staff, tools, systems, test environments, test data, and other materials required.
- Test items: the state that the items to be tested must be in to start and to finish testing.

Typical factors for exit criteria are:

- Defects: the number known to be present, the arrival rate, the number predicted to remain, and the number resolved.
- Tests: the number prepared, run, passed, failed, blocked, skipped, and so forth.
- Coverage: the extent to which the test basis, risk, functionality, supported configurations, and the software code have been tested – or have not.
- Quality: the status of the important quality characteristics for the system, the estimated number of defects present or remaining, and other attributes.
- Money: the cost of finding the next defect in the current level of testing compared to the cost of finding it in the next level of testing (or in production).
- Schedule: the project schedule implications of starting or ending testing.
- Risk: the undesirable outcomes that could result from shipping too early (such as latent defects or untested areas) – or too late (such as loss of market share).

When writing exit criteria, we try to remember that a successful project is a balance of quality, budget, schedule and feature considerations. This is even more important when applying exit criteria at the end of the project.

5.2.3 Estimating what testing will involve and what it will cost

The testing work to be done can often be seen as a subproject within the larger project. So, we can adapt fundamental techniques of estimation for testing. We could start with a work-breakdown structure that identifies the stages, activities and tasks.

Starting at the highest level, we can break down a testing project into phases using the fundamental test process identified in the ISTQB Syllabus: planning and control; analysis and design; implementation and execution; evaluating exit criteria and reporting; and test closure. Within each phase we identify activities and within each activity we identify tasks and perhaps subtasks. To identify the activities and tasks, we work both forward and backward. When we say we work forward, we mean that we start with the planning activities and then move forward in time step by step, asking, 'Now, what comes next?'

Working backward means that we consider the risks that we identified during risk analysis (which we'll discuss in Section 5.5). For those risks which you intend to address through testing, ask yourself, 'So, what activities and tasks are required in each stage to carry out this testing?' Let's look at an example of how you might work backward.

Suppose that you've identified performance as a major area of risk for your product. So, performance testing is an activity in the test execution phase. You now estimate the tasks involved with running a performance test, how long those tasks will take and how many times you'll need to run the performance tests.

Now, those tests didn't just appear out of thin air: someone had to develop them. So, performance test development entails activities in test analysis, design and implementation. You now estimate the tasks involved in developing a performance test, such as writing test scripts and creating test data.

Typically, performance tests need to be run in a special test environment that is designed to look like the production or field environment, at least in those ways which would affect response time and resource utilization and performance tests need special tools to generate load and check response. So, performance test environment acquisition and configuration is an activity in the test implementation phase. You now estimate tasks involved in acquiring and configuring such a test environment, such as simulating performance based on the production environment design to look for potential bottlenecks, getting the right hardware, software and tools and setting up hardware, software and tools.

Not everyone knows how to use performance-testing tools or to design performance tests. So, performance-testing training or staffing is an activity in the test planning phase. Depending on the approach you intend to take, you now estimate the time required to identify and hire a performance test professional or to train one or more people in your organization to do the job.

Finally, in many cases a detailed test plan is written for performance testing, due to its differences from other test types. So, performance-testing planning is an activity in the test planning phase. You now estimate the time required to draft, review and finalize a performance test plan.

When you are creating your work-breakdown structure, remember that you will want to use it for both estimation (at the beginning) and monitoring and control (as the project continues). To ensure accuracy of the estimate and precise control, make sure that you subdivide the work finely enough. This means that tasks should be short in duration, say one to three days. If they are much longer – say two weeks – then you run the risk that long and complex sub-tasks are 'hiding' within the larger task, only to be discovered later. This can lead to nasty surprises during the project.

5.2.4 Estimation techniques

There are two techniques for estimation covered by the ISTQB Foundation Syllabus. One involves consulting the people who will do the work and other people with expertise on the tasks to be done. The other involves analyzing metrics from past projects and from industry data. Let's look at each in turn.

Asking the individual contributors and experts involves working with experienced staff members to develop a work-breakdown structure for the project. With that done, you work together to understand, for each task, the effort, duration, dependencies, and resource requirements. The idea is to draw on the collective wisdom of the team to create your test estimate. Using a tool such as Microsoft Project or a whiteboard and sticky-notes, you and the team can then predict the testing end-date and major milestones. This technique is often called 'bottom up' estimation because you start at the lowest level of the hierarchical breakdown in the work-breakdown structure – the task – and let the duration, effort, dependencies and resources for each task add up across all the tasks.

Analyzing metrics can be as simple or sophisticated as you make it. The simplest approach is to ask, 'How many testers do we typically have per developer on a project?' A somewhat more reliable approach involves classifying the project in terms of size (small, medium or large) and complexity (simple, moderate or complex) and then seeing on average how long projects of a particular size and complexity combination have taken in the past. Another simple and reliable approach we have used is to look at the average effort per test case in similar past projects and to use the estimated number of test cases to estimate the total effort. Sophisticated approaches involve building mathematical models in a spreadsheet that look at historical or industry averages for certain key parameters – number of tests run by tester per day, number of defects found by tester per day, etc. – and then plugging in those parameters to predict duration and effort for key tasks or activities on your project. The tester-to-developer ratio is an example of a top-down estimation technique, in that the entire estimate is derived at the project level, while the parametric technique is bottom-up, at least when it is used to estimate individual tasks or activities.

We prefer to start by drawing on the team's wisdom to create the work-breakdown structure and a detailed bottom-up estimate. We then apply models and rules of thumb to check and adjust the estimate bottom-up and top-down using past history. This approach tends to create an estimate that is both more accurate and more defensible than either technique by itself.

Even the best estimate must be negotiated with management. Negotiating sessions exhibit amazing variety, depending on the people involved. However, there are some classic negotiating positions. It's not unusual for the test leader or manager to try to sell the management team on the value added by the testing or to alert management to the potential problems that would result from not testing enough. It's not unusual for management to look for smart ways to accelerate the schedule or to press for equivalent coverage in less time or with fewer resources. In between these positions, you and your colleagues can reach compromise, if the parties are willing. Our experience has been that successful negotiations about estimates are those where the focus is less on winning and losing and more about figuring out how best to balance competing pressures in the realms of quality, schedule, budget and features.

5.2.5 Factors affecting test effort

Testing is a complex endeavour on many projects and a variety of factors can influence it. When creating test plans and estimating the testing effort and schedule, you must keep these factors in mind or your plans and estimates will deceive you at the beginning of the project and betray you at the middle or end.

The test strategies or approaches you pick will have a major influence on the testing effort. This factor is so influential that we'll come back to it in Section 5.2.6. In this section, let's look at factors related to the product, the process and the results of testing.

Product factors start with the presence of sufficient project documentation so that the testers can figure out what the system is, how it is supposed to work and what correct behaviour looks like. In other words, adequate and high-quality information about the test basis will help us do a better, more efficient job of defining the tests.

The importance of non-functional quality characteristics such as usability, reliability, security, performance, and so forth also influences the testing effort. These test targets can be expensive and time consuming.

Complexity is another major product factor. Examples of complexity considerations include:

- The difficulty of comprehending and correctly handling the problem the system is being built to solve (e.g. avionics and oil exploration software).
- The use of innovative technologies, especially those long on hyperbole and short on proven track records.
- The need for intricate and perhaps multiple test configurations, especially when these rely on the timely arrival of scarce software, hardware and other supplies.
- The prevalence of stringent security rules, strictly regimented processes or other regulations.
- The geographical distribution of the team, especially if the team crosses time-zones (as many outsourcing efforts do).

While good project documentation is a positive factor, it's also true that having to produce detailed documentation, such as meticulously specified test cases, results in delays. During test execution, having to maintain such detailed documentation requires lots of effort, as does working with fragile test data that must be maintained or restored frequently during testing.

Finally, increasing the size of the product leads to increases in the size of the project and the project team. Increases in the project and project team increases the difficulty of predicting and managing them. This leads to the disproportionate rate of collapse of large projects.

Process factors include the availability of test tools, especially those that reduce the effort associated with test execution, which is on the critical path for release. On the development side, debugging tools and a dedicated debugging environment (as opposed to debugging in the test environment) also reduce the time required to complete testing.

The life cycle itself is an influential process factor, as the V-model tends to be more fragile in the face of late change while incremental models tend to have high regression testing costs. Process maturity, including test process maturity, is another factor, especially the implication that mature processes involve carefully managing change in the middle and end of the project, which reduces test execution cost.

Time pressure is another factor to be considered. Pressure should not be an excuse to take unwarranted risks. However, it is a reason to make careful, considered decisions and to plan and re-plan intelligently throughout the process, which is another hallmark of mature processes.

People execute the process, and people factors are as important or more important than any other. Indeed, even when many troubling things are true about a project, an excellent team can often make good things happen on the project and in testing. Important people factors include the skills of the individuals and the team as a whole, and the alignment of those skills with the project's needs. Since a project team is a team, solid relationships, reliable execution of agreed-upon commitments and responsibilities and a determination to work together towards a common goal are important. This is especially important for testing, where so much of what we test, use, and produce either comes from, relies upon or goes to people outside the testing group. Because of the importance of trusting relationships and the lengthy learning curves involved in software and system engineering, the stability of the project team is an important people factor, too.

The test results themselves are important in the total amount of test effort during test execution. The delivery of good-quality software at the start of test execution and quick, solid defect fixes during test execution prevents delays in the test execution process. A defect, once identified, should not have to go through multiple cycles of fix/retest/re-open, at least not if the initial estimate is going to be held to.

You probably noticed from this list that we included a number of factors outside the scope and control of the test leader or manager. Indeed, events that occur before or after testing can bring these factors about. For this reason, it's important that testers, especially test leaders or managers, be attuned to the overall context in which they operate. Some of these contextual factors result in specific project risks for testing, which should be addressed in the test plan. Project risks are discussed in more detail in Section 5.5.

5.2.6 Test approaches and strategies

A test strategy is the general way in which testing will happen, within each of the levels of testing, independent of project, across the organization. The test approach is the name the ISTQB gives to the implementation of the test strategy on a specific project. Since the test approach is specific to a project, you should define and document the approach in the test plans, and refine and document the test approach, providing further details, in the test designs.

Deciding on the test approach involves careful consideration of the testing objectives, the project's goals, and overall risk assessment. These decisions provide the starting point for planning the test process, for selecting the test design techniques and test types to be applied, and for defining the entry and exit criteria. In your decision-making on the approach, you should take into account the project, product, and organization context, issues related to risks, hazards and safety, the available resources, the team's level of skills, the technology involved, the nature of the system under test, considerations related to whether the system is custom built or assembled from commercial off the shelf components (COTS), the organization's test objectives, and any applicable regulations.

The choice of test approaches or strategies is one powerful factor in the success of the test effort and the accuracy of the test plans and estimates. This factor is under the control of the testers and test leaders. Of course, having choices also means that you can make mistakes, so we'll go into more detail about how to pick the right test strategies in a minute. First, though, let's survey the major types of test strategies that are commonly found.[1]

● Analytical: For example, the risk-based strategy involves performing a risk analysis using project documents and stakeholder input, then planning, estimating, designing, and prioritizing the tests based on risk. (We'll talk more about risk analysis later in this chapter.) Another analytical test strategy is the requirements-based strategy, where an analysis of the requirements specification forms the basis for planning, estimating and designing tests. Analytical test strategies have in common the use of some formal or informal analytical technique, usually during the requirements and design stages of the project.

● Model-based: For example, you can build mathematical models for loading and response for e-commerce servers, and test based on that model. If the behaviour of the system under test conforms to that predicted by the model, the system is deemed to be working. Model-based test strategies have in common the creation or selection of some formal or informal model for critical system behaviours, usually during the requirements and design stages of the project.

● Methodical: For example, you might have a checklist that you have put together over the years that suggests the major areas of testing to run or you might follow an industry-standard for software quality, such as ISO 9126, for your outline of major test areas. You then methodically design, implement and execute tests following this outline. Methodical test strategies have in common the adherence to a pre-planned, systematized approach that has been developed in-house, assembled from various concepts developed in-house and gathered from outside, or adapted significantly from outside ideas and may have an early or late point of involvement for testing.

● Process- or standard-compliant: For example, you might adopt the IEEE 829 standard for your testing, using books such as [Craig and Jaskiel 2002] or [Drabick 2004] to fill in the methodological gaps. Alternatively, you might adopt an agile methodology. Process- or standard-compliant strategies have in common reliance upon an externally developed approach to testing, often with little – if any – customization and may have an early or late point of involvement for testing.

● Dynamic: For example, you might create a lightweight set of testing guidelines that focus on rapid adaptation or known weaknesses in software. Dynamic strategies, such as exploratory testing, have in common concentrating on finding as many defects as possible during test execution and adapting to the realities of the system under test as it is when delivered, and they typically emphasize the later stages of testing. See, for example, the attack-based approach of [Whittaker 2002] and [Whittaker and Thompson 2003] and the exploratory approach of [Kaner et al. 2002].

---

[1]The catalogue of testing strategies that has been included in the ISTQB Foundation Syllabus grew out of an email discussion between Rex Black, Ross Collard, Kathy Iberle and Cem Kaner. We thank them for their thought-provoking comments.

- Consultative or directed: For example, you might ask the users or developers of the system to tell you what to test or even rely on them to do the testing. Consultative or directed strategies have in common the reliance on a group of non-testers to guide or perform the testing effort and typically emphasize the later stages of testing simply due to the lack of recognition of the value of early testing.

- Regression-averse: For example, you might try to automate all the tests of system functionality so that, whenever anything changes, you can re-run every test to ensure nothing has broken. Regression-averse strategies have in common a set of procedures – usually automated – that allow them to detect regression defects. A regression-averse strategy may involve automating functional tests prior to release of the function, in which case it requires early testing, but sometimes the testing is almost entirely focused on testing functions that already have been released, which is in some sense a form of post-release test involvement.

Some of these strategies are more preventive, others more reactive. For example, analytical test strategies involve upfront analysis of the test basis, and tend to identify problems in the test basis prior to test execution. This allows the early – and cheap – removal of defects. That is a strength of preventive approaches.

Dynamic test strategies focus on the test execution period. Such strategies allow the location of defects and defect clusters that might have been hard to anticipate until you have the actual system in front of you. That is a strength of reactive approaches.

Rather than see the choice of strategies, particularly the preventive or reactive strategies, as an either/or situation, we'll let you in on the worst-kept secret of testing (and many other disciplines): There is no one best way. We suggest that you adopt whatever test approaches make the most sense in your particular situation, and feel free to borrow and blend.

How do you know which strategies to pick or blend for the best chance of success? There are many factors to consider, but let us highlight a few of the most important:

- Risks: Testing is about risk management, so consider the risks and the level of risk. For a well-established application that is evolving slowly, regression is an important risk, so regression-averse strategies make sense. For a new application, a risk analysis may reveal different risks if you pick a risk-based analytical strategy.

- Skills: Strategies must not only be chosen, they must also be executed. So, you have to consider which skills your testers possess and lack. A standard-compliant strategy is a smart choice when you lack the time and skills in your team to create your own approach.

- Objectives: Testing must satisfy the needs of stakeholders to be successful. If the objective is to find as many defects as possible with a minimal amount of up-front time and effort invested – for example, at a typical independent test lab – then a dynamic strategy makes sense.

- Regulations: Sometimes you must satisfy not only stakeholders, but also regulators. In this case, you may need to devise a methodical test strategy that satisfies these regulators that you have met all their requirements.

● Product: Some products such as weapons systems and contract-development software tend to have well-specified requirements. This leads to synergy with a requirements-based analytical strategy.

● Business: Business considerations and business continuity are often important. If you can use a legacy system as a model for a new system, you can use a model-based strategy.

We mentioned above that a good team can sometimes triumph over a situation where materials, process and delaying factors are ranged against its success. However, talented execution of an unwise strategy is the equivalent of going very fast down a highway in the wrong direction. Therefore, you must make smart choices in terms of testing strategies. Furthermore, you must choose testing strategies with an eye towards the factors mentioned earlier, the schedule, budget, and feature constraints of the project and the realities of the organization and its politics.

5.3 TEST PROGRESS MONITORING AND CONTROL

SYLLABUS LEARNING OBJECTIVES FOR 5.3 TEST PROGRESS MONITORING AND CONTROL (K2)

LO-5.3.1 Recall common metrics used for monitoring test preparation and execution. (K1)

LO-5.3.2 Explain and compare test metrics for test reporting and test control (e.g. defects found and fixed, and tests passed and failed) related to purpose and use. (K2)

LO-5.3.3 Summarize the purpose and content of the test summary report document according to the 'Standard for Software Test Documentation' (IEEE Std 829-1998). (K2)

In this section, we'll review techniques and metrics that are commonly used for monitoring test preparation and execution. We'll focus especially on the use and interpretation of such test metrics for reporting, controlling and analyzing the test effort, including those based on defects and those based on test data. We'll also look at options for reporting test status using such metrics and other information.

As you read, remember to watch for the glossary terms **defect density** and **failure rate.**

5.3.1 Monitoring the progress of test activities

Having developed our plans, defined our test strategies and approaches and estimated the work to be done, we must now track our testing work as we carry it out. Test monitoring can serve various purposes during the project, including the following:

● Give the test team and the test manager feedback on how the testing work is going, allowing opportunities to guide and improve the testing and the project.

- Provide the project team with visibility about the test results.
- Measure the status of the testing, test coverage and test items against the exit criteria to determine whether the test work is done.
- Gather data for use in estimating future test efforts.

Especially for small projects, the test leader or a delegated person can gather test progress monitoring information manually using documents, spreadsheets and simple databases. When working with large teams, distributed projects and long-term test efforts, we find that the efficiency and consistency of data collection is aided by the use of automated tools (see Chapter 6).

One way to gather test progress information is to use the IEEE 829 test log template. While much of the information related to logging events can be usefully captured in a document, we prefer to capture the test-by-test information in spreadsheets (see Figure 5.1).

IEEE 829 STANDARD: TEST LOG TEMPLATE

Test log identifier

Description (items being tested, environment in which the testing is conducted)

Activity and event entries (execution description, procedure results, environmental information, anomalous events, incident report identifiers)

In Figure 5.1, columns A and B show the test ID and the test case or test suite name. The state of the test case is shown in column C ('Warn' indicates a test that resulted in a minor failure). Column D shows the tested configuration, where the codes A, B and C correspond to test environments described in detail in the test plan. Columns E and F show the defect (or bug) ID number (from the defect-tracking database) and the risk priority number of the defect (ranging from 1, the worst, to 25, the least risky). Column G shows the initials of the tester who ran the test. Columns H through L capture data for each test related to dates, effort and duration (in hours). We have metrics for planned and actual effort and dates completed which would allow us to summarize progress against the planned schedule and budget. This spreadsheet can also be summarized in terms of the percentage of tests which have been run and the percentage of tests which have passed and failed.

Figure 5.1 might show a snapshot of test progress during the test execution period, or perhaps even at test closure if it were deemed acceptable to skip some of the tests. During the analysis, design and implementation of the tests, such a worksheet would show the state of the tests in terms of their state of development.

In addition to test case status, it is also common to monitor test progress during the test execution period by looking at the number of defects found and fixed. Figure 5.2 shows a graph that plots the total number of defects opened and closed over the course of the test execution so far.

Test ID	Test Suite/Case	Status	System Config	Bug ID	Bug RPN	Run By	Plan Date	Act Date	Plan Effort	Actual Effort	Test Duration	Comment
	System Test Case Summary											
	Cycle One											
1.000	*Functionality*											
1.001	File	Fail	A	701	1	LTW	1/8	1/8	4	6	6	
1.002	Edit	Fail	A	709	1	LTW	1/9	1/10	4	8	8	
				710	5							
				718	3							
				722	4							
1.003	Font	Pass	B			JHB	1/10	1/10	4	4	4	
1.004	Tables	Warn	B	708	15	JHB	1/8	1/9	4	5	5	
1.005	Printing	Skip					1/10		4			Out of runway
	Suite Summary						1/10	1/10	20	23	23	
2.000	*Performance/Stress*											
2.001	Solaris Server	Warn	A,B,C	701	1	EM	1/10	1/13	4	8	24	Replan 1/11
2.002	NT Server	Fail	A,B,C	724	2	EM	1/11	1/14	4	4	24	Replan 1/12
				713	2							
				725	1							
2.003	Linux Server	Skip					1/12		4			Out of runway
	Suite Summary						1/12	1/14	12	12	48	
3.000	*Error Handling/Recovery*											
3.001	Corrupt File	Fail	A	701	1	LTW	1/8	1/9	4	8	8	
				706	2							
				707	4							
				709	1							
				710	5							
				713	2							
3.002	Server Crash	Fail	A	712	6	LTW	1/9	1/10	4	6	6	
				713	2							
				717	1							
	Suite Summary						1/9	1/10	8	14	14	
4.000	*Localization*											
4.001	Spanish	Skip										
4.002	French	Skip										
4.003	Japanese	Skip										
4.004	Chinese	Skip										
	Suite Summary						1/0	1/0	0	0	0	

FIGURE 5.1 Test case summary worksheet

failure rate The ratio of the number of failures of a given category to a given unit of measure, e.g. failures per unit of time, failures per number of transactions, failures per number of computer runs.

defect density The number of defects identified in a component or system divided by the size of the component or system (expressed in standard measurement terms, e.g. lines-of-code, number of classes or function points).

It also shows the planned test period end date and the planned number of defects that will be found. Ideally, as the project approaches the planned end date, the total number of defects opened will settle in at the predicted number and the total number of defects closed will converge with the total number opened. These two outcomes tell us that we have found enough defects to feel comfortable that we're done testing, that we have no reason to think many more defects are lurking in the product, and that all known defects have been resolved.

Charts such as Figure 5.2 can also be used to show **failure rates** or **defect density**. When reliability is a key concern, we might be more concerned with the frequency with which failures are observed than with how many defects are causing the failures. In organizations that are looking to produce ultra-reliable software, they may plot the number of unresolved defects normalized by the size of the product, either in thousands of source lines of code (KSLOC), function points (FP) or some other metric of code size. Once the number of unresolved defects falls below some predefined threshold – for example, three per million lines of code – then the product may be deemed to have met the defect density exit criteria.

Measuring test progress based on defects found and fixed is common and useful – if used with care. Avoid using defect metrics alone, as it is possible to achieve a flat defect find rate and to fix all the known defects by stopping any further testing, by deliberately impeding the reporting of defects and by allowing programmers to reject, cancel, or close defect reports without any independent review.

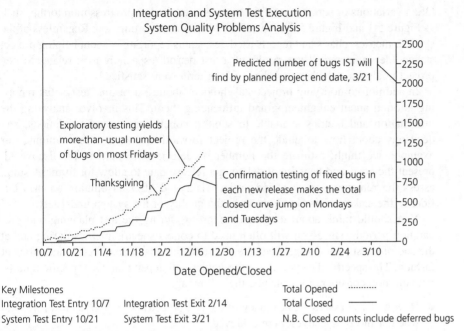

Integration and System Test Execution
System Quality Problems Analysis

Predicted number of bugs IST will
find by planned project end date, 3/21

Exploratory testing yields
more-than-usual number
of bugs on most Fridays

Thanksgiving

Confirmation testing of fixed bugs in
each new release makes the total
closed curve jump on Mondays
and Tuesdays

10/7   10/21   11/4   11/18   12/2   12/16   12/30   1/13   1/27   2/10   2/24   3/10

Date Opened/Closed

Key Milestones

Integration Test Entry 10/7   Integration Test Exit 2/14

System Test Entry 10/21   System Test Exit 3/21

Total Opened   ···········

Total Closed   ————

N.B. Closed counts include deferred bugs

FIGURE 5.2   Total defects opened and closed chart

That said, test progress monitoring techniques vary considerably depending on the preferences of the testers and stakeholders, the needs and goals of the project, regulatory requirements, time and money constraints and other factors. In addition to the kinds of information shown in the IEEE 829 Test Log Template, Figures 5.1 and Figure 5.2, other common metrics for test progress monitoring include:

- The extent of completion of test environment preparation.
- The extent of test coverage achieved, measured against requirements, risks, code, configurations or other areas of interest.
- The status of the testing (including analysis, design and implementation) compared to various test milestones.
- The economics of testing, such as the costs and benefits of continuing test execution in terms of finding the next defect or running the next test.

As a complementary monitoring technique, you might assess the subjective level of confidence the testers have in the test items. However, avoid making important decisions based on subjective assessments alone, as people's impressions have a way of being inaccurate and coloured by bias.

5.3.2 Reporting test status

Test progress monitoring is about gathering detailed test data; reporting test status is about effectively communicating our findings to other project stake-holders. As with test progress monitoring, in practice there is wide variability observed in how people report test status, with the variations driven by the preferences of the testers and stakeholders, the needs and goals of the project, regulatory requirements, time and money constraints and limitations of the tools available for test status reporting.

Often variations or summaries of the metrics used for test progress monitoring, such as Figure 5.1 and Figure 5.2, are used for test status reporting, too. Regardless of the specific metrics, charts and reports used, test status reporting is about helping project stakeholders understand the results of a test period, especially as it relates to key project goals and whether (or when) exit criteria were satisfied.

In addition to notifying project stakeholders about test results, test status reporting is often about enlightening and influencing them. This involves analyzing the information and metrics available to support conclusions, recommendations, and decisions about how to guide the project forward or to take other actions. For example, we might estimate the number of defects remaining to be discovered, present the costs and benefits of delaying a release date to allow for further testing, assess the remaining product and project risks and offer an opinion on the confidence the stakeholders should have in the quality of the system under test.

You should think about test status reporting during the test planning and preparation periods, since you will often need to collect specific metrics during and at the end of a test period to generate the test status reports in an effective and efficient fashion. The specific data you'll want to gather will depend on your specific reports, but common considerations include the following:

● How will you assess the adequacy of the test objectives for a given test level and whether those objectives were achieved?
● How will you assess the adequacy of the test approaches taken and whether they support the achievement of the project's testing goals?
● How will you assess the effectiveness of the testing with respect to these objectives and approaches?

For example, if you are doing risk-based testing, one main test objective is to subject the important product risks to the appropriate extent of testing. Table 5.1 shows an example of a chart that would allow you to report your test coverage and unresolved defects against the main product risk areas you identified in your risk analysis. If you are doing requirements-based testing, you could measure coverage in terms of requirements or functional areas instead of risks.

On some projects, the test team must create a test summary report. Such a report, created either at a key milestone or at the end of a test level, describes the results of a given level or phase of testing. The IEEE 829 Standard Test Summary Report Template provides a useful guideline for what goes into such a report. In addition to including the kind of charts and tables shown earlier, you might discuss important events (especially problematic ones) that occurred during testing, the objectives of testing and whether they were achieved, the test strategy followed and how well it worked, and the overall effectiveness of the test effort.

5.3.3 Test control

Projects do not always unfold as planned. In fact, any human endeavour more complicated than a family picnic is likely to vary from plan. Risks become occurrences. Stakeholder needs evolve. The world around us changes. When plans and reality diverge, we must act to bring the project back under control.

In some cases, the test findings themselves are behind the divergence; for example, suppose the quality of the test items proves unacceptably bad and delays test progress. In other cases, testing is affected by outside events; for example, testing can be delayed when the test items show up late or the test environment is

TABLE 5.1   Risk coverage by defects and tests

Test targets (product risk areas)	Unresolved defects		Test cases to be run		
	#	%	Planned	Actual	%
Performance, load, reliability	304	27	3843	1512	39
Robustness, operations, security	234	21	1032	432	42
Functionality, data, dates	224	20	4744	2043	43
Use cases, user interfaces, localization	160	14	498	318	64
Interfaces	93	8	193	153	79
Compatibility	71	6	1787	939	53
Other	21	2	0	0	0
	1107	*100*	*12857*	*5703*	*44*

IEEE 829 STANDARD: TEST SUMMARY REPORT TEMPLATE

Test summary report identifier

Summary

Variances

Comprehensive assessment

Summary of results

Evaluation

Summary of activities

Approvals

---

unavailable. Test control is about guiding and corrective actions to try to achieve the best possible outcome for the project.

The specific corrective or guiding actions depend, of course, on what we are trying to control. Consider the following hypothetical examples:

● A portion of the software under test will be delivered late, after the planned test start date. Market conditions dictate that we cannot change the release date. Test control might involve re-prioritizing the tests so that we start testing against what is available now.

● For cost reasons, performance testing is normally run on weekday evenings during off-hours in the production environment. Due to unanticipated high demand for your products, the company has temporarily adopted an evening shift that keeps the production environment in use 18 hours a day, five days a week. Test control might involve rescheduling the performance tests for the weekend.

While these examples show test control actions that affect testing, the project team might also have to take other actions that affect others on the project. For example, suppose that the test completion date is at risk due to a high number of defect fixes that fail confirmation testing in the test environment. In this case, test control might involve requiring the programmers making the fixes to thoroughly retest the fixes prior to checking them in to the code repository for inclusion in a test build.

5.4 CONFIGURATION MANAGEMENT

SYLLABUS LEARNING OBJECTIVES FOR 5.4 CONFIGURATION MANAGEMENT (K2)

LO-5.4.1   Summarize how configuration management supports testing. (K2)

In this brief section, we'll look at how configuration management relates to and supports testing. You will come across the glossary terms **configuration control, configuration management** and **version control**.

configuration management A discipline applying technical and administrative direction and surveillance to: identify and document the functional and physical characteristics of a configuration item, control changes to those characteristics, record and report change processing and implementation status, and verify compliance with specified requirements.

Configuration control (version control) An element of configuration management, consisting of the evaluation, co-ordination, approval or disapproval, and implementation of changes to configuration items after formal establishment of their configuration identification.

Configuration management is a topic that often perplexes new practitioners, but, if you ever have the bad luck to work as a tester on a project where this critical activity is handled poorly, you'll never forget how important it is. Briefly put, configuration management is in part about determining clearly what the items are that make up the software or system. These items include source code, test scripts, third-party software (including tools that support testing), hardware, data and both development and test documentation. Configuration management is also about making sure that these items are managed carefully, thoroughly and attentively throughout the entire project and product life cycle.

Configuration management has a number of important implications for testing. For one thing, it allows the testers to manage their testware and test results using the same configuration management mechanisms, as if they were as valuable as the source code and documentation for the system itself – which of course they are.

For another thing, configuration management supports the build process, which is essential for delivery of a test release into the test environment. Simply sending Zip archives by e-mail will not suffice, because there are too many opportunities for such archives to become polluted with undesirable contents or to harbour left-over previous versions of items. Especially in later phases of testing, it is critical to have a solid, reliable way of delivering test items that work and are the proper version.

Last but not least, configuration management allows us to map what is being tested to the underlying files and components that make it up. This is absolutely critical. For example, when we report defects, we need to report them *against* something, something which is **configuration controlled** or **version controlled**. If it's not clear what we found the defect in, the programmers will have a very tough time of finding the defect in order to fix it. For the kind of test reports discussed earlier to have any meaning, we must be able to trace the test results back to what exactly we tested.

Ideally, when testers receive an organized, version-controlled test release from a change-managed source code repository, it is accompanied by a test item transmittal report or release notes. [IEEE 829] provides a useful guideline for what goes into such a report. Release notes are not always so formal and do not always contain all the information shown.

While our description was brief, configuration management is a topic that is as complex as test environment management. So, advanced planning is critical to making this work. During the project planning stage – and perhaps as part of your own test plan – make sure that configuration management procedures and tools are selected. As the project proceeds, the configuration process and mechanisms must be implemented, and the key interfaces to the rest of the development process should be documented. Come test execution time, this will allow you and the rest of the project team to avoid nasty surprises like testing the wrong software, receiving uninstallable builds and reporting irreproducible defects against versions of code that don't exist anywhere but in the test environment.

IEEE 829 STANDARD: TEST ITEM TRANSMITTAL REPORT TEMPLATE

Transmittal report identifier	Status
Transmitted items	Approvals
Location	

5.5 RISK AND TESTING

SYLLABUS LEARNING OBJECTIVES FOR 5.5 RISK AND TESTING (K2)

LO-5.5.1   Describe a risk as a possible problem that would threaten the achievement of one or more stakeholders' project objectives. (K2)

LO-5.5.2   Remember that the level of risk is determined by likelihood (of happening) and impact (harm resulting if it does happen). (K1)

LO-5.5.3   Distinguish between the project and product risks. (K2)

LO-5.5.4   Recognize typical product and project risks. (K1)

LO-5.5.5   Describe, using examples, how risk analysis and risk management may be used for test planning. (K2)

This section covers a topic that we believe is critical to testing: risk. Let's look closely at risks, the possible problems that might endanger the objectives of the project stakeholders. We'll discuss how to determine the level of risk using likelihood and impact. We'll see that there are risks related to the product and risks related to the project, and look at typical risks in both categories. Finally – and most important – we'll look at various ways that risk analysis and risk management can help us plot a course for solid testing

As you read this section, make sure to attend carefully to the glossary terms **product risk, project risk,** and **risk-based testing**.

5.5.1 Risks and levels of risk

Risk is a word we all use loosely, but what exactly is risk? Simply put, it's the possibility of a negative or undesirable outcome. In the future, a risk has some likelihood between 0% and 100%; it is a possibility, not a certainty. In the past, however, either the risk has materialized and become an outcome or issue or it has not; the likelihood of a risk in the past is either 0% or 100%.

The likelihood of a risk becoming an outcome is one factor to consider when thinking about the level of risk associated with its possible negative consequences. The more likely the outcome is, the worse the risk. However, likelihood is not the only consideration.

For example, most people are likely to catch a cold in the course of their lives, usually more than once. The typical healthy individual suffers no serious consequences. Therefore, the overall level of risk associated with colds is low for this person. But the risk of a cold for an elderly person with breathing difficulties would be high. The potential consequences or impact is an important consideration affecting the level of risk, too.

Remember that in Chapter 1 we discussed how system context, and especially the risk associated with failures, influences testing. Here, we'll get into more detail about the concept of risks, how they influence testing, and specific ways to manage risk.

We can classify risks into project risks (factors relating to the way the work is carried out, i.e. the test project) and product risks (factors relating to what is produced by the work, i.e. the thing we are testing). We will look at product risks first.

5.5.2 Product risks

product risk A risk directly related to the test object.

You can think of a **product risk** as the possibility that the system or software might fail to satisfy some reasonable customer, user, or stakeholder expectation. (Some authors refer to 'product risks' as 'quality risks' as they are risks to the quality of the product.) Unsatisfactory software might omit some key function that the customers specified, the users required or the stakeholders were promised. Unsatisfactory software might be unreliable and frequently fail to behave normally. Unsatisfactory software might fail in ways that cause financial or other damage to a user or the company that user works for. Unsatisfactory software might have problems with data integrity and data quality, such as data migration issues, data conversion problems, data transport problems, and violations of data standards such as field and referential integrity. Unsatisfactory software might have problems related to a particular quality characteristic. The problems might not involve functionality, but rather security, reliability, usability, maintainability or performance. Generally, the software could fail to perform its intended functions, dissatisfying users and customers.

risk-based testing An approach to testing to reduce the level of product risks and inform stakeholders of their status, starting in the initial stages of a project. It involves the identification of product risks and the use of risk levels to guide the test process.

Risk-based testing is the idea that we can organize our testing efforts in a way that reduces the residual level of product risk when the system ships. Risk-based testing uses risk to prioritize and emphasize the appropriate tests during test execution, but it's about more than that. Risk-based testing starts early in the project, identifying risks to system quality and using that knowledge of risk to guide testing planning, specification, preparation and execution. Risk-based testing involves both mitigation – testing to provide opportunities to reduce the likelihood of defects, especially high-impact defects – and contingency – testing to identify work-arounds to make the defects that do get past us less painful. Risk-based testing also involves measuring how well we are doing at finding and removing defects in critical areas, as was shown in Table 5.1. Risk-based testing can also involve using risk analysis to identify proactive opportunities to remove or prevent defects through non-testing activities and to help us select which test activities to perform.

Mature test organizations use testing to reduce the risk associated with delivering the software to an acceptable level [Beizer 1990], [Hetzel 1988]. In the middle of the 1990s, a number of testers, including us, started to explore various techniques for risk-based testing. In doing so, we adapted well-accepted risk management concepts to software testing. Applying and refining risk assessment and management techniques are discussed in [Black 2001] and [Black 2004]. For two alternative views, see Chapter 11 of [Pol *et al.* 2002] and Chapter 2 of [Craig and Jaskiel 2002]. The origin of the risk-based testing concept can be found in Chapter 1 of [Beizer 1990] and Chapter 2 of [Hetzel 1988].

Risk-based testing starts with product risk analysis. One technique for risk analysis is a close reading of the requirements specification, design specifications, user documentation and other items. Another technique is brainstorming with many of the project stakeholders. Another is a sequence of one-on-one or small-group sessions with the business and technology experts in the company. Some people use all these techniques when they can. To us, a team-based approach that involves the key stakeholders and experts is preferable to a purely document-based approach, as team approaches draw on the knowledge, wisdom and insight of the entire team to determine what to test and how much.

While you could perform the risk analysis by asking, 'What should we worry about?' usually more structure is required to avoid missing things. One way to provide that structure is to look for specific risks in particular product risk categories. You could consider risks in the areas of functionality, localization, usability, reliability, performance and supportability. Alternatively, you could use the quality characteristics and sub-characteristics from ISO 9126 (introduced in Chapter 1), as each sub-characteristic that matters is subject to risks that the system might have troubles in that area. You might have a checklist of typical or past risks that should be considered. You might also want to review the tests that failed and the bugs that you found in a previous release or a similar product. These lists and reflections serve to jog the memory, forcing you to think about risks of particular kinds, as well as helping you structure the documentation of the product risks.

When we talk about specific risks, we mean a particular kind of defect or failure that might occur. For example, if you were testing the calculator utility that is bundled with Microsoft Windows, you might identify 'incorrect calculation' as a specific risk within the category of functionality. However, this is too broad. Consider incorrect addition. This is a high-impact kind of defect, as everyone who uses the calculator will see it. It is unlikely, since addition is not a complex algorithm. Contrast that with an incorrect sine calculation. This is a low-impact kind of defect, since few people use the sine function on the Windows calculator. It is more likely to have a defect, though, since sine functions are hard to calculate.

After identifying the risk items, you and, if applicable, the stakeholders, should review the list to assign the likelihood of problems and the impact of problems associated with each one. There are many ways to go about this assignment of likelihood and impact. You can do this with all the stakeholders at once. You can have the business people determine impact and the technical people determine likelihood, and then merge the determinations. Either way, the reason for identifying risks first and then assessing their level, is that the risks are relative to each other.

The scales used to rate likelihood and impact vary. Some people rate them high, medium and low. Some use a 1–10 scale. The problem with a 1–10 scale is that it's often difficult to tell a 2 from a 3 or a 7 from an 8, unless the differences between each rating are clearly defined. A five-point scale (very high, high, medium, low and very low) tends to work well.

Given two classifications of risk levels, likelihood and impact, we have a problem, though: We need a single, aggregate risk rating to guide our testing effort. As with rating scales, practices vary. One approach is to convert each risk classification into a number and then either add or multiply the numbers to calculate a risk priority number. For example, suppose a particular risk has a high likelihood and a medium impact. The risk priority number would then be 6 (2 times 3).

Armed with a risk priority number, we can now decide on the various risk-mitigation options available to us. Do we use formal training for programmers or analysts, rely on cross-training and reviews or assume they know enough? Do we perform extensive testing, cursory testing or no testing at all? Should we ensure unit testing and system testing coverage of this risk? These options and more are available to us.

As you go through this process, make sure you capture the key information in a document. We're not fond of excessive documentation but this quantity of information simply cannot be managed in your head. We recommend a lightweight table like the one shown in Table 5.2; we usually capture this in a spreadsheet.

Let's finish this section with two quick tips about product risk analysis. First, remember to consider both likelihood and impact. While it might make you feel like a hero to find lots of defects, testing is also about building confidence in key functions. We need to test the things that probably won't break but would be catastrophic if they did.

Second, risk analyzes, especially early ones, are educated guesses. Make sure that you follow up and revisit the risk analysis at key project milestones. For example, if you're following a V-model, you might perform the initial analysis during the

TABLE 5.2 A risk analysis template

Product risk	Likelihood	Impact	Risk priority #	Mitigation
Risk category 1				
Risk 1				
Risk 2				
Risk n				

requirements phase, then review and revise it at the end of the design and implementation phases, as well as prior to starting unit test, integration test, and system test. We also recommend revisiting the risk analysis during testing. You might find you have discovered new risks or found that some risks weren't as risky as you thought and increased your confidence in the risk analysis.

5.5.3 Project risks

We just discussed the use of testing to manage risks to product quality. However, testing is an activity like the rest of the project and thus it is subject to risks that endanger the project. To deal with the **project risks** that apply to testing, we can use the same concepts we apply to identifying, prioritizing and managing product risks.

project risk A risk related to management and control of the (test) project, e.g. lack of staffing, strict deadlines, changing requirements, etc.

Remembering that a risk is the possibility of a negative outcome, what project risks affect testing? There are direct risks such as the late delivery of the test items to the test team or availability issues with the test environment. There are also indirect risks such as excessive delays in repairing defects found in testing or problems with getting professional system administration support for the test environment.

Of course, these are merely four examples of project risks; many others can apply to your testing effort. To discover these risks, ask yourself and other project participants and stakeholders, 'What could go wrong on the project to delay or invalidate the test plan, the test strategy and the test estimate? What are unacceptable outcomes of testing or in testing? What are the likelihoods and impacts of each of these risks?' You can see that this process is very much like the risk analysis process for products. Checklists and examples can help you identify test project risks [Black 2004].

For any risk, product or project, you have four typical options:

● Mitigate: Take steps in advance to reduce the likelihood (and possibly the impact) of the risk.

● Contingency: Have a plan in place to reduce the impact should the risk become an outcome.

● Transfer: Convince some other member of the team or project stakeholder to reduce the likelihood or accept the impact of the risk.

● Ignore: Do nothing about the risk, which is usually a smart option only when there's little that can be done or when the likelihood and impact are low.

There is another typical risk-management option, buying insurance, which is not usually pursued for project or product risks on software projects, though it is not unheard of.

Here are some typical risks along with some options for managing them:

● Logistics or product quality problems that block tests: These can be mitigated through careful planning, good defect triage and management, and robust test design.

● Test items that won't install in the test environment: These can be mitigated through smoke (or acceptance) testing prior to starting test phases or as part of a nightly build or continuous integration. Having a defined uninstall process is a good contingency plan.

● Excessive change to the product that invalidates test results or requires updates to test cases, expected results and environments: These can be mitigated through good change-control processes, robust test design and light-weight test documentation. When severe incidents occur, transference of the risk by escalation to management is often in order.

- Insufficient or unrealistic test environments that yield misleading results: One option is to transfer the risks to management by explaining the limits on test results obtained in limited environments. Mitigation – sometimes complete alleviation – can be achieved by outsourcing tests such as performance tests that are particularly sensitive to proper test environments.

Here are some additional risks to consider and perhaps to manage:

- Organizational issues such as shortages of people, skills or training, problems with communicating and responding to test results, bad expectations of what testing can achieve and complexity of the project team or organization.

- Supplier issues such as problems with underlying platforms or hardware, failure to consider testing issues in the contract or failure to properly respond to the issues when they arise.

- Technical problems related to ambiguous, conflicting or unprioritized requirements, an excessively large number of requirements given other project constraints, high system complexity and quality problems with the design, the code or the tests.

There may be other risks that apply to your project and not all projects are subject to the same risks. See Chapter 2 of [Black 2009], Chapters 6 and 7 of [Black 2004] and Chapter 3 of [Craig and Jaskiel 2002] for a discussion on managing project risks during testing and in the test plan.

Finally, don't forget that test items can also have risks associated with them. For example, there is a risk that the test plan will omit tests for a functional area or that the test cases do not exercise the critical areas of the system.

5.5.4 Tying it all together for risk management

We can deal with test-related risks to the project and product by applying some straightforward, structured risk management techniques. The first step is to assess or analyze risks early in the project. Like a big ocean liner, projects, especially large projects, require steering well before the iceberg is in plain sight. By using a test plan template like the IEEE 829 template shown earlier, you can remind yourself to consider and manage risks during the planning phase.

It's worth repeating here that early risk analyzes are educated guesses. Some of those guesses will be wrong. Make sure that you plan to re-assess and adjust your risks at regular intervals in the project and make appropriate course corrections to the testing or the project itself.

One common problem people have when organizations first adopt risk-based testing is a tendency to be excessively alarmed by some of the risks once they are clearly articulated. Do not confuse impact with likelihood or vice versa. You should manage risks appropriately, based on likelihood and impact. Triage the risks by understanding how much of your overall effort can be spent dealing with them.

It's very important to maintain a sense of perspective, a focus on the point of the exercise. As with life, the goal of risk-based testing should not be – cannot practically be – a risk-free project. What we can accomplish with risk-based testing is the marriage of testing with best practices in risk management to achieve a project outcome that balances risks with quality, features, budget and schedule.

5.6 INCIDENT MANAGEMENT

SYLLABUS LEARNING OBJECTIVES FOR 5.6 INCIDENT MANAGEMENT (K3)

LO-5.6.1   Recognize the content of an incident report according to the 'Standard for Software Test Documentation' (IEEE Std 829-1998). (K1)

LO-5.6.2   Write an incident report covering the observation of a failure during testing. (K3)

Let's wind down this chapter on test management with an important subject: how we can document and manage the incidents that occur during testing. One of the objectives of testing is to find defects, which reveal themselves as discrepancies between actual and expected outcomes. These discrepancies are called anomalies. When we observe an anomaly, we need to log the details as incidents. We have to investigate these incidents, as some will be due to defects. Proper test management involves establishing appropriate actions to investigate and dispose of incidents. This includes tracking incidents (and any underlying defects) from initial discovery and classification through to resolution, confirmation testing, and ultimate disposition, with the incidents following a clearly established set of rules and processes for **incident management** and classification. We'll look at what topics we should cover when reporting incidents and defects. At the end of this section, you'll be ready to write a thorough incident report.

Keep your eyes open for the Syllabus terms in this section, **defect detection percentage, defect report, incident logging, incident management, incident report, priority, root cause** and **severity**.

> **incident management** The process of recognizing, investigating, taking action and disposing of incidents. It involves logging incidents, classifying them and identifying the impact.

5.6.1 What are incident reports for and how do I write good ones?

When running a test, you might observe actual results that vary from expected results. This is not a bad thing – one of the major goals of testing is to find problems. Different organizations have different names to describe such situations. Commonly, they're called incidents, bugs, defects, problems or issues.

To be precise, we sometimes draw a distinction between incidents on the one hand and defects or bugs on the other. An incident is any situation where the system exhibits questionable behaviour, but often we refer to an incident as a defect only when the root cause is some problem in the item we're testing.

Other causes of incidents include misconfiguration or failure of the test environment, corrupted test data, bad tests, invalid expected results and tester mistakes. (However, in some cases the policy is to classify as a defect any incident that arises from a test design, the test environment or anything else which is under formal configuration management.) We talk about incidents to indicate the possibility that a questionable behaviour is not necessarily a true defect. We log these incidents so that we have a record of what we observed and can follow up the incident and track what is done to correct it.

While it is most common to find **incident logging** or **defect reporting** processes and tools in use during formal, independent test phases, you can also log, report, track, and manage incidents found during development and reviews. In fact, this is a good idea, because it gives useful information on the extent to which early – and cheaper – defect detection and removal activities are happening.

Of course, we also need some way of reporting, tracking, and managing incidents that occur in the field or after deployment of the system. While many of these incidents will be user error or some other behaviour not related to a defect, some percentage of defects do escape from quality assurance and testing activities. The **defect detection percentage**, which compares field defects with test defects, is an important metric of the effectiveness of the test process.

Here is an example of a DDP formula that would apply for calculating DDP for the last level of testing prior to release to the field:

$$DDP = \frac{\text{defects (testers)}}{\text{defects (testers)} + \text{defects (field)}}$$

It is most common to find defects reported against the code or the system itself. However, we have also seen cases where defects are reported against requirements and design specifications, user and operator guides and tests. Often, it aids the effectiveness and efficiency of reporting, tracking and managing defects when the defect-tracking tool provides an ability to vary some of the information captured depending on what the defect was reported against.

In some projects, a very large number of defects are found. Even on smaller projects where 100 or fewer defects are found, you can easily lose track of them unless you have a process for reporting, classifying, assigning and managing the defects from discovery to final resolution.

An **incident report** contains a description of the misbehaviour that was observed and classification of that misbehaviour. As with any written communication, it helps to have clear goals in mind when writing. One common goal for such reports is to provide programmers, managers and others with detailed information about the behaviour observed and the defect. Another is to support the analysis of trends in aggregate defect data, either for understanding more about a particular set of problems or tests or for understanding and reporting the overall level of system quality. Finally, defect reports, when analyzed over a project and even across projects, give information that can lead to development and test process improvements.

When writing an incident, it helps to have the readers in mind, too. The programmers need the information in the report to find and fix the defects. Before that happens, though, managers should review and prioritize the defects so that scarce testing and developer resources are spent fixing and confirmation testing the most important defects. Since some defects may be deferred – perhaps to be fixed later or perhaps, ultimately, not to be fixed at all – we should include work-arounds and other helpful information for help desk or technical support teams. Finally, testers often need to know what their colleagues are finding so that they can watch for similar behaviour elsewhere and avoid trying to run tests that will be blocked.

A good incident report is a technical document. In addition to being clear for its goals and audience, any good report grows out of a careful approach to researching and writing the report. We have some rules of thumb that can help you write a better incident report.

First, use a careful, attentive approach to running your tests. You never know when you're going to find a problem. If you're pounding on the keyboard while gossiping with office mates or daydreaming about a movie you just saw, you might not notice strange behaviours. Even if you see the incident, how much do you really know about it? What can you write in your incident report?

Intermittent or sporadic symptoms are a fact of life for some defects and it's always discouraging to have an incident report bounced back as 'irreproducible'. So, it's a good idea to try to reproduce symptoms when you see them and we have found three times to be a good rule of thumb. If a defect has intermittent symptoms, we would still report it, but we would be sure to include as much information as possible, especially how many times we tried to reproduce it and how many times it did in fact occur.

You should also try to isolate the defect by making carefully chosen changes to the steps used to reproduce it. In isolating the defect, you help guide the programmer to the problematic part of the system. You also increase your own knowledge of how the system works – and how it fails.

Some test cases focus on boundary conditions, which may make it appear that a defect is not likely to happen frequently in practice. We have found that it's a good idea to look for more generalized conditions that cause the failure to occur, rather than simply relying on the test case. This helps prevent the infamous incident report rejoinder, 'No real user is ever going to do that'. It also cuts down on the number of duplicate reports that get filed.

As there is often a lot of testing going on with the system during a test period, there are lots of other test results available. Comparing an observed problem against other test results and known defects found is a good way to find and document additional information that the programmer is likely to find very useful. For example, you might check for similar symptoms observed with other defects, the same symptom observed with defects that were fixed in previous versions or similar (or different) results seen in tests that cover similar parts of the system.

Many readers of incident reports, managers especially, will need to understand the **priority** and **severity** of the defect. So, the impact of the problem on the users, customers and other stakeholders is important. Most defect-tracking systems have a title or summary field and that field should mention the impact, too.

> **priority** The level of (business) importance assigned to an item, e.g. defect.
>
> **severity** The degree of impact that a defect has on the development or operation of a component or system.

Choice of words definitely matters in incident reports. You should be clear and unambiguous. You should also be neutral, fact-focused and impartial, keeping in mind the testing-related interpersonal issues discussed in Chapter 1 and earlier in this chapter. Finally, keeping the report concise helps keep people's attention and avoids the problem of losing them in the details.

As a last rule of thumb for incident reports, we recommend that you use a review process for all reports filed. It works if you have the lead tester review reports and we have also allowed testers – at least experienced ones – to review other testers' reports. Reviews are proven quality assurance techniques and incident reports are important project deliverables.

5.6.2 What goes in an incident report?

An incident report describes some situation, behaviour or event that occurred during testing that requires further investigation. In many cases, an incident report consists of one or two screens – full of information gathered by a defect-tracking tool and stored in a database.

As mentioned above, you often document narrative information such as the summary, the steps to reproduce, the isolation steps tried and the impact of the problem. These fields should mention the inputs given and outputs observed, the discrepancy or variance from expectations, the different ways you could – and couldn't – make the problem recur and the impact. Classification information that a tester would provide includes the date and time of the failure, what phase of the project the failure was found in, the test case that produced the incident, references to specifications or other documents that provide information about correct behaviour, the name of the tester (and perhaps the reviewer), the test environment and any additional information about the configuration of the software, system or environment. Sometimes testers classify the scope, severity and priority of the defect, though sometimes managers or a bug triage committee handle that role.

As the incident is managed to resolution, managers might assign a level of priority to the report. The change control board or bug triage committee might document the risks, costs, opportunities and benefits associated with fixing or not fixing the defect. The programmer, when fixing the defect, can capture the **root cause**, the phase of introduction and the phase of removal.

After the defect has been resolved, managers, programmers or others may want to capture conclusions and recommendations. Throughout the life cycle of the incident report, from discovery to resolution, the defect-tracking system should allow each person who works on the incident report to enter status and history information. IEEE 829 gives a template for test incident reports.

> **root cause** A source of a defect such that if it is removed, the occurrence of the defect type is decreased or removed.

IEEE 829 STANDARD: TEST INCIDENT REPORT TEMPLATE

Test incident report identifier
Summary
Incident description (inputs, expected results, actual results, anomalies, date and time, procedure step, environment, attempts to repeat, testers and observers)
Impact

5.6.3 What happens to incident reports after you file them?

As we mentioned earlier, incident reports are managed through a life cycle from discovery to resolution. The incident report life cycle is often shown as a state transition diagram (see Figure 5.3). While your defect-tracking system may use a different life cycle, let's take this one as an example to illustrate how an incident report life cycle might work.

In the incident report life cycle shown in Figure 5.3, all incident reports move through a series of clearly identified states after being reported. Some of these state transitions occur when a member of the project team completes some assigned task related to closing an incident report. Some of these state transitions occur when the project team decides not to repair a defect during this project, leading to the deferral of the incident report. Some of these state transitions occur when an incident report

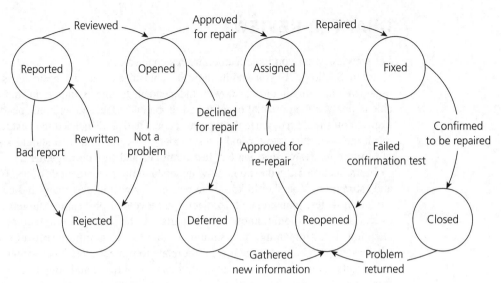

FIGURE 5.3 Incident report life cycle

is poorly written or describes behaviour which is actually correct, leading to the rejection of that report.

Let's focus on the path taken by incident reports which are ultimately fixed. After an incident is reported, a peer tester or test manager reviews the report. If successful in the review, the incident report becomes opened, so now the project team must decide whether or not to repair the defect. If the defect is to be repaired, a programmer is assigned to repair it.

Once the programmer believes the repairs are complete, the incident report returns to the tester for confirmation testing. If the confirmation test fails, the incident report is re-opened and then re-assigned. Once the tester confirms a good repair, the incident report is closed. No further work remains to be done.

In any state other than rejected, deferred or closed, further work is required on the incident prior to the end of this project. In such a state, the incident report has a clearly identified owner. The owner is responsible for transitioning the incident into an allowed subsequent state. The arrows in the diagram show these allowed transitions.

In a rejected, deferred or closed state, the incident report will not be assigned to an owner. However, certain real-world events can cause an incident report to change state even if no active work is occurring on the incident report. Examples include the recurrence of a failure associated with a closed incident report and the discovery of a more serious failure associated with a deferred incident report.

Ideally, only the owner can transition the incident report from the current state to the next state and ideally the owner can only transition the incident report to an allowed next state. Most defect-tracking systems support and enforce the life cycle and life cycle rules. Good defect-tracking systems allow you to customize the set of states, the owners, and the transitions allowed to match your actual workflows. And, while a good defect-tracking system is helpful, the actual defect workflow should be monitored and supported by project and company management.

CHAPTER REVIEW

Let's review what you have learned in this chapter.

From Section 5.1, you should now be able to explain the basic ideas of test organization. You should know why independent testing is important, but also be able to analyze the potential benefits and problems associated with independent test teams. You should recognize the types of people and skills needed in a test team and recall the tasks that a tester and a test leader will carry out. You should know the glossary terms **tester, test leader, test manager** and **test management**.

From Section 5.2, you should now understand the fundamentals of test planning and estimation. You should know the reasons for writing test plans and be able to explain how test plans relate to projects, test levels or phases, test targets and test execution. You should know which parts of the test process require special attention in test planning. You should be able to explain the justification behind various entry and exit criteria that might relate to projects, test levels or phases and test targets. You should be able to distinguish the purpose and content of test plans from that of test design specifications, test cases and test procedures, and know the IEEE 829 outline for a test plan. You should know the factors that affect the effort involved in testing, including especially test strategies (approaches) and how they affect testing. You should be able to explain how metrics, expertise and negotiation are used for estimating. There are no extra glossary terms for this section.

From Section 5.3, you should be able to explain the essentials of test progress monitoring and control. You should know the common metrics that are captured, logged and used for monitoring, as well as ways to present these metrics. You should be able to analyze, interpret and explain test metrics that can be useful for reporting test status and for making decisions about how to control test progress. You should be able to explain a typical test status report and know the IEEE 829 test summary report and test log. You should know the glossary terms **defect density** and **failure rate**.

From Section 5.4, you should now understand the basics of configuration management that relate to testing. You should be able to summarize how good configuration management helps us do our testing work better. You should know the glossary terms **configuration control, configuration management** and **version control**.

From Section 5.5, you should now be able to explain how risk and testing relate. You should know that a risk is a potential undesirable or negative outcome and that most of the risks we are interested in relate to the achievement of project objectives. You should know about likelihood and impact as factors that determine the importance of a risk. You should be able to compare and contrast risks to the product (and its quality) and risks to the project itself and know typical risks to the product and project. You should be able to describe how to use risk analysis and risk management for testing and test planning. You should know the glossary terms **product risk, project risk and risk-based testing**.

From Section 5.6, you should now understand incident logging and be able to use incident management on your projects. You should know the content of an incident report according to the IEEE 829 standard. You should be able to write a high-quality report based on test results and manage that report through its life cycle. You should know the glossary terms **defect detection percentage, defect report, incident logging, incident management, incident report, priority, root cause** and **severity**.

SAMPLE EXAM QUESTIONS

Question 1 Why is independent testing important?

a. Independent testing is usually cheaper than testing your own work.

b. Independent testing is more effective at finding defects.

c. Independent testers should determine the processes and methodologies used.

d. Independent testers are dispassionate about whether the project succeeds or fails.

Question 2 Which of the following is among the typical tasks of a test leader?

a. Develop system requirements, design specifications and usage models.

b. Handle all test automation duties.

c. Keep tests and test coverage hidden from programmers.

d. Gather and report test progress metrics.

Question 3 According to the ISTQB Glossary, what do we mean when we call someone a test manager?

a. A test manager manages a collection of test leaders.

b. A test manager is the leader of a test team or teams.

c. A test manager gets paid more than a test leader.

d. A test manager reports to a test leader.

Question 4 What is the primary difference between the test plan, the test design specification, and the test procedure specification?

a. The test plan describes one or more levels of testing, the test design specification identifies the associated high-level test cases and a test procedure specification describes the actions for executing a test.

b. The test plan is for managers, the test design specification is for programmers and the test procedure specification is for testers who are automating tests.

c. The test plan is the least thorough, the test procedure specification is the most thorough and the test design specification is midway between the two.

d. The test plan is finished in the first third of the project, the test design specification is finished in the middle third of the project and the test procedure specification is finished in the last third of the project.

Question 5 Which of the following factors is an influence on the test effort involved in most projects?

a. Geographical separation of tester and programmers.

b. The departure of the test manager during the project.

c. The quality of the information used to develop the tests.

d. Unexpected long-term illness by a member of the project team.

Question 6 The ISTQB Foundation Syllabus establishes a fundamental test process where test planning occurs early in the project, while test execution occurs later. Which of the following elements of the test plan, while specified during test planning, are assessed during test execution?

a. Test tasks

b. Environmental needs

c. Exit criteria

d. Test team training

Question 7 Consider the following exit criteria which might be found in a test plan:

I. No known customer-critical defects.

II. All interfaces between components tested.

III. 100% code coverage of all units.

IV. All specified requirements satisfied.

V. System functionality matches legacy system for all business rules.

Which of the following statements is true about whether these exit criteria belong in an acceptance test plan?

a. All statements belong in an acceptance test plan.

b. Only statement I belongs in an acceptance test plan.

c. Only statements I, II, and V belong in an acceptance test plan.

d. Only statements I, IV, and V belong in an acceptance test plan.

Question 8 According to the ISTQB Glossary, what is a test level?

a. A group of test activities that are organized together.

b. One or more test design specification documents.

c. A test type.

d. An ISTQB certification.

Question 9 Which of the following metrics would be most useful to monitor during test execution?

a. Percentage of test cases written.

b. Number of test environments remaining to be configured.

c. Number of defects found and fixed.

d. Percentage of requirements for which a test has been written.

Question 10 During test execution, the test manager describes the following situation to the project team: '90% of the test cases have been run. 20% of the test cases have identified defects. 127 defects have been found. 112 defects have been fixed and have passed confirmation testing. Of the remaining 15 defects, project management has decided that they do not need to be fixed prior to release.' Which of the following is the most reasonable interpretation of this test status report?

a. The remaining 15 defects should be confirmation tested prior to release.

b. The remaining 10% of test cases should be run prior to release.

c. The system is now ready for release with no further testing or development effort.

d. The programmers should focus their attention on fixing the remaining known defects prior to release.

Question 11 In a test summary report, the project's test leader makes the following statement, 'The payment processing subsystem fails to accept payments from American Express cardholders, which

is considered a must-work feature for this release.' This statement is likely to be found in which of the following sections?

a. Evaluation

b. Summary of activities

c. Variances

d. Incident description

Question 12 During an early period of test execution, a defect is located, resolved and confirmed as resolved by re-testing, but is seen again later during subsequent test execution. Which of the following is a testing-related aspect of configuration management that is most likely to have broken down?

a. Traceability

b. Confirmation testing

c. Configuration control

d. Test documentation management

Question 13 You are working as a tester on a project to develop a point-of-sales system for grocery stores and other similar retail outlets. Which of the following is a product risk for such a project?

a. The arrival of a more-reliable competing product on the market.

b. Delivery of an incomplete test release to the first cycle of system test.

c. An excessively high number of defect fixes fail during re-testing.

d. Failure to accept allowed credit cards.

Question 14 A product risk analysis meeting is held during the project planning period. Which of the following determines the level of risk?

a. Difficulty of fixing related problems in code.

b. The harm that might result to the user.

c. The price for which the software is sold.

d. The technical staff in the meeting.

Question 15 You are writing a test plan using the IEEE 829 template and are currently completing the Risks and Contingencies section. Which of the following is most likely to be listed as a project risk?

a. Unexpected illness of a key team member.

b. Excessively slow transaction-processing time.

c. Data corruption under network congestion.

d. Failure to handle a key use case.

Question 16 You and the project stakeholders develop a list of product risks and project risks during the planning stage of a project. What else should you do with those lists of risks during test planning?

a. Determine the extent of testing required for the product risks and the mitigation and contingency actions required for the project risks.

b. Obtain the resources needed to completely cover each product risk with tests and transfer responsibility for the project risks to the project manager.

c. Execute sufficient tests for the product risks, based on the likelihood and impact of each product risk and execute mitigation actions for all project risks.

d. No further risk management action is required at the test planning stage.

Question 17 According to the ISTQB Glossary, a product risk is related to which of the following?

a. Control of the test project

b. The test object

c. A single test item

d. A potential negative outcome

Question 18 In an incident report, the tester makes the following statement, 'At this point, I expect to receive an error message explaining the rejection of this invalid input and asking me to enter a valid input. Instead the system accepts the input, displays an hourglass for between one and five seconds and finally terminates abnormally, giving the message, "Unexpected data type: 15. Click to continue".' This statement is likely to be found in which of the following sections of an IEEE 829 standard incident report?

a. Summary

b. Impact

c. Item pass/fail criteria

d. Incident description

Question 19 According to the ISTQB Glossary, what do we call a document that describes any event that occurred during testing which requires further investigation?

a. A bug report

b. A defect report

c. An incident report

d. A test summary report

Question 20 A product risk analysis is performed during the planning stage of the test process. During the execution stage of the test process, the test manager directs the testers to classify each defect report by the known product risk it relates to (or to 'other'). Once a week, the test manager runs a report that shows the percentage of defects related to each known product risk and to unknown risks. What is one possible use of such a report?

a. To identify new risks to system quality.

b. To locate defect clusters in product subsystems.

c. To check risk coverage by tests.

d. To measure exploratory testing.

EXERCISE: INCIDENT REPORT

Assume you are testing a maintenance release which will add a new supported model to a browser-based application that allows car dealers to order custom-configured cars from the maker. You are working with a selected number of dealers who are performing beta testing. When they find problems, they send you an e-mail describing the failure. You use that e-mail to create an IEEE 829 compliant incident report in your incident management system.

You receive the following e-mail from one of the dealers:

I entered an order for a Racinax 917X in midnight violet. During the upload, I got an 'unexpected return value' error message. I then checked the order and it was in the system. I think the Internet connection might have gone down for a moment our cable television went blank at the same time and we use a cable modem for Internet access.

Write an IEEE 829 compliant incident report based on this e-mail, and note any elements of such a report which might not be available based on this e-mail alone.

Note that this scenario, including the name of the car model, is entirely fictitious.

EXERCISE SOLUTION

Here is an example of an incident report:

Test incident report identifier: This would be assigned by the incident tracking tool.

Summary: System returns confusing error message if Internet connectivity is interrupted.

Incident description:
  Steps to reproduce

  1 Entered an order for a Racinax 917X in midnight violet.

  2 During the order upload, the system displayed an 'unexpected return value' error message.

  3 Verified that, in spite of the error message, the order was in the system.

Suspected cause Given that a brief interruption in the Internet connection (provided through a cable modem) may have occurred during order transmission, the suspected cause of the failure is a lack of robust handling of slow or unreliable Internet connections.

Impact assessment The message in step 2 is not helpful to the user, because it gives the user no clues about what to do next. A user encountering the message described in step 2 might decide to re-enter the order, which in this case would result in a redundant order.
Some car dealerships will have unreliable Internet connections, with the frequency of connection loss depending on location, wireless infrastructure available in the dealership, type of Internet connection hardware used in the dealers' computers, and other such factors. Therefore, we can expect that some number of incidents such as this will occur in widespread use. (Indeed, this beta test incident proves that this is a likely event in the real world.) Since a careless or rushed dealer might decide to resubmit the order based on the error message, this will result in redundant orders, which will cause significant loss of profitability for the dealerships and the salespeople themselves.

This report addresses the inputs, the expected results, the actual results, the difference between the expected and actual results (the anomalies), and the procedure steps in which the tester identified the unexpected results. Here's some additional information needed to improve the report:

- The failure needs to be reproduced at least two more times. By doing the failure replication in the test environment, the tester will be able to control whether the Internet connection goes down during the order and for how long the connection is down.

- Is the problem in any way specific to the Racinax 917X model and/or the colour? Isolation of the failure is needed, and then the report can be updated.

- Is the problem in any way specific to a cable modem connection? We would guess not, but checking with different types of connections (during the isolation and replication discussed above) would make sense. If it proves independent of the type of connection, we would know that the problem is more general than just for cable modems.

- The incident report should also include information about the date and time of the test, the beta test environment, and the name of the beta tester and the tester entering the defect.

CHAPTER SIX

Tool support for testing

You may be wishing that you had a magic tool that would automate all of the testing for you. If so, you will be disappointed. However, there are a number of very useful tools that can bring significant benefits. In this chapter we will see that there is tool support for many different aspects of software testing. We will see that success with tools is not guaranteed, even if an appropriate tool is acquired – there are also risks in using tools. There are some special considerations mentioned in the Syllabus for certain types of tool: test execution tools, performance testing tools, static analysis tools and test management tools.

6.1 TYPES OF TEST TOOL

SYLLABUS LEARNING OBJECTIVES FOR 6.1 TYPES OF TEST TOOL (K2)

LO-6.1.1   Classify different types of test tools according to their purpose and to the activities of the fundamental test process and the software life cycle. (K2)

LO-6.1.3   Explain the term test tool and the purpose of tool support for testing. (K2)

(Please note that a learning objective, LO-6.1.2, was deleted in the 2010 release, which results in the gap in numbering here.)

In this section, we will describe the various tool types in terms of their general functionality, rather than going into lots of detail. The reason for this is that, in general, the types of tool will be fairly stable over a longer period, even though there will be new vendors in the market, new and improved tools, and even new types of tool in the coming years.

We will not mention any commercial tools in this chapter. If we did, this book would date very quickly! Tool vendors are acquired by other vendors, change their names, and change the names of the tools quite frequently, so we will not mention the names of any tools or vendors.

As we go through this section, watch for the Syllabus terms **capture/playback tool, configuration management tool, coverage tool, debugging tool, dynamic analysis tool, incident management tool, load testing tool, modelling tool, monitoring tool, performance testing tool, probe effect, requirements management tool, review tool, security testing tool, security tool, static analysis tool, static code**

analysis, static code analyzer, stress testing tool, test comparator, test comparison, test data preparation tool, test design tool, test framework, test execution tool, test management tool, unit test framework tool and **volume testing**. You'll find these terms defined in the glossary.

6.1.1 Understanding the Meaning and Purpose of Tool Support for Testing

There are a number of ways in which tools can be used for testing, though most of the time people think of automated test execution when they think of test tools. What can tools do for us as testers?

1 To start with the most visible use, we can use tools directly in testing. This includes test execution tools (including via so-called **test frameworks**), test data generation tools and result comparison tools.

2 We can use tools to help us manage the testing process. This includes tools that manage tests, test results, test data, requirements, incidents, and defects, as well as tools that assist with reporting and monitoring test execution progress.

3 We can use tools as part of what's called reconnaissance, or, to use a simpler term, exploration. For example, we can use tools to monitor file activity for an application.

4 We can use tools in a number of other ways, in the form of any tool that aids in testing. This would include spreadsheets when used to manage test assets or progress, or as a way to document manual or automated tests.

What are we trying to achieve with tools? What are the motivations? As you can imagine, these vary depending on the activity, but common objectives for the use of tools include the following:

- We might want to improve the efficiency of our testing. This can involve automating repetitive tasks such as regression testing, or supporting manual test activities such test planning, test design, test reporting and monitoring.

- We might want to automate activities that would otherwise require significant resources to do manually. Static testing of code, as discussed in Chapter 3, is an example of this motivation.

- We might need to carry out activities that simply cannot be done manually, but which can be done via automated tools. Examples include large scale performance testing of client-server or e-commerce applications.

- We might want to increase the reliability of our testing. Examples include automation of large data comparisons, simulating user behaviour, or repeating large numbers of tests (which can lead to mistakes due to tedium of the work).

Clearly understanding the objectives for automation and tool support for testing is essential for success, but so is a good business case, the right skills, and management support.

test framework As mentioned in the Syllabus, the term 'test framework' is frequently used in the software testing profession. However, it can have three very distinct meanings: 1) Reusable and extensible testing libraries that can be used to build testing tools (which are also called **test harnesses)**; 2) A type of design of test automation (e.g., **data-driven** and **keyword-driven**); and, 3) An overall process of execution of testing. In the Foundation syllabus, and in this book, especially in this chapter, we use the term **test frameworks** in its first two meanings.

6.1.2 Test tool classification

The tools are grouped by the testing activities or areas that are supported by a set of tools, for example, tools that support management activities, tools to support static testing, etc.

There is not necessarily a one-to-one relationship between a type of tool described here and a tool offered by a commercial tool vendor or an open source tool. Some tools perform a very specific and limited function (sometimes called a 'point solution'), but many of the commercial tools provide support for a number of different functions (tool suites or families of tools). For example a 'test management' tool may provide support for managing testing (progress monitoring), configuration management of testware, incident management, and requirements management and traceability; another tool may provide both coverage measurement and test design support.

There are some things that people can do much better or easier than a computer can do. For example, when you see a friend in an unexpected place, say in an airport, you can immediately recognize their face. This is an example of pattern recognition that people are very good at, but it is not easy to write software that can recognize a face.

There are other things that computers can do much better or more quickly than people can do. For example, can you add up 20 three-digit numbers quickly? This is not easy for most people to do, so you are likely to make some mistakes even if the numbers are written down. A computer does this accurately and very quickly. As another example, if people are asked to do exactly the same task over and over, they soon get bored and then start making mistakes.

The point is that it's a good idea to use computers to do things that computers are really good at and that people are not very good at. So tool support is very useful for repetitive tasks – the computer doesn't get bored and will be able to exactly repeat what was done before. Because the tool will be fast, this can make those activities much more efficient and more reliable. The tools can also do things that might overload a person, such as comparing the contents of a large data file or simulating how the system would behave.

A tool that measures some aspect of software may have unexpected side-effects on that software. For example, a tool that measures timings for non-functional (performance) testing needs to interact very closely with that software in order to measure it. A performance tool will set a start time and a stop time for a given transaction in order to measure the response time, for example. But the act of taking that measurement, i.e. storing the time at those two points, could actually make the whole transaction take slightly longer than it would do if the tool wasn't measuring the response time. Of course, the extra time is very small, but it is still there. This effect is called the '**probe effect**'.

probe effect The effect on the component or system by the measurement instrument when the component or system is being measured, e.g. by a performance testing tool or monitor. For example performance may be slightly worse when performance testing tools are being used.

Another example of the probe effect occurs with coverage tools. In order to measure coverage, the tool must first identify all of the structural elements that might be exercised to see whether a test exercises it or not. This is called 'instrumenting the code'. The tests are then run through the instrumented code so that the tool can tell (through the instrumentation) whether or not a given branch (for example) has been exercised. But the instrumented code is not the same as the real code – it also includes the instrumentation code. In theory the code is the same, but in practice, it isn't. Because different coverage tools work in slightly different ways, you may get a slightly different coverage measure on the same program because of the probe effect. For example different tools may count branches in different ways, so the percentage of coverage would be compared to a different total number of branches. The response time of the instrumented code may also be significantly worse than the code without instrumentation. (There are also non-intrusive coverage tools that observe the blocks of memory containing the object code to get a rough measurement without instrumentation, e.g. for embedded software.)

One further example of the probe effect is when a debugging tool is used to try to find a particular defect. If the code is run with the debugger, then the bug disappears; it only reappears when the debugger is turned off (thereby making it much more difficult to find). These are sometimes known as 'Heisenbugs' (after Heisenberg's uncertainty principle).

In the descriptions of the tools below, we will indicate the tools that are more likely to be used by developers during component testing and component integration testing. For example coverage measurement tools are most often used in component testing, but performance testing tools are more often used at system testing, system integration testing and acceptance testing.

Note that for the Foundation Certificate exam, you only need to recognize the different types of tools and what they do; you do not need a detailed understanding of them (or know how to use them).

6.1.3 Tool support for management of testing and tests

What does 'test management' mean? It could be 'the management of tests' or it could be 'managing the testing process'. The tools in this broad category provide support for either or both of these. The management of testing applies over the whole of the software development life cycle, so a test management tool could be among the first to be used in a project. A test management tool may also manage the tests, which would begin early in the project and would then continue to be used throughout the project and also after the system had been released. In practice, test management tools are typically used by specialist testers or test managers at system or acceptance test level.

Test management tools

The features provided by **test management tools** include those listed below. Some tools will provide all of these features; others may provide one or more of the features, however such tools would still be classified as test management tools.

Features or characteristics of test management tools include support for:

> **Test management tool** A tool that provides support to the test management and control part of a test process. It often has several capabilities, such as testware management, scheduling of tests, the logging of results, progress tracking, incident management and test reporting.

- management of tests or testware management (e.g. keeping track of the associated data for a given set of tests, knowing which tests need to run in a common environment, number of tests planned, written, run, passed or failed);
- scheduling of tests to be executed (manually or by a test execution tool);
- management of testing activities (time spent in test design, test execution, whether we are on schedule or on budget);
- interfaces to other tools, such as
  - test execution tools (test running tools);
  - incident management tools;
  - requirement management tools;
  - configuration management tools;
- traceability of tests, test results and defects to requirements or other sources;
- logging test results (note that the test management tool does not run tests, but could summarize results from test execution tools that the test management tool interfaces with);
- preparing progress reports based on metrics (quantitative analysis), such as:
  - tests run and tests passed;
  - incidents raised, defects fixed and outstanding.

This information can be used to monitor the testing process and decide what actions to take (test control), as described in Chapter 5. The tool also gives information about the component or system being tested (the test object). Test management tools help to gather, organize, and communicate information about the testing on a project.

Requirements management tools

Are **requirements management tools** really testing tools? Some people may say they are not, but they do provide some features that are very helpful to testing. Because tests are based on requirements, the better the quality of the requirements, the easier it will be to write tests from them. It is also important to be able to trace tests to requirements and requirements to tests, as we saw in Chapter 2.

Some requirements management tools are able to find defects in the requirements, for example by checking for ambiguous or forbidden words, such as 'might', 'and/or', 'as needed' or '(to be decided)'.

Features or characteristics of requirements management tools include support for:

- storing requirement statements;
- storing information about requirement attributes;
- checking consistency of requirements;
- identifying undefined, missing or 'to be defined later' requirements;
- prioritizing requirements for testing purposes;
- traceability of requirements to tests and tests to requirements, functions or features;
- traceability through levels of requirements;
- interfacing to test management tools;
- coverage of requirements by a set of tests (sometimes).

Incident management tools

This type of tool is also known as a defect-tracking tool, a defect-management tool, a bug-tracking tool or a bug-management tool. However, '**incident management tool**' is probably a better name for it because not all of the things tracked are actually defects or bugs; incidents may also be perceived problems, anomalies (that aren't necessarily defects) or enhancement requests. Also what is normally recorded is information about the failure (not the defect) that was generated during testing – information about the defect that caused that failure would come to light when someone (e.g. a developer) begins to investigate the failure.

Incident reports go through a number of stages from initial identification and recording of the details, through analysis, classification, assignment for fixing, fixed, re-tested and closed, as described in Chapter 5. Incident management tools make it much easier to keep track of the incidents over time.

Features or characteristics of incident management tools include support for:

- storing information about the attributes of incidents (e.g. severity);
- storing attachments (e.g. a screen shot);
- prioritizing incidents;
- assigning actions to people (fix, confirmation test, etc.);
- status (e.g. open, rejected, duplicate, deferred, ready for confirmation test, closed);
- reporting of statistics/metrics about incidents (e.g. average time open, number of incidents with each status, total number raised, open or closed).

Incident management tool functionality may be included in commercial test management tools.

Configuration management tools

An example: A test group began testing the software, expecting to find the usual fairly high number of problems. But to their surprise, the software seemed to be much better than usual this time – very few defects were found. Before they celebrated the great quality of this release, they just made an additional check to see if they had the right version and discovered that they were actually testing the version from two months earlier (which had been debugged) with the tests for that earlier version. It was nice to know that this was still OK, but they weren't actually testing what they thought they were testing or what they should have been testing.

Configuration management tools are not strictly testing tools either, but good configuration management is critical for controlled testing, as was described in Chapter 5. We need to know exactly what it is that we are supposed to test, such as the exact version of all of the things that belong in a system. It is possible to perform configuration management activities without the use of tools, but the tools make life a lot easier, especially in complex environments.

Testware needs to be under configuration management and the same tool may be able to be used for testware as well as for software items. Testware also has different versions and is changed over time. It is important to run the correct version of the tests as well, as our earlier example shows.

Features or characteristics of configuration management tools include support for:

- storing information about versions and builds of the software and testware;
- traceability between software and testware and different versions or variants;
- keeping track of which versions belong with which configurations (e.g. operating systems, libraries, browsers);
- build and release management;
- baselining (e.g. all the configuration items that make up a specific release);
- access control (checking in and out).

> **Configuration management tool**
> A tool that provides support for the identification and control of configuration items, their status over changes and versions, and the release of baselines consisting of configuration items.

6.1.4 Tool support for static testing

The tools described in this section support the testing activities described in Chapter 3.

Review tools

The value of different types of review was discussed in Chapter 3. For a very informal review, where one person looks at another's document and gives a few comments about it, a tool such as this might just get in the way. However, when the review process is more formal, when many people are involved, or when the people involved are in different geographical locations, then tool support becomes far more beneficial.

It is possible to keep track of all the information for a review process using spreadsheets and text documents, but a **review tool** that is designed for the purpose is more likely to do a better job. For example, one thing that should be monitored for each review is that the reviewers have not gone over the document too quickly, i.e. that the checking rate (number of pages checked per hour) was close to that

> **Review tool** A tool that provides support to the review process. Typical features include review planning and tracking support, communication support, collaborative reviews and a repository for collecting and reporting of metrics.

recommended for that review cycle. A review tool could automatically calculate the checking rate and flag exceptions. The review tools can normally be tailored for the particular review process or type of review being done.

Features or characteristics of review tools include support for:

- a common reference for the review process or processes to use in different situations;
- storing and sorting review comments;
- communicating comments to relevant people;
- coordinating online reviews;
- keeping track of comments, including defects found, and providing statistical information about them;
- providing traceability between comments, documents reviewed and related documents;
- a repository for rules, procedures and checklists to be used in reviews, as well as entry and exit criteria;
- monitoring the review status (passed, passed with corrections, requires re-review);
- collecting metrics and reporting on key factors.

Static analysis tools (D)

The '(D)' after this (and other types of tool) indicates that these tools are more likely to be used by developers. Static analysis by tools was discussed in Chapter 3. In this section we give a summary of what the tools do.

Static analysis tool (static analyzer) A tool that carries out static analysis.

Static analysis tools are normally used by developers as part of the development and component testing process. The key aspect is that the code (or other artefact) is not executed or run. Of course the tool itself is executed, but the source code we are interested in is the input data to the tool.

Static analysis tools are an extension of compiler technology – in fact some compilers do offer static analysis features. It is worth checking what is available from existing compilers or development environments before looking at purchasing a more sophisticated static analysis tool.

Static analysis can also be carried out on things other than software code, for example static analysis of requirements or static analysis of websites (for example, to assess for proper use of accessibility tags or the following of HTML standards).

Static code analyzer A tool that carries out static code analysis. The tool checks source code, for certain properties such as conformance to coding standards, quality metrics or data flow anomalies.

Static analysis tools for **code** can help the developers to understand the structure of the **code**, and can also be used to enforce coding standards. See Section 6.2.3 for special considerations when introducing static analysis tools into an organization.

Features or characteristics of static analysis tools include support to:

Static code analysis Analysis of source code carried out without execution of that software.

- calculate metrics such as cyclomatic complexity or nesting levels (which can help to identify where more testing may be needed due to increased risk);
- enforce coding standards;
- analyze structures and dependencies;
- aid in code understanding;
- identify anomalies or defects in the code (as described in Chapter 3).

Modelling tools (D)

Modelling tools help to validate models of the system or software. For example a tool can check consistency of data objects in a database and can find inconsistencies and defects. These may be difficult to pick up in testing – you may have tested with one data item and not realize that in another part of the database there is conflicting information related to that item. Modelling tools can also check state models or object models.

Modelling tools are typically used by developers and can help in the design of the software.

One strong advantage of both modelling tools and static analysis tools is that they can be used before dynamic tests can be run. This enables any defects that these tools can find to be identified as early as possible, when it is easier and cheaper to fix them. There are also fewer defects left to propagate into later stages, so development can be speeded up and there is less rework. (Of course this is difficult to show, since those defects aren't there now!)

Note that 'model-based testing tools' are actually tools that generate test inputs or test cases from stored information about a particular model (e.g. a state diagram), so are classified as test design tools (see Section 6.1.5).

Features or characteristics of modelling tools include support for:

- identifying inconsistencies and defects within the model;

- helping to identify and prioritize areas of the model for testing;

- predicting system response and behaviour under various situations, such as level of load;

- helping to understand system functions and identify test conditions using a modelling language such as UML.

> **Modelling tool** A tool that supports the creation, amendment and verification of models of the software or system.

6.1.5 Tool support for test specification

The tools described in this section support the testing activities described in Chapter 4.

Test design tools

Test design tools help to construct test cases, or at least test inputs (which is part of a test case). If an automated oracle is available, then the tool can also construct the expected result, so it can actually generate test cases (rather than just test inputs).

For example, if the requirements are kept in a requirements management or test management tool, then it is possible to identify the input fields, including the range of valid values. This range information can be used to identify boundary values and equivalence partitions. If the valid range is stored, the tool can distinguish between values that should be accepted and those that should generate an error message. If the error messages are stored, then the expected result can be checked in detail. If the expected result of the input of a valid value is known, then that expected result can also be included in the test case constructed by the test design tool.

Another type of test design tool is one that helps to select combinations of possible factors to be used in testing, to ensure that all pairs of combinations of operating system and browser are tested, for example. Some of these tools may use orthogonal arrays. See [Copeland 2003] for a description of these combination techniques.

> **Test design tool** A tool that supports the test design activity by generating test inputs from a specification that may be held in a CASE tool repository, e.g. requirements management tool, from specified test conditions held in the tool itself, or from code.

Note that the test design tool may have only a partial oracle – that is, it may know which input values are to be accepted and rejected, but it may not know the exact error message or resulting calculation for the expected result of the test. Thus the test design tool can help us to get started with test design and will identify all of the fields, but it will not do the whole job of test design for us – there will be more verification that may need to be done.

Another type of test design tool is sometimes called a 'screen scraper', a structured template or a test frame. The tool looks at a window of the graphical user interface and identifies all of the buttons, lists and input fields, and can set up a test for each thing that it finds. This means that every button will be clicked for example and every list box will be selected. This is a good start for a thorough set of tests and it can quickly and easily identify non-working buttons. However, unless the tool has access to an oracle, it may not know what should actually happen as a result of the button click.

Yet another type of test design tool may be bundled with a coverage tool. If a coverage tool has identified which branches have been covered by a set of existing tests for example, it can also identify the path that needs to be taken in order to cover the untested branches. By identifying which of the previous decision outcomes need to be True or False, the tool can calculate an input value that will cause execution to take a particular path in order to increase coverage. Here the test is being designed from the code itself. In this case the presence of an oracle is less likely, so it may only be the test inputs that are constructed by the test design tool.

Features or characteristics of test design tools include support for:

- generating test input values from:
  - requirements;
  - design models (state, data or object);
  - code;
  - graphical user interfaces;
  - test conditions;
- generating expected results, if an oracle is available to the tool.

The benefit of this type of tool is that it can easily and quickly identify the tests (or test inputs) that will exercise all of elements, e.g. input fields, buttons, branches. This helps the testing to be more thorough (if that is an objective of the test!)

Then we may have the problem of having too many tests and need to find a way of identifying the most important tests to run. Cutting down an unmanageable number of tests can be done by risk analysis (see Chapter 5). Using a combination technique such as orthogonal arrays can also help.

Test data preparation tools

Test data preparation tool A type of test tool that enables data to be selected from existing databases or created, generated, manipulated and edited for use in testing.

Setting up test data can be a significant effort, especially if an extensive range or volume of data is needed for testing. **Test data preparation tools** help in this area. They may be used by developers, but they may also be used during system or acceptance testing. They are particularly useful for performance and reliability testing, where a large amount of realistic data is needed.

Test data preparation tools enable data to be selected from an existing database or created, generated, manipulated and edited for use in tests. The most sophisticated tools can deal with a range of files and database formats.

Features or characteristics of test data preparation tools include support to:

- extract selected data records from files or databases;
- 'massage' data records to make them anonymous or not able to be identified with real people (for data protection);
- enable records to be sorted or arranged in a different order;
- generate new records populated with pseudo-random data, or data set up according to some guidelines, e.g. an operational profile;
- construct a large number of similar records from a template, to give a large set of records for volume tests, for example.

6.1.6 Tool support for test execution and logging

Test execution tools

When people think of a 'testing tool', it is usually a **test execution tool** that they have in mind, a tool that can run tests. This type of tool is also referred to as a 'test running tool'. Most tools of this type offer a way to get started by capturing or recording manual tests; hence they are also known as **'capture/playback' tools**, 'capture/replay' tools or 'record/playback' tools. The analogy is with recording a television programme, and playing it back. However, the tests are not something which is played back just for someone to watch!

Test execution tools use a scripting language to drive the tool. The scripting language is actually a programming language. So any tester who wishes to use a test execution tool directly will need to use programming skills to create and modify the scripts. The advantage of programmable scripting is that tests can repeat actions (in loops) for different data values (i.e. test inputs), they can take different routes depending on the outcome of a test (e.g. if a test fails, go to a different set of tests) and they can be called from other scripts giving some structure to the set of tests.

When people first encounter a test execution tool, they tend to use it to 'capture/playback', which sounds really good when you first hear about it. However, the approach breaks down when you try to replay the captured tests – this approach does not scale up for large numbers of tests as described in Section 6.2.3. The main reason for this is that a captured script is very difficult to maintain because:

- It is closely tied to the flow and interface presented by the GUI.
- It may rely on the circumstances, state and context of the system at the time the script was recorded. For example, a script will capture a new order number assigned by the system when a test is recorded. When that test is played back, the system will assign a different order number and reject subsequent requests that contain the previously captured order number.
- The test input information is 'hard-coded', i.e. it is embedded in the individual script for each test.

Any of these things can be overcome by modifying the scripts, but then we are no longer just recording and playing back! If it takes more time to update a captured test than it would take to run the same test again manually, the scripts tend to be abandoned and the tool becomes 'shelf-ware'.

There are better ways to use test execution tools to make them work well and actually deliver the benefits of unattended automated test running. There are at least five

test execution tool
A type of test tool that is able to execute other software using an automated test script, e.g. capture/playback.

Capture/playback tool (capture/replay tool)
A type of test execution tool where inputs are recorded during manual testing in order to generate automated test scripts that can be executed later (i.e. replayed). These tools are often used to support automated regression testing.

levels of scripting and also different comparison techniques. Data-driven scripting is an advance over captured scripts but keyword-driven scripts give significantly more benefits [Fewster and Graham 1999], [Buwalda *et al.* 2001]. [Mosley and Posey 2002] describe 'control synchronized data-driven testing'. See also Section 6.2.3.

There are many different ways to use a test execution tool and the tools themselves are continuing to gain new useful features. For example, a test execution tool can help to identify the input fields that will form test inputs and may construct a table which is the first step towards data-driven scripting.

Although they are commonly referred to as testing tools, they are often used for regression testing, where tests are run that have been run before, such as in Continuous Integration. One of the most significant benefits of using this type of tool is that whenever an existing system is changed (e.g. for a defect fix or an enhancement), *all* of the tests that were run earlier could potentially be run again, to make sure that the changes have not disturbed the existing system by introducing or revealing a defect.

Features or characteristics of test execution tools include support for:

- capturing (recording) test inputs while tests are executed manually;
- storing an expected result in the form of a screen or object to compare to, the next time the test is run;
- executing tests from stored scripts and optionally data files accessed by the script (if data-driven or keyword-driven scripting is used);
- dynamic comparison (while the test is running) of screens, elements, links, controls, objects and values;
- ability to initiate post-execution comparison;
- logging results of tests run (pass/fail, differences between expected and actual results);
- masking or filtering of subsets of actual and expected results, for example excluding the screen-displayed current date and time which is not of interest to a particular test;
- measuring timings for tests;
- synchronizing inputs with the application under test, e.g. wait until the application is ready to accept the next input, or insert a fixed delay to represent human interaction speed;
- sending summary results to a test management tool.

Test harness/unit test framework tools (D)

These two types of tool are grouped together because they are variants of the type of support needed by developers when testing individual components or units of software. A test harness provides stubs and drivers, which are small programs that interact with the software under test (e.g. for testing middle-ware and embedded software). See Chapter 2 for more detail of how these are used in integration testing. Some **unit test framework tools** provide support for object-oriented software, others for other development paradigms. Unit test frameworks can be used in agile development to automate tests in parallel with development. Both types of tool enable the developer to test, identify and localize any defects. The framework or the stubs and drivers supply any information needed by the software being tested (e.g. an input that would have come from a user) and also receive any information sent by the software (e.g. a value to be displayed on a screen). Stubs may also be referred to as 'mock objects'.

Unit test framework tool A tool that provides an environment for unit or component testing in which a component can be tested in isolation or with suitable stubs and drivers. It also provides other support for the developer, such as debugging capabilities. [Note: This is actually the definition for *unit test framework*. The term *unit test framework tool* is not defined in the ISTQB Glossary.]

Test harnesses or drivers may be developed in-house for particular systems. Advice on designing test drivers can be found in [Hoffman and Strooper 1995].

There are a large number of 'xUnit' tools for different programming languages, e.g. JUnit for Java, NUnit for .Net applications, etc. There are both commercial tools and also open-source tools. Unit test framework tools are very similar to test execution tools, since they include facilities such as the ability to store test cases and monitor whether tests pass or fail, for example. The main difference is that there is no capture/playback facility and they tend to be used at a lower level, i.e. for component or component integration testing, rather than for system or acceptance testing.

Features or characteristics of test harnesses and unit test framework tools include support for:

- supplying inputs to the software being tested;
- receiving outputs generated by the software being tested;
- executing a set of tests within the framework or using the test harness;
- recording the pass/fail results of each test (framework tools);
- storing tests (framework tools);
- support for debugging (framework tools);
- coverage measurement at code level (framework tools).

Test comparators

Is it really a test if you put some inputs into some software, but never look to see whether the software produces the correct result? The essence of testing is to check whether the software produces the correct result, and to do that, we must compare what the software produces to what it should produce. **A test comparator** helps to automate aspects of that comparison.

> **Test comparator** A test tool to perform automated test comparison of actual results with expected results.

There are two ways in which actual results of a test can be compared to the expected results for the test. Dynamic comparison is where the comparison is done dynamically, i.e. while the test is executing. The other way is post-execution comparison, where the comparison is performed after the test has finished executing and the software under test is no longer running.

Test execution tools include the capability to perform dynamic comparison while the tool is executing a test. This type of comparison is good for comparing the wording of an error message that pops up on a screen with the correct wording for that error message. Dynamic comparison is useful when an actual result does not match the expected result in the middle of a test – the tool can be programmed to take some recovery action at this point or go to a different set of tests.

> **Test comparison** The process of identifying differences between the actual results produced by the component or system under test and the expected results for a test. Test comparison can be performed during test execution (dynamic comparison) or after test execution.

Post-execution comparison is usually best done by a separate tool (i.e. not the test execution tool). This is the type of tool that we mean by a test comparator or **test comparison** tool and is typically a 'stand-alone' tool. Operating systems normally have file comparison tools available that can be used for post-execution comparison and often a comparison tool will be developed in-house for comparing a particular type of file or test result.

Post-execution comparison is best for comparing a large volume of data, such as comparing the contents of an entire file with the expected contents of that file, or comparing a large set of records from a database with the expected content of those records. For example, comparing the result of a batch run (e.g. overnight processing of the day's online transactions) is probably impossible to do without tool support.

Whether a comparison is dynamic or post-execution, the test comparator needs to know what the correct result is. This may be stored as part of the test case itself or it may be computed using a test oracle. See Chapter 4 for information about test oracles.

Features or characteristics of test comparators include support for:

- dynamic comparison of transient events that occur during test execution;
- post-execution comparison of stored data, e.g. in files or databases;
- masking or filtering of subsets of actual and expected results.

Coverage measurement tools (D)

Coverage tool A tool that provides objective measures of what structural elements, e.g. statements, branches have been exercised by a test suite.

How thoroughly have you tested? **Coverage tools** can help answer this question.

A coverage tool first identifies the elements or coverage items that can be counted, and where the tool can identify when a test has exercised that coverage item. At component testing level, the coverage items could be lines of code or code statements or decision outcomes (e.g. the True or False exit from an IF statement). At component integration level, the coverage item may be a call to a function or module. Although coverage can be measured at system or acceptance testing levels, e.g. where the coverage item may be a requirement statement, there aren't many (if any) commercial tools at this level; there is more tool support at component testing level or to some extent at component integration level.

The process of identifying the coverage items at component test level is called 'instrumenting the code', as described in Chapter 4. A suite of tests is then run through the instrumented code, either automatically using a test execution tool or manually. The coverage tool then counts the number of coverage items that have been executed by the test suite, and reports the percentage of coverage items that have been exercised, and may also identify the items that have not yet been exercised (i.e. not yet tested). Additional tests can then be run to increase coverage (the tool reports accumulated coverage of all the tests run so far).

The more sophisticated coverage tools can provide support to help identify the test inputs that will exercise the paths that include as-yet unexercised coverage items (or link to a test design tool to identify the unexercised items). For example, if not all decision outcomes have been exercised, the coverage tool can identify the particular decision outcome (e.g. a False exit from an IF statement) that no test has taken so far, and may then also be able to calculate the test input required to force execution to take that decision outcome.

Features or characteristics of coverage measurement tools include support for:

- identifying coverage items (instrumenting the code);
- calculating the percentage of coverage items that were exercised by a suite of tests;
- reporting coverage items that have not been exercised as yet;
- identifying test inputs to exercise as yet uncovered items (test design tool functionality);
- generating stubs and drivers (if part of a unit test framework).

Note that the coverage tools only measure the coverage of the items that they can identify. Just because your tests have achieved 100% statement coverage, this does not mean that your software is 100% tested!

Security testing tools

There are a number of tools that protect systems from external attack, for example firewalls, which are important for any system.

Security testing tools can be used to test **security** by trying to break into a system, whether or not it is protected by a **security tool**. The attacks may focus on the network, the support software, the application code or the underlying database.

Features or characteristics of security testing tools include support for:

- identifying viruses;
- detecting intrusions such as denial of service attacks;
- simulating various types of external attacks;
- probing for open ports or other externally visible points of attack;
- identifying weaknesses in password files and passwords;
- security checks during operation, e.g. for checking integrity of files, and intrusion detection, e.g. checking results of test attacks.

Security testing tool A tool that provides support for testing security characteristics and vulnerabilities.

Security Attributes of software products that bear on its ability to prevent unauthorized access, whether accidental or deliberate, to programs and data.

security tool A tool that supports operational security.

6.1.7 Tool support for performance and monitoring

The tools described in this section support testing that can be carried out on a system when it is operational, i.e. while it is running. This can be during testing or could be after a system is released into live operation.

Dynamic analysis tools (D)

Dynamic analysis tools are 'dynamic' because they require the code to be running. They are 'analysis' rather than 'testing' tools because they analyze what is happening 'behind the scenes' while the software is running (whether being executed with test cases or being used in operation).

An analogy with a car may be useful here. If you go to look at a car to buy, you might sit in it to see if is comfortable and see what sound the doors make – this would be static analysis because the car is not being driven. If you take a test drive, then you would check that the car performs as you expect (e.g. turns right when you turn the steering wheel clockwise) – this would be a test. While the car is running, if you were to check the oil pressure or the brake fluid, this would be dynamic analysis – it can only be done while the engine is running, but it isn't a test case.

When your PC's response time gets slower and slower over time, but is much improved after you re-boot it, this may well be due to a 'memory leak', where the programs do not correctly release blocks of memory back to the operating system. Eventually the system will run out of memory completely and stop. Rebooting restores all of the memory that was lost, so the performance of the system is now restored to its normal state.

Features or characteristics of dynamic analysis tools include support for:

- detecting memory leaks;
- identifying pointer arithmetic errors such as null pointers;
- identifying time dependencies.

These tools would typically be used by developers in component testing and component integration testing, e.g. when testing middleware, when testing security or when looking for robustness defects.

Dynamic analysis tool A tool that provides run-time information on the state of the software code. These tools are most commonly used to identify unassigned pointers, check pointer arithmetic and to monitor the allocation, use and de-allocation of memory and to flag memory leaks.

Another form of dynamic analysis for websites is to check whether each link does actually link to something else (this type of tool may be called a 'web spider'). The tool doesn't know if you have linked to the correct page, but at least it can find dead links, which may be helpful.

Performance-testing, load-testing and stress-testing tools

Performance-testing tool (load-testing tool) A tool to support performance testing that usually has two main facilities: load generation and test transaction measurement. Load generation can simulate either multiple users or high volumes of input data. During execution, response time measurements are taken from selected transactions and these are logged. Performance testing tools normally provide reports based on test logs and graphs of load against response times.

Volume testing Testing where the system is subjected to large volumes of data.

Stress testing tool A tool that supports stress testing.

Performance-testing tools are concerned with testing at system level to see whether or not the system will stand up to a high volume of usage. A 'load' test checks that the system can cope with its expected number of transactions. **A 'volume' test** checks that the system can cope with a large amount of data, e.g. many fields in a record, many records in a file, etc. **A 'stress' test** is one that goes beyond the normal expected usage of the system (to see what would happen outside its design expectations), with respect to load or volume.

In performance testing, many test inputs may be sent to the software or system where the individual results may not be checked in detail. The purpose of the test is to measure characteristics, such as response times, throughput or the mean time between failures (for reliability testing).

In order to assess performance, the **tool** needs to generate some kind of activity on the system, and this can be done in different ways. At a very simple level the same transaction could be repeated many times, but this is not realistic. There are many levels of realism that could be set, depending on the tool, such as different user profiles, different types of activity, timing delays and other parameters. Adequately replicating the end-user environments or user profiles is usually key to realistic results.

Analyzing the output of a performance-testing tool is not always straightforward and it requires time and expertise. If the performance is not up to the standard expected, then some analysis needs to be performed to see where the problem is and to know what can be done to improve the performance.

Features or characteristics of performance-testing tools include support for:

- generating a load on the system to be tested;
- measuring the timing of specific transactions as the load on the system varies;
- measuring average response times;
- producing graphs or charts of responses over time.

Monitoring tools

Monitor (monitoring tool) A software tool or hardware device that runs concurrently with the component or system under test and supervises, records and/or analyzes the behaviour of the component or system.

Monitoring tools are used to continuously keep track of the status of the system in use, in order to have the earliest warning of problems and to improve service. There are monitoring tools for servers, networks, databases, security, performance, website and internet usage, and applications.

Features or characteristics of monitoring tools include support for:

- identifying problems and sending an alert message to the administrator (e.g. network administrator);
- logging real-time and historical information;
- finding optimal settings;
- monitoring the number of users on a network;
- monitoring network traffic (either in real time or covering a given length of time of operation with the analysis performed afterwards).

6.1.8 Tool support for specific application areas (K1)

In this chapter, we have described tools according to their general functional classifications. There are also further specializations of tools within these classifications. For example there are web-based performance-testing tools as well as performance-testing tools for back-office systems. There are static analysis tools for specific development platforms and programming languages, since each programming language and every platform has distinct characteristics. There are dynamic analysis tools that focus on security issues, as well as dynamic analysis tools for embedded systems.

Commercial tool sets may be bundled for specific application areas such as web-based or embedded systems.

6.1.9 Tool support using other tools

The tools described in this chapter are not the only tools that a tester can make use of. You may not normally think of a word processor or a spreadsheet as a testing tool, but they are often used to store test designs, test scripts or test data. Testers may also use SQL to set up and query databases containing test data. Tools used by developers when debugging, to help localize defects and check their fixes, are also testing tools.

Developers use **debugging tools** when identifying and fixing defects. The debugging tools enable them to run individual and localized tests to ensure that they have correctly identified the cause of a defect and to confirm that their change to the code will indeed fix the defect.

> **Debugging tool** A tool used by programmers to reproduce failures, investigate the state of programs and find the corresponding defect. Debuggers enable programmers to execute programs step by step, to halt a program at any program statement and to set and examine program variables.

6.1.10 Tool support for specific testing needs

We can also use tools for data quality assessment. In many IT-centric organizations, systems and systems of systems manage tremendous volumes of complex, inter-related data. This puts data at the centre of many projects in these organizations, including data conversion and migration projects and data warehouse projects. The data involved can vary in terms of criticality and volume. You can – and often should – use tools as part of the data quality assessment, including reviewing and verifying data conversion and migration rules. Tools can help ensure that the processed data is correct, and complete, and that it complies to pre-defined, context-specific standards, even when the volume of data is large.

You can also use tools for usability testing. These can include general-purpose tools such as video recorders and screen-capture utilities.

6.2 EFFECTIVE USE OF TOOLS: POTENTIAL BENEFITS AND RISKS

SYLLABUS LEARNING OBJECTIVES FOR 6.2 EFFECTIVE USE OF TOOLS: POTENTIAL BENEFITS AND RISKS(K2)

LO-6.2.1 Summarize the potential benefits and risks of test automation and tool support for testing. (K2)

LO-6.2.2 Remember special considerations for test execution tools, static analysis, and test management tools. (K1)

The reason for acquiring tools to support testing is to gain benefits, by using a software program to do certain tasks that are better done by a computer than by a person.

Advice on introducing tools into an organization can be found in web articles, magazines and books such as [Siteur 2005] and [Fewster and Graham 1999].

As we go through this section, watch for the Syllabus term **scripting language**. You'll find these terms defined in the glossary.

6.2.1 Potential benefits of using tools

There are many benefits that can be gained by using tools to support testing, whatever the specific type of tool. Benefits include:

- reduction of repetitive work;
- greater consistency and repeatability;
- objective assessment;
- ease of access to information about tests or testing.

Repetitive work is tedious to do manually. People become bored and make mistakes when doing the same task over and over. Examples of this type of repetitive work include running regression tests, entering the same test data over and over again (both of which can be done by a test execution tool), checking against coding standards (which can be done by a static analysis tool) or creating a specific test database (which can be done by a test data preparation tool).

People tend to do the same task in a slightly different way even when they think they are repeating something exactly. A tool will exactly reproduce what it did before, so each time it is run the result is consistent. Examples of where this aspect is beneficial include checking to confirm the correctness of a fix to a defect (which can be done by a debugging tool or test execution tool), entering test inputs (which can be done by a test execution tool) and generating tests from requirements (which can be done by a test design tool or possibly a requirements management tool).

If a person calculates a value from the software or incident reports, they may inadvertently omit something, or their own subjective prejudices may lead them to interpret that data incorrectly. Using a tool means that subjective bias is removed and the assessment is more repeatable and consistently calculated. Examples include assessing the cyclomatic complexity or nesting levels of a component (which can be done by a static analysis tool), coverage (coverage measurement tool), system behaviour (monitoring tools) and incident statistics (test management tool or incident management tool).

Having lots of data doesn't mean that information is communicated. Information presented visually is much easier for the human mind to take in and interpret. For example, a chart or graph is a better way to show information than a long list of numbers – this is why charts and graphs in spreadsheets are so useful. Special purpose tools give these features directly for the information they process. Examples include statistics and graphs about test progress (test execution or test management tool), incident rates (incident management or test management tool) and performance (performance testing tool).

In addition to these general benefits, each type of tool has specific benefits relating to the aspect of testing that the particular tool supports. These benefits are normally prominently featured in the information available for the type of tool. It is worth investigating a number of different tools to get a general view of the benefits.

6.2.2 Risks of using tools

Although there are significant benefits that can be achieved using tools to support testing activities, there are many organizations that have not achieved the benefits they expected.

Simply purchasing a tool is no guarantee of achieving benefits, just as buying membership in a gym does not guarantee that you will be fitter. Each type of tool requires investment of effort and time in order to achieve the potential benefits.

There are many risks that are present when tool support for testing is introduced and used, whatever the specific type of tool. Risks include:

- unrealistic expectations for the tool;
- underestimating the time, cost and effort for the initial introduction of a tool;
- underestimating the time and effort needed to achieve significant and continuing benefits from the tool;
- underestimating the effort required to maintain the test assets generated by the tool;
- over-reliance on the tool, including relying on tools for test design or test execution where manual testing would work better;
- failing to use proper configuration management and version control facilities for the test assets created for and by the tool;
- failing to consider and manage issues related to relationships and interoperability between critical tools, such as requirements management tools, version control tools, incident management tools, defect tracking tools and tools from multiple vendors;
- possibility of the tool vendor going out of business, retiring the tool, or selling the tool to a different vendor, or in the open-source world, the possibility of orphanage of the tool or suspension of the project by the open-source community;
- poor or completely non-existent vendor response, whether for support, upgrades, or defect fixes;
- various uncertainties and unforeseen problems, such as the inability to support a new platform.

Unrealistic expectations may be one of the greatest risks to success with tools. The tools are only software and we all know that there are many problems with any kind of software! It is important to have clear objectives for what the tool can do and that those objectives are realistic.

Introducing something new into an organization is seldom straightforward. Having purchased a tool, you will want to move from opening the box to having a number of people being able to use the tool in a way that will bring benefits. There will be technical problems to overcome, but there will also be resistance from other people – both need to be addressed in order to succeed in introducing a tool.

Think back to the last time you did something new for the very first time (learning to drive, riding a bike, skiing). Your first attempts were unlikely to be very good but with more experience you became much better. Using a testing tool for the first time will not be your best use of the tool either. It takes time to develop ways of using the tool in order to achieve what is possible. Fortunately there are some short-cuts (e.g. reading books and articles about other people's experiences and learning from them). See also Section 6.3 for more detail on introducing a tool into an organization.

Insufficient planning for maintenance of the assets that the tool produces is a strong contributor to tools that end up as 'shelf-ware', along with the previously listed risks. Although particularly relevant for test execution tools, planning for maintenance is also a factor with other types of tool.

Tools are definitely not magic! They can do very well what they have been designed to do (at least a good quality tool can), but they cannot do everything. A tool can certainly help, but it does not replace the intelligence needed to know how best to use it, and how to evaluate current and future uses of the tool. For example, a test execution tool does not replace the need for good test design and should not be used for every test – some tests are still better executed manually. A test that takes a very long time to automate and will not be run very often is better done manually.

This list of risks is not exhaustive. Two other important factors are:

● the skill needed to create good tests;

● the skill needed to use the tools well, depending on the type of tool.

The skills of a tester are not the same as the skills of the tool user. The tester concentrates on what should be tested, what the test cases should be and how to prioritize the testing. The tool user concentrates on how best to get the tool to do its job effectively and how to give increasing benefit from tool use.

6.2.3 Special considerations for some types of tools

Test execution tools

In order to know what tests to execute and how to run them, the test execution tool must have some way of knowing what to do – this is the script for the tool. But since the tool is only software, the script must be completely exact and unambiguous to the computer (which has no common sense). This means that the script becomes a program, written in a programming language. **The scripting language** may be specific to a particular tool, or it may be a more general language. Scripting languages are not used just by test execution tools, but the scripts used by the tool are stored electronically to be run when the tests are executed under the tool's control.

> **scripting language**
> A programming language in which executable test scripts are written, used by a test execution tool (e.g. a capture/playback tool).

There are tools that can generate scripts by identifying what is on the screen rather than by capturing a manual test, but they still generate scripts to be used in execution; they are not script-free.

There are different levels of scripting. Five are described in [Fewster and Graham 1999]:

● linear scripts (which could be created manually or captured by recording a manual test);

● structured scripts (using selection and iteration programming structures);

● shared scripts (where a script can be called by other scripts so can be re-used – shared scripts also require a formal script library under configuration management);

● data-driven scripts (where test data is in a file or spreadsheet to be read by a control script);

● keyword-driven scripts (where all of the information about the test is stored in a file or spreadsheet, with a single control scripts that implements the tests described in the file using shared and keyword scripts).

Capturing a manual test seems like a good idea to start with, particularly if you are currently running tests manually anyway. But a captured test (a linear script) is not a good solution, for a number of reasons, including:

- The script doesn't know what the expected result is until you program it in – it only stores inputs that have been recorded, not test cases.
- A small change to the software may invalidate dozens or hundreds of scripts.
- The recorded script can only cope with exactly the same conditions as when it was recorded. Unexpected events (e.g. a file that already exists) will not be interpreted correctly by the tool.

However, there are some times when capturing test inputs (i.e. recording a manual test) is useful. For example, if you are doing exploratory testing or if you are running unscripted tests with experienced business users, it can be very helpful simply to log everything that is done, as an audit trail. This serves as a form of documentation of what was tested (although analyzing it may not be easy). This audit trail can also be very useful if a failure occurs which cannot be easily reproduced – the recording of the specific failure can be played to the developer to see exactly what sequence caused the problem.

Captured test inputs can be useful in the short term, where the context remains valid. Just don't expect to replay them as regression tests (when the context of the test may be different). Captured tests may be acceptable for a few dozen tests, where the effort to update them when the software changes is not very large. Don't expect a linear-scripting approach to scale to hundreds or thousands of tests.

So capturing tests does have a place, but it is not a large place in terms of automating test execution.

Data driven scripts allow the data, i.e. the test inputs and expected outcomes, to be stored separately from the script. This can include situations where, instead of the testing putting hard-coded data combinations in a spreadsheet, a tool generates and supplies data in real time, based on configurable parameters. For example, a tool may generate a random user ID for accounts, and can take advantage of random-number seeding to ensuring repeatability in the pattern of user IDs. Whichever way data-driven scripts are implemented, they have the advantage that a tester who doesn't know how to use a scripting language can populate a file or spreadsheet with the data for a specific test. This is particularly useful when there are a large number of data values that need to be tested using the same control script.

Keyword-driven scripts include not just data but also keywords in the data file or spreadsheet. In other words, the spreadsheet or data file contains keywords that describe the actions to be taken and the test data. ('Action words' is another term used for keywords.) Keyword-driven (or action-word) automation enables a tester (who is not a script programmer) to devise a great variety of tests (not just the test input data for essentially the same test, as in data-driven scripts). The tester needs to know what keywords are currently available to use (by someone having written a script for it) and what data the keyword is expecting, but the tester can then write tests, not just test data. The tester can also request additional keywords to be added to the available programmed set of scripts as needed. Keywords can deal with both test inputs and expected outcomes.

Of course, someone still needs to be able to use the tool directly and be able to program in the tool's scripting language in order to write and debug the scripts that will use the data tables or keyword tables. A small number of automation specialists

> **data-driven** A scripting technique that stores test input and expected results in a table or spreadsheet, so that a single control script can execute all of the tests in the table. Data driven testing is often used to support the application of test execution tools such as capture/playback tools.

can support a larger number of testers, who then don't need to learn to be script programmers (unless they want to).

The data files (data-driven or keyword-driven) include the expected results for the tests. The actual results from each test run also need to be stored, at least until they are compared to the expected results and any differences are logged.

More information on data-driven and keyword-driven scripting can be found in [Fewster and Graham 1999].

Performance testing tools

Performance testing is developing into a specialized discipline of its own. With functional testing, the types of defect that we are looking for are functionality – does the system or component produce the correct result for given inputs? In performance testing, we are not normally concerned so much with functional correctness, but with non-functional quality characteristics. When using a performance testing tool we are looking at the transaction throughput, the degree of accuracy of a given computation, the computer resources being used for a given level of transactions, the time taken for certain transactions or the number of users that can use the system at once.

In order to get the best from a performance-testing tool, it is important to understand what the tool can and cannot do for you. Although this is true for other types of tool as well, there are particular issues with performance-testing tools, including:

- the design of the load to be generated by the tool (e.g. random input or according to user profiles);
- timing aspects (e.g. inserting delays to make simulated user input more realistic);
- the length of the test and what to do if a test stops prematurely;
- narrowing down the location of a bottleneck;
- exactly what aspects to measure (e.g. user interaction level or server level);
- how to present the information gathered.

Static analysis tools

Static analysis tools are very useful to developers, as they can identify potential problems in code before the code is executed and they can also help to check that the code is written to coding standards.

When a static analysis tool is first introduced, there can be some problems. For example, if the tool checks the current coding standard against code written several years ago, there may be a number of things found in the old code that fail to meet the new coding standard now in place. If the old code has been working well for years, it is probably not a good idea to change it just to satisfy the new coding standard (unless changes are necessary for some other reason). There is a risk that the changes to meet the new standard may have inadvertent side-effects which may not be picked up by regression testing.

Static analysis tools can generate a large number of messages, for example by finding the same thing every few lines. This can be rather annoying, especially if the things found are not considered important now, for example warnings rather than potential defects.

The aim of the static analysis tool is to produce code that will be easier to maintain in the future, so it would be a good idea to implement higher standards on new code that is still being tested, before it is released into use, but to allow older code to be less stringently checked. There is still a risk that the changes to conform to the new standard will introduce an unexpected side-effect, but there is a much greater likelihood that it will be found in testing and there is time to fix it before the system is released.

A filter on the output of the static analysis tool could eliminate some of the less important messages and make the more important messages more likely to be noticed and fixed.

Test management tools

Test management tools can provide a lot of useful information, but the information as produced by the tool may not be in the form that will be most effective within your own context. Some additional work may be needed to produce interfaces to other tools or a spreadsheet in order to ensure that the information is communicated in the most effective way.

A report produced by a test management tool (either directly or indirectly through another tool or spreadsheet) may be a very useful report at the moment, but may not be useful in three or six months. It is important to monitor the information produced to ensure it is the most relevant now.

It is important to have a defined test process before test management tools are introduced. If the testing process is working well manually, then a test management tool can help to support the process and make it more efficient. If you adopt a test management tool when your own testing processes are immature, one option is to follow the standards and processes that are assumed by the way the tool works. This can be helpful; but it is not necessary to follow the vendor-specific processes. The best approach is to define your own processes, taking into account the tool you will be using, and then adapt the tool to provide the greatest benefit to your organization.

6.3 INTRODUCING A TOOL INTO AN ORGANIZATION

> **SYLLABUS LEARNING OBJECTIVES FOR 6.3 INTRODUCING A TOOL INTO AN ORGANIZATION (K1)**
>
> **LO-6.3.1** State the main principles of introducing a tool into an organization. (K1)
>
> **LO-6.3.2** State the goals of a proof-of-concept for tool evaluation and a piloting phase for tool implementation. (K1)
>
> **LO-6.3.3** Recognize that factors other than simply acquiring a tool are required for good tool support. (K1)

In this section, we discuss the principles and process of introducing automated testing tools into your organization. We look at the process of tool selection. We'll talk about how to carry out tool pilot programs. We'll conclude with thoughts on what makes tool introduction successful.

There are no Syllabus terms for this section.

6.3.1 Main principles

The place to start when introducing a tool into an organization is not with the tool – it is with the organization. In order for a tool to provide benefit, it must match a need within the organization, and solve that need in a way that is both effective and efficient. The tool should help to build on the strengths of the organization and address its weaknesses. The organization needs to be ready for the changes that will come with the new tool. If the current testing practices are not good and the organization is not mature, then it is generally more cost-effective to improve testing practices rather than to try to find tools to support poor practices. Automating chaos just gives faster chaos!

Of course, we can sometimes improve our own processes in parallel with introducing a tool to support those practices and we can pick up some good ideas for improvement from the ways that the tools work. However, be aware that the tool should not take the lead, but should provide support to what your organization defines.

The following factors are important in selecting a tool:

- assessment of the organization's maturity (e.g. readiness for change);
- identification of the areas within the organization where tool support will help to improve testing processes;
- evaluation of tools against clear requirements and objective criteria;
- proof-of-concept to see whether the product works as desired and meets the requirements and objectives defined for it;
- evaluation of the vendor (training, support and other commercial aspects) or open-source network of support;
- identifying and planning internal implementation (including training, coaching and mentoring for those new to the use of the tool);
- estimation of the return on investment (cost-benefit ratio) based on a concrete and realistic business case.

6.3.2 Pilot project

One of the ways to do a proof-of-concept is to have a pilot project as the first thing done with a new tool. This will use the tool in earnest but on a small scale, with sufficient time to explore different ways of using the tool. Objectives should be set for the pilot in order to assess whether or not the concept *is* proven, i.e. that the tool can accomplish what is needed within the current organizational context.

A pilot tool project should expect to encounter problems – they should be solved in ways that can be used by everyone later on. The pilot project should experiment with different ways of using the tool. For example, different settings for a static analysis tool, different reports from a test management tool, different scripting and comparison techniques for a test execution tool or different load profiles for a performance-testing tool.

The objectives for a pilot project for a new tool are:

- to learn more about the tool (more detail, more depth);
- to see how the tool would fit with existing processes or documentation, how those would need to change to work well with the tool and how to use the tool to streamline existing processes;

- to decide on standard ways of using the tool that will work for all potential users (e.g. naming conventions, creation of libraries, defining modularity, where different elements will be stored, how they and the tool itself will be maintained);
- to evaluate the pilot project against its objectives (have the benefits been achieved at reasonable cost?).

6.3.3 Success factors

Success is not guaranteed or automatic when implementing a testing tool, but many organizations have succeeded. Here are some of the factors that have contributed to success:

- incremental roll-out (after the pilot) to the rest of the organization;
- adapting and improving processes, testware and tool artefacts to get the best fit and balance between them and the use of the tool;
- providing adequate support, training, coaching and mentoring of new users;
- defining and communicating guidelines for the use of the tool, based on what was learned in the pilot;
- implementing a continuous improvement mechanism as tool use spreads through more of the organization;
- monitoring the use of the tool and the benefits achieved and adapting the use of the tool to take account of what is learned;
- provide continuing support for anyone using test tools, such as the test team; for example, technical expertise is needed to help non-programmer testers who use keyword-driven test automation;
- continuous improvement of tool use should be based on information gathered from all teams who are using test tools.

More information and advice about selecting and implementing tools can be found in [Fewster and Graham 1999].

CHAPTER REVIEW

Let's review what you have learned in this chapter.

From Section 6.1, you should now be able to classify different types of test tools according to the test process activities that they support. You should also recognize the tools that may help developers in their testing (shown by '(D)' below). In addition to the list below, you should recognize that there are tools that support specific application areas and that general-purpose tools can also be used to support testing. The tools you should now recognize are:

Tools that support the management of testing and tests:

- test management tool;
- requirements management tool;
- incident management tool;
- configuration management tool.

Tools that support static testing:

- review tool;
- static analysis tool (D);
- modelling tool (D).

Tools that support test specification:

- test design tool;
- test data preparation tool.

Tools that support test execution and logging:

- test execution tool;
- test harness and unit test framework tool (D);
- test comparator;
- coverage measurement tool (D);
- security tool.

Tools that support performance and monitoring:

- dynamic analysis tool;
- performance-testing, load-testing and stress-testing tool;
- monitoring tool.

In addition to the tools already listed, you should know the glossary terms **capture/playback tool**, configuration management tool, coverage tool, debugging tool, dynamic analysis tool, incident management tool, load testing tool, modelling tool, monitoring tool, performance testing tool, probe effect, requirements management tool, review tool, **security testing tool,** security tool, static analysis tool, **static code analysis, static code analyzer,** stress testing tool, test comparator, **test comparison,** test data preparation tool, test design tool, **test framework,** test execution tool, test management tool, unit test framework tool and **volume testing**.

From Section 6.2, you should be able to summarize the potential benefits and potential risks of tool support for testing in general. You should recognize that some tools have special considerations, including test execution tools, performance-testing tools, static analysis tools and test management tools. You should know the glossary term **scripting language** and recognize these as associated with test execution tools.

From Section 6.3, you should be able to state the main principles of introducing a tool into an organization (e.g. assessing organizational maturity, clear requirements and objective criteria, proof-of-concept, vendor evaluation, coaching and mentoring). You should be able to state the goals of a proof-of-concept or piloting phase for tool evaluation (e.g. learn about the tool, assess fit with current practices, decide on standards, assess benefits). You should recognize that simply acquiring a tool is not the only factor in achieving good tool support; there are many other factors that are important for success (e.g. incremental roll-out, adapting processes, training and coaching, defining usage guidelines, learning lessons and monitoring benefits). There are no specific definitions for this section.

SAMPLE EXAM QUESTIONS

Question 1 Which tools help to support static testing?

a. Static analysis tools, and test execution tools.

b. Review tools, static analysis tools, and coverage measurement tools.

c. Dynamic analysis tools, and modelling tools.

d. Review tools, static analysis tools, and modelling tools.

Question 2 Which test activities are supported by test harness or unit test framework tools?

a. Test management and control.

b. Test specification and design.

c. Test execution and logging.

d. Performance and monitoring.

Question 3 What are the potential benefits from using tools in general to support testing?

a. Greater quality of code, reduction in the number of testers needed, better objectives for testing.

b. Greater repeatability of tests, reduction in repetitive work, objective assessment.

c. Greater responsiveness of users, reduction of tests run, objectives not necessary.

d. Greater quality of code, reduction in paperwork, fewer objections to the tests.

Question 4 What is a potential risk in using tools to support testing?

a. Unrealistic expectations, expecting the tool to do too much.

b. Insufficient reliance on the tool, i.e. still doing manual testing when a test execution tool has been purchased.

c. The tool may find defects that aren't there.

d. The tool will repeat exactly the same thing it did the previous time.

Question 5 Which of the following are advanced scripting techniques for test execution tools?

a. Data-driven and keyword-driven.

b. Data-driven and capture-driven.

c. Capture-driven and keyhole-driven.

d. Playback-driven and keyword-driven.

Question 6 Which of the following would NOT be done as part of selecting a tool for an organization?

a. Assess organizational maturity, strengths, and weaknesses.

b. Roll out the tool to as many users as possible within the organization.

c. Evaluate the tool features against clear requirements and objective criteria.

d. Identify internal requirements for coaching and mentoring in the use of the tool.

Question 7 Which of the following is a goal for a proof-of-concept or pilot phase for tool evaluation?

a. Decide which tool to acquire.

b. Decide on the main objectives and requirements for this type of tool.

c. Evaluate the tool vendor including training, support, and commercial aspects.

d. Decide on standard ways of using, managing, storing, and maintaining the tool and the test assets.

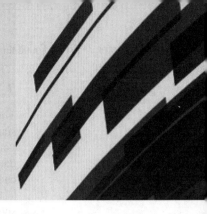

CHAPTER SEVEN
ISTQB Foundation Exam

We wrote (and re-wrote and re-wrote) this book specifically to cover the International Software Testing Qualification Board (ISTQB) Foundation Syllabus 2011. As such, mastery of the previous six chapters should ensure that you master the exam, too. Here are some thoughts on how to make sure you show how much you know when taking the exam.

7.1 PREPARING FOR THE EXAM

7.1.1 Studying for the exam

Whether you have taken a preparatory course along with reading this book or just read the book, we have some study tips for certification candidates who intend to take an exam under one of the ISTQB-recognized National Boards or Exam Boards.

Of course, you should carefully study the Syllabus. If you encounter any statements or concepts you do not *completely* understand, refer back to this book and to any course materials used, to prepare for the exam. Exam questions often turn on *precise* understanding of a concept.

While you should study the whole Syllabus, scrutinize the learning objectives in the Syllabus one by one. Ask yourself if you have achieved that learning objective to the given level of knowledge. If not, go back and review the appropriate material in the section corresponding to that learning objective.

Going beyond the Syllabus, notice that a number of international standards are referred to in the Syllabus. You should obtain copies of those standards and read them. Some exam questions will be about the standards and glossary terms, and often even experienced testers are unfamiliar with them.

We recommend that you try all of the sample exam questions in this book. If you have understood the material in a chapter, you should have no trouble with the questions. Make sure you understand why the right answer is the right answer and why the wrong answers are wrong. If you cannot answer a question and don't understand why, review that section.

We also recommend that you try all of the exercises in the book. If you can answer them correctly, you probably understand the concepts. If you have not done the exercises, you may well fail the exam.

Finally, be sure to take the mock exam we have provided at the end of this chapter. If you have understood the material in the book, you should have no trouble with most, if not all, of the questions on the mock exam. Make sure you carefully review the book sections corresponding to any questions that you do not answer correctly.

7.1.2 The exam and the Syllabus

The ISTQB Foundation exam is designed to assess your knowledge and under-standing of basic testing ideas and terms, which provides a solid starting point for your future testing efforts. These exams are not perfect. Even well-qualified candidates often fail a few questions or disagree with some answers. Study hard, so you can take the exam in a relaxed and confident way.

If you take the exam unprepared, you should expect your lack of preparation to show in your score. Since you'll pay to take the exam, consider preparation time an investment in protecting your exam fee.

The ISTQB Foundation Syllabus 2011 is the current syllabus. It replaces the 2010 version, which in turn replaced the 2007 version, which in turn replaced the 2005 version. Do not refer to the old syllabi, as the exam covers the new Syllabus.

7.1.3 Where should you take the exam?

If you have taken an accredited training course, it's quite likely the exam will occur on the last day of the course. The exam fee may have been included in the course fee. If so, you should plan to study each evening during the course, including material that will be covered on the last day. Any topic covered in the Syllabus may be in an exam. You might even want to read this book before starting the course.

You might be taking an on-line course. Again, we recommend that you study the materials as you cover each section. Consider reading the book during or even before taking the course.

If you have studied on your own, without taking a course, then you'll need to find a place open to the general public to take the exam. Many conferences around the world offer the exam this way. Otherwise the website for the testing board for your country (the National Board) should be able to help you find the right venue for a public exam.

In addition, the Foundation Certification exam is available in electronic versions; e.g. via Kryterion, Pearson-Vue, Prometric and other commercial electronic test centres. This is a real advantage for those who live or work away from those cities where in-person courses and exams are offered. The price is competitive with the in-person exam fee, so you won't pay a big premium for convenience.

Regardless of which National Board administers the exam, all National Boards are bound by the ISTQB Constitution to recognize the certification granted. In addition, ISTQB-recognized Exam Boards such as DLGI, GASQ, ISEB, iSQI and SAQ will provide you with ISTQB-branded certificates, as they work in close cooperation with the ISTQB and its National Boards. The ISTQB and each ISTQB-recognized National Board and Exam Board are constitutionally obliged to support a single, universally accepted, international qualification scheme. Therefore, you are free to choose ISTQB-accredited trainers, if desired, and ISTQB-accredited exam providers based on factors like convenience, competence, suitability of the training to your immediate professional and business needs and price.

7.2 TAKING THE EXAM

All the National Boards offer the same type of Foundation exam. It is a multiple-choice exam that conforms to the guidelines established by the ISTQB. For some of us, it's been a while since we last took an exam and you may not remember all the tricks and techniques for taking a multiple-choice exam. Here are a few paragraphs that will give you some ideas on how to take the exam.

7.2.1 How to approach multiple-choice questions

Remember that there are two aspects to correctly answering a multiple-choice exam question. First, you must understand the question and decide what the right answer should be. Second, you must correctly communicate your answer by selecting the most correct option from the choices listed.

Each question has one correct answer. This answer is always or most frequently true, given the stated context and conditions in the question. The other answers are intended to mislead people who don't completely understand the concept, and are called 'distracters' in the examination business.

So, read the question carefully and make sure you understand it before you decide on your answer. It may help to underline the key words or concepts stated in the question. Some questions may be ambiguous or ask which is the best or worst alternative. You should choose the best answer based on what you've learned in this book. Remember that your own situation may be different from the most common situation.

Some of the distracters may distract you. In other words, you might be unsure about the correct answers to all of the questions. So, make two passes through the exam. On your first pass, answer all of the questions you are sure of. Come back to the others later.

If a question will take a long time to answer, come back to it later. For example, questions that require you to draw flow charts to understand code coverage often take much longer to answer. Come back to them later when you feel confident that you have enough time.

It's important to pace yourself. We suggest that you spend 45–60 seconds on each question; that way your first pass will take less than 40 minutes. You can then use the remaining time to have a one-minute break, then double-check your answers on the answer sheet, and then finally go back to any questions you have left blank.

The answer sheets for the exams vary slightly from one National Board or Exam Board to another. However, you should make sure that each answer corresponds to the correct question number. Especially if you have skipped a question, it's easy to get confused and mark the answer option above or below the question you are trying to answer. Also, make sure you have an answer for every question. In addition, double-check that you have selected the answer you want, as it is easy to select the wrong answer.

7.2.2 On 'trick' questions

There are no deliberately designed trick questions in the ISTQB exams, but some can seem quite difficult if you are not completely sure of the right answer. Remember, just because it's hard to answer doesn't make it a trick. Here are some ideas for dealing with the tough questions.

First, read the question and each of the options very thoroughly. It is easy to read what you expect to be there rather than what is there.

If you are tempted to change your answer, do so only if you are quite sure. When you are vacillating, it is usually best to go with your first instinct. Remember that the correct answer is the one always or most often true. Simply because you can imagine a circumstance under which an answer might not be true does not make it wrong, just as knowing a 95-year-old cigarette smoker does not prove that cigarette smoking is not risky.

For most exams, you are allowed to write on the question paper. In addition, there is typically no penalty for the wrong answer. So, feel free to guess!

While the ISTQB guidelines call for straightforward questions, some topics are difficult to cover without some amount of complexity. Be especially careful with negative questions and complex questions. If the question asks which is false (or true), mark them T or F first. This will make it easier to see which is the odd one out. If the question requires matching a list of definitions, draw lines between the definitions and the words they define. And remember to put the process of elimination to work for you whenever possible. Use what you know to eliminate wrong answers and cross them out up front to avoid mistakes.

Finally, remember that the ISTQB exam is about the theory of good practice, not what you typically do in practice. The ISTQB syllabus was developed by an international working group of testing experts based on the best practices they have seen in the real world. In testing, best practices lead typical practices by about 20 years at this point. Some organizations are struggling to implement even basic testing principles, such as convincing managers that exhaustive testing is impossible, while other organizations may already be doing most of the things discussed in the Syllabus; still other organizations may do things well but differently to what is described in the Syllabus. So, remember to apply what you've learned in this book to the exam. When an exam question calls into conflict what you've learned here and what you typically have done in the past, rely on what you've learned to answer the exam question. And then go back to your workplace and put the good ideas that you've learned into practice!

7.2.3 Last but not least

We wish you good luck with your certification exam and best of success in your career as a test professional! We stand poised on the brink of great forward progress in the field of testing and are happy that you will be a part of it.

MOCK EXAM

On the real exam, you will have 60 minutes to work through 40 questions of approximately the same difficulty mix and Syllabus distribution as shown in the following mock exam. After you have taken this mock exam, check your answers with the answer key. (The answers to all exam questions in this book are in the section after the Glossary.)

Question 1 What is a key characteristic of specification-based testing techniques?

a. Tests are derived from information about how the software is constructed.

b. Tests are derived from models (formal or informal) that specify the problem to be solved by the software or its components.

c. Tests are derived based on the skills and experience of the tester.

d. Tests are derived from the extent of the coverage of structural elements of the system or components.

Question 2 An exhaustive test suite would include:

a. All combinations of input values and preconditions.

b. All combinations of input values and output values.

c. All pairs of input value and preconditions.

d. All states and state transitions.

Question 3 Which statement about testing is true?

a. Testing is started as early as possible in the life cycle.

b. Testing is started after the code is written so that we have a system with which to work.

c. Testing is most economically done at the end of the life cycle.

d. Testing can only be done by an independent test team.

Question 4 For a test procedure that is checking modifications of customers on a database, which of the following two steps would be the lowest priority if we didn't have time to execute all of the steps?

1 Open database and confirm existing customer.

2 Change customer's marital status from single to married.

3 Change customer's street name from Parks Road to Park Road.

4 Change customer's credit limit from 500 to 750.

5 Replace customer's first name with exactly the same first name.

6 Close the customer record and close the database.

a. Test steps 1 and 4.

b. Test steps 2 and 3.

c. Test steps 5 and 6.

d. Test steps 3 and 5.

Question 5 Consider the following list of either product or project risks:

I An incorrect calculation of fees might short-change the organization.

II A vendor might fail to deliver a system component on time.

III A defect might allow hackers to gain administrative privileges.

IV A skills gap might occur in a new technology used in the system.

V A defect-prioritization process might overload the development team.

Which of the following statements is true?

a. I is primarily a product risk and II, III, IV and V are primarily project risks.

b. II and V are primarily product risks and I, III and V are primarily project risks.

c. I and III are primarily product risks, while II, IV and V are primarily project risks.

d. III and V are primarily product risks, while I, II and IV are primarily project risks.

Question 6 Consider the following statements about regression tests:

I   They may usefully be automated if they are well designed.

II They are the same as confirmation tests (re-tests).

III They are a way to reduce the risk of a change having an adverse affect elsewhere in the system.

IV They are only effective if automated.

Which pair of statements is true?

a. I and II

b. I and III

c. II and III

d. II and IV

Question 7 Which of the following could be used to assess the coverage achieved for structure-based (white-box) test techniques?

V Decision outcomes exercised.

W Partitions exercised.

X Boundaries exercised.

Y Conditions or multiple conditions exercised.

Z Statements exercised.

a. V, W or Y

b. W, X or Y

c. V, Y or Z

d. W, X or Z

Question 8 Review the following portion of an incident report.

1 I place any item in the shopping cart.

2 I place any other (different) item in the shopping cart.

3 I remove the first item from the shopping cart, but leave the second item in the cart.

4 I click the <Checkout> button.

5 I expect the system to display the first checkout screen. Instead, it gives the pop-up error message, 'No items in shopping cart. Click <Okay> to continue shopping.'

6 I click <Okay>.

7 I expect the system to return to the main window to allow me to continue adding and removing items from the cart. Instead, the browser terminates.

8 The failure described in steps 5 and 7 occurred in each of three attempts to perform steps 1, 2, 3, 4 and 6.

Assume that no other narrative information is included in the report. Which of the following important aspects of a good incident report is missing from this incident report?

a. The steps to reproduce the failure.

b. The summary.

c. The check for intermittence.

d. The use of an objective tone.

Question 9 Which of the following are benefits and which are risks of using tools to support testing?

1 Over-reliance on the tool.

2 Greater consistency and repeatability.

3 Objective assessment.

4 Unrealistic expectations.

5 Underestimating the effort required to maintain the test assets generated by the tool.

6 Ease of access to information about tests or testing.

7 Repetitive work is reduced.

a. Benefits: 3, 4, 6 and 7. Risks: 1, 2 and 5.

b. Benefits: 1, 2, 3 and 7, Risks: 4, 5 and 6.

c. Benefits: 2, 3, 6 and 7. Risks: 1, 4 and 5.

d. Benefits: 2, 3, 5 and 6. Risks: 1, 4 and 7.

Question 10 Which of the following encourages objective testing?

a. Unit testing.

b. System testing.

c. Independent testing.

d. Destructive testing.

Question 11 Of the following statements about reviews of specifications, which statement is true?

a. Reviews are not generally cost effective as the meetings are time consuming and require preparation and follow up.

b. There is no need to prepare for or follow up on reviews.

c. Reviews must be controlled by the author.

d. Reviews are a cost effective early static test on the system.

Question 12 Consider the following list of test process activities:

I Analysis and design.

II Test closure activities.

III Evaluating exit criteria and reporting.

IV Planning and control.

V Implementation and execution.

Which of the following places these in their logical sequence?

a. I, II, III, IV and V.

b. IV, I, V, III and II.

c. IV, I, V, II and III.

d. I, IV, V, III and II.

Question 13 Test objectives vary between projects and so must be stated in the test plan. Which one of the following test objectives might conflict with the proper tester mindset?

a. Show that the system works before we ship it.

b. Find as many defects as possible.

c. Reduce the overall level of product risk.

d. Prevent defects through early involvement.

Question 14 Which test activities are supported by test data preparation tools?

a. Test management and control.

b. Test specification and design.

c. Test execution and logging.

d. Performance and monitoring.

Question 15 If you are flying with an economy ticket, there is a possibility that you may get upgraded to business class, especially if you hold a gold card in the airline's frequent flyer programme. If you don't hold a gold card, there is a possibility that you will get 'bumped' off the flight if it is full and you check in late. This is shown in Figure 7.1. Note that each box (i.e. statement) has been numbered.

  Three tests have already been run:

Test 1: Gold card holder who gets upgraded to business class.

Test 2: Non-gold card holder who stays in economy.

Test 3: A person who is bumped from the flight.

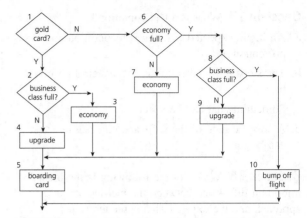

FIGURE 7.1 Control flow diagram for flight check-in

What additional tests would be needed to achieve 100% decision coverage?

a. A gold card holder who stays in economy and a non-gold card holder who gets upgraded to business class.

b. A gold card holder and a non-gold card holder who are both upgraded to business class.

c. A gold card holder and a non-gold card holder who both stay in economy class.

d. A gold card holder who is upgraded to business class and a non-gold card holder who stays in economy class.

Question 16 Consider the following types of tools:

V Test management tools.

W Static analysis tools.

X Modelling tools.

Y Dynamic analysis tools.

Z Performance testing tools.

Which of the following of these tools is most likely to be used by developers?

a. W, X and Y

b. V, Y and Z

c. V, W and Z

d. X, Y and Z

Question 17 What is a test condition?

a. An input, expected outcome, precondition and postcondition.

b. The steps to be taken to get the system to a given point.

c. Something that can be tested.

d. A specific state of the software, e.g. before a test can be run.

Question 18 Which of the following is the most important difference between the metrics-based approach and the expert-based approach to test estimation?

a. The metrics-based approach is more accurate than the expert-based approach.

b. The metrics-based approach uses calculations from historical data while the expert-based approach relies on team wisdom.

c. The metrics-based approach can be used to verify an estimate created using the expert-based approach, but not vice versa.

d. The expert-based approach takes longer than the metrics-based approach.

Question 19 If the temperature falls below 18 degrees, the heating is switched on. When the temperature reaches 21 degrees, the heating is switched off. What is the minimum set of test input values to cover all valid equivalence partitions?

a. 15, 19 and 25 degrees.

b. 17, 18, 20 and 21 degrees.

c. 18, 20 and 22 degrees.

d. 16 and 26 degrees.

Question 20 Which of these statements about functional testing is true?

a. Structural testing is more important than functional testing as it addresses the code.

b. Functional testing is useful throughout the life cycle and can be applied by business analysts, testers, developers and users.

c. Functional testing is more powerful than static testing as you actually run the system and see what happens.

d. Inspection is a form of functional testing.

Question 21 What is the purpose of confirmation testing?

a. To confirm the users' confidence that the system will meet their business needs.

b. To confirm that a defect has been fixed correctly.

c. To confirm that no unexpected changes have been introduced or uncovered as a result of changes made.

d. To confirm that the detailed logic of a component conforms to its specification.

Question 22 Which success factors are required for good tool support within an organization?

a. Acquiring the best tool and ensuring that all testers use it.

b. Adapting processes to fit with the use of the tool and monitoring tool use and benefits.

c. Setting ambitious objectives for tool benefits and aggressive deadlines for achieving them.

d. Adopting practices from other successful organizations and ensuring that initial ways of using the tool are maintained.

Question 23 Which of the following best describes integration testing?

a. Testing performed to expose faults in the interfaces and in the interaction between integrated components.

b. Testing to verify that a component is ready for integration.

c. Testing to verify that the test environment can be integrated with the product.

d. Integration of automated software test suites with the product.

Question 24 According to the ISTQB Glossary, debugging:

a. Is part of the fundamental testing process.

b. Includes the repair of the cause of a failure.

c. Involves intentionally adding known defects.

d. Follows the steps of a test procedure.

Question 25 Which of the following could be a root cause of a defect in financial software in which an incorrect interest rate is calculated?

a. Insufficient funds were available to pay the interest rate calculated.

b. Insufficient calculations of compound interest were included.

c. Insufficient training was given to the developers concerning compound interest calculation rules.

d. Inaccurate calculators were used to calculate the expected results.

Question 26 Assume postal rates for 'light letters' are:

$0.25 up to 10 grams;

$0.35 up to 50 grams;

$0.45 up to 75 grams;

$0.55 up to 100 grams.

Which test inputs (in grams) would be selected using boundary value analysis?

a. 0, 9, 19, 49, 50, 74, 75, 99, 100

b. 10, 50, 75, 100, 250, 1000

c. 0, 1, 10, 11, 50, 51, 75, 76, 100, 101

d. 25, 26, 35, 36, 45, 46, 55, 56

Question 27 Consider the following decision table.

TABLE 7.1 Decision table for car rental

Conditions	Rule 1	Rule 2	Rule 3	Rule 4
Over 23?	F	T	T	T
Clean driving record?	Don't care	F	T	T
On business?	Don't care	Don't care	F	T
Actions				
Supply rental car?	F	F	T	T
Premium charge?	F	F	F	T

Given this decision table, what is the expected result for the following test cases?

TC1: A 26-year-old on business but with violations or accidents on his driving record.

TC2: A 62-year-old tourist with a clean driving record.

a. TC1: Don't supply car; TC2: Supply car with premium charge.

b. TC1: Supply car with premium charge; TC2: Supply car with no premium charge.

c. TC1: Don't supply car; TC2: Supply car with no premium charge.

d. TC1: Supply car with premium charge; TC2: Don't supply car.

Question 28 What is exploratory testing?

a. The process of anticipating or guessing where defects might occur.

b. A systematic approach to identifying specific equivalent classes of input.

c. The testing carried out by a chartered engineer.

d. Concurrent test design, test execution, test logging and learning.

Question 29 What does it mean if a set of tests has achieved 90% statement coverage?

a. 9 out of 10 decision outcomes have been exercised by this set of tests.

b. 9 out of 10 statements have been exercised by this set of tests.

c. 9 out of 10 tests have been run on this set of software.

d. 9 out of 10 requirements statements about the software are correct.

Question 30 A test plan is written specifically to describe a level of testing where the primary goal is establishing confidence in the system. Which of the following is a likely name for this document?

a. Master test plan.

b. System test plan.

c. Acceptance test plan.

d. Project plan.

Question 31 Requirement 24.3. A 'Postage Assistant' will calculate the amount of postage due for letters and small packages up to 1 kilogram in weight. The inputs are: the type of item (letter, book or other package) and the weight in grams. Which of the following conform to the required contents of a test case?

a. Test the three types of item to post and three different weights [Req 24.3].

b. Test 1: letter, 10 grams, postage €0.25. Test 2: book, 500 grams, postage €1.00. Test 3: package, 999 grams, postage €2.53 [Req 24.3].

c. Test 1: letter, 10 grams to Belgium. Test 2: book 500 grams to USA. Test 3: package, 999 grams to South Africa [Req 24.3].

d. Test 1: letter 10 grams, Belgium, postage €0.25. Test 2: package 999 grams to South Africa, postage €2.53.

Question 32 What is the best description of static analysis?

a. The analysis of batch programs.

b. The reviewing of test plans.

c. The analysis of program code or other software artefacts.

d. The use of black-box testing.

Question 33 System test execution on a project is planned for eight weeks. After a week of testing, a tester suggests that the test objective stated in the test plan of 'finding as many defects as possible during system test' might be more closely met by redirecting the test effort according to which test principle?

a. Impossibility of exhaustive testing.

b. Importance of early testing.

c. The absence of errors fallacy.

d. Defect clustering.

Question 34 Consider the following activities that might relate to configuration management:

I   Identify and document the characteristics of a test item.

II Control changes to the characteristics of a test item.

III Check a test item for defects introduced by a change.

IV Record and report the status of changes to test items.

V   Confirm that changes to a test item fixed a defect.

Which of the following statements is true?

a. Only I is a configuration management task.

b. All are configuration management tasks.

c. I, II and III are configuration management tasks.

d. I, II and IV are configuration management tasks.

Question 35 Consider the following state transition diagram.

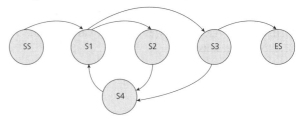

FIGURE 7.2   State transition diagram

Given this diagram, which test case below covers every valid transition?

a. SS – S1 – S2 – S4 – S1 – S3 – ES

b. SS – S1 – S2 – S3 – S4 – S3 – S4 – ES

c. SS – S1 – S2 – S4 – S1 – S3 – S4 – S1 – S3 – ES

d. SS – S1 – S4 – S2 – S1 – S3 – ES

Question 36 A test plan included the following clauses among the exit criteria:

● System test shall continue until all significant product risks have been covered to the extent specified in the product risk analysis document.

● System test shall continue until no must-fix defects remain against any significant product risks specified in the product risk analysis document.

During test execution, the test team detects 430 must-fix defects prior to release and all must-fix defects are resolved. After release, the customers find 212 new defects, none of which were detected during testing. This means that only 67% of the important defects were found prior to release, a percentage which is well below average in your industry. You are asked to find the root cause for the high number of field failures. Consider the following list of possible root causes:

I   Not all the tests planned for the significant product risks were executed.

II The organization has unrealistic expectations of the percentage of defects that testing can find.

III A version-control issue has resulted in the release of a version of the software that was used during early testing.

IV The product risk analysis failed to identify all the important risks from a customer point of view.

V The product risk analysis was not updated during the project as new information became available.

Which of the following statements indicate which explanations are possible root causes?

a. II, III and IV are possible root causes, but I and V are not possible root causes.

b. All five are possible root causes.

c. I, IV and V are possible root causes, but II and III are not possible root causes.

d. III, IV and V are possible root causes, but I and II are not possible root causes.

Question 37 What is the most important factor for successful performance of reviews?

a. A separate scribe during the logging meeting.

b. Trained participants and review leaders.

c. The availability of tools to support the review process.

d. A reviewed test plan.

Question 38 Consider the following statements about maintenance testing:

I It requires both re-test and regression test and may require additional new tests.

II It is testing to show how easy it will be to maintain the system.

III It is difficult to scope and therefore needs careful risk and impact analysis.

IV It need not be done for emergency bug fixes.

Which of the statements are true?

a. I and III

b. I and IV

c. II and III

d. II and IV

Question 39 Which two specification-based testing techniques are most closely related to each other?

a. Decision tables and state transition testing.

b. Equivalence partitioning and state transition testing.

c. Decision tables and boundary value analysis.

d. Equivalence partitioning and boundary value analysis.

Question 40 Which of the following is an advantage of independent testing?

a. Independent testers don't have to spend time communicating with the project team.

b. Programmers can stop worrying about the quality of their work and focus on producing more code.

c. The others on a project can pressure the independent testers to accelerate testing at the end of the schedule.

d. Independent testers sometimes question the assumptions behind requirements, designs and implementations.

GLOSSARY

This glossary provides the complete definition set of software testing terms, as defined by ISTQB.

The glossary has been arranged in a single section of definitions ordered alphabetically. Some terms are preferred to other synonymous ones, in which case the definition of the preferred term appears, with the synonymous ones referring to that. For example *structural testing* refers to *white-box testing*. For synonyms, the 'See' indicator is used.

'See also' cross-references are also used. They assist the user to quickly navigate to the right index term. 'See also' cross-references are constructed for relationships such as broader term to a narrower term and overlapping meanings between two terms.

Finally, note that the terms that are underlined are those that are specifically mentioned in the Syllabus, either as listed definitions or terms used in the Syllabus. These are the terms that you should know for the exam.

abstract test case: See *high level test case.*

acceptance: See *acceptance testing.*

acceptance criteria: The exit criteria that a component or system must satisfy in order to be accepted by a user, customer or other authorized entity. [IEEE 610]

acceptance testing: Formal testing with respect to user needs, requirements and business processes conducted to determine whether or not a system satisfies the acceptance criteria and to enable the user, customers or other authorized entity to determine whether or not to accept the system. [After IEEE 610]

accessibility testing: Testing to determine the ease by which users with disabilities can use a component or system. [Gerrard]

accuracy: The capability of the software product to provide the right or agreed results or effects with the needed degree of precision. [ISO 9126] See also *functionality testing.*

accuracy testing: The process of testing to determine the accuracy of a software product.

acting (IDEAL):   The phase within the IDEAL model where the improvements are developed, put into practice, and deployed across the organization. The acting phase consists of the activities: create solution, pilot/test solution, refine solution and implement solution. See also *IDEAL.*

action word driven testing: See *keyword driven testing.*

actual outcome: See *actual result.*

actual result: The behavior produced/observed when a component or system is tested.

ad hoc review: See *informal review.*

ad hoc testing: Testing carried out informally; no formal test preparation takes place, no recognized test design technique is used, there are no expectations for results and arbitrariness guides the test execution activity.

adaptability: The capability of the software product to be adapted for different specified environments without applying actions or means other than those provided for this purpose for the software considered. [ISO 9126] See also *portability.*

agile manifesto: A statement on the values that underpin agile software development. The values are:
- individuals and interactions over processes and tools
- working software over comprehensive documentation
- customer collaboration over contract negotiation
- responding to change over following a plan.

agile software development: A group of software development methodologies based on iterative incremental development, where requirements and solutions evolve through collaboration between self-organizing cross-functional teams.

agile testing: Testing practice for a project using agile methodologies, such as extreme programming (XP), treating development as the customer of testing and emphasizing the test-first design paradigm. See also *test driven development.*

algorithm test: [TMap] See *branch testing.*

alpha testing: Simulated or actual operational testing by potential users/customers or an independent test team at the developers' site, but outside the development organization. Alpha testing is often employed for off-the-shelf software as a form of internal acceptance testing.

analyzability: The capability of the software product to be diagnosed for deficiencies or causes of failures in the software, or for the parts to be modified to be identified. [ISO 9126] See also *maintainability.*

analyzer: See *static analyzer.*

anomaly: Any condition that deviates from expectation based on requirements specifications, design documents, user documents, standards, etc. or from someone's perception or experience. Anomalies may be found during, but not limited to, reviewing, testing, analysis, compilation, or use of software products or applicable documentation. [IEEE 1044] See also *bug, defect, deviation, error, fault, failure, incident, problem.*

arc testing: See *branch testing.*

assessment report: A document summarizing the assessment results, e.g. conclusions, recommendations and findings. See also *process assessment.*

assessor: A person who conducts an assessment; any member of an assessment team.

attack: Directed and focused attempt to evaluate the quality, especially reliability, of a test object by attempting to force specific failures to occur. See also *negative testing.*

attractiveness: The capability of the software product to be attractive to the user. [ISO 9126] See also *usability.*

audit: An independent evaluation of software products or processes to ascertain compliance to standards, guidelines, specifications, and/or procedures based on objective criteria, including documents that specify:
1 the form or content of the products to be produced
2 the process by which the products shall be produced
3 how compliance to standards or guidelines shall be measured. [IEEE 1028]

audit trail: A path by which the original input to a process (e.g. data) can be traced back through the process, taking the process output as a starting point. This facilitates defect analysis and allows a process audit to be carried out. [After TMap]

automated testware: Testware used in automated testing, such as tool scripts.

availability: The degree to which a component or system is operational and accessible when required for use. Often expressed as a percentage. [IEEE 610]

back-to-back testing: Testing in which two or more variants of a component or system are executed with the same inputs, the outputs compared, and analyzed in cases of discrepancies. [IEEE 610]

balanced scorecard: A strategic performance management tool for measuring whether the operational activities of a company are aligned with its objectives in terms of business vision and strategy. See also *corporate dashboard, scorecard.*

baseline: A specification or software product that has been formally reviewed or agreed upon, that thereafter serves as the basis for further development, and that can be changed only through a formal change control process. [After IEEE 610]

basic block: A sequence of one or more consecutive executable statements containing no branches. Note: A node in a control flow graph represents a basic block.

basis test set: A set of test cases derived from the internal structure of a component or specification to ensure that 100% of a specified coverage criterion will be achieved.

bebugging: [Abbott] See *fault seeding.*

behavior: The response of a component or system to a set of input values and preconditions.

benchmark test: (1) A standard against which measurements or comparisons can be made. (2) A test that is be used to compare components or systems to each other or to a standard as in (1). [After IEEE 610]

bespoke software: Software developed specifically for a set of users or customers. The opposite is off-the-shelf software.

best practice: A superior method or innovative practice that contributes to the improved performance of an organization under given context, usually recognized as 'best' by other peer organizations.

beta testing: Operational testing by potential and/or existing users/customers at an external site not otherwise involved with the developers, to determine whether or not a component or system satisfies the user/customer needs and fits within the business processes. Beta testing is often employed as a form of external acceptance testing for off-the-shelf software in order to acquire feedback from the market.

big-bang testing: A type of integration testing in which software elements, hardware elements, or both are combined all at once into a component or an overall system, rather than in stages. [After IEEE 610] See also *integration testing.*

black box technique: See *black box test design technique.*

black box test design technique: Procedure to derive and/or select test cases based on an analysis of the specification, either functional or non-functional, of a component or system without reference to its internal structure.

black box testing: Testing, either functional or non-functional, without reference to the internal structure of the component or system.

blocked test case: A test case that cannot be executed because the preconditions for its execution are not fulfilled.

bottom-up testing: An incremental approach to integration testing where the lowest level components are tested first, and then used to facilitate the testing of higher level components. This process is repeated until the component at the top of the hierarchy is tested. See also *integration testing.*

boundary value: An input value or output value which is on the edge of an equivalence partition or at the smallest incremental distance on either side of an edge, for example the minimum or maximum value of a range.

boundary value analysis: A black box test design technique in which test cases are designed based on boundary values. See also *boundary value.*

boundary value coverage: The percentage of boundary values that have been exercised by a test suite.

boundary value testing: See *boundary value analysis.*

branch: A basic block that can be selected for execution based on a program construct in which one of two or more alternative program paths is available, e.g. case, jump, go to, if-then-else.

branch condition: See *condition.*

branch condition combination coverage: See *multiple condition coverage.*

branch condition combination testing: See *multiple condition testing.*

branch condition coverage: See *condition coverage.*

branch coverage: The percentage of branches that have been exercised by a test suite. One-hundred % branch coverage implies both 100% decision coverage and 100% statement coverage.

branch testing: A white box test design technique in which test cases are designed to execute branches.

buffer: A device or storage area used to store data temporarily for differences in rates of data flow, time or occurrence of events, or amounts of data that can be handled by the devices or processes involved in the transfer or use of the data. [IEEE 610]

buffer overflow: A memory access failure due to the attempt by a process to store data beyond the boundaries of a fixed length buffer, resulting in overwriting of adjacent memory areas or the raising of an overflow exception. See also *buffer.*

bug: See *defect.*

bug report: See *defect report.*

bug taxonomy: See *defect taxonomy.*

bug tracking tool: See *defect management tool.*

business process-based testing: An approach to testing in which test cases are designed based on descriptions and/ or knowledge of business processes.

call graph: An abstract representation of calling relationships between subroutines in a program.

Capability Maturity Model (CMM): A five level staged framework that describes the key elements of an effective software process. The Capability Maturity Model covers best-practices for planning, engineering and managing software development and maintenance. [CMM] See also *Capability Maturity Model Integration (CMMI).*

Capability Maturity Model Integration (CMMI): A framework that describes the key elements of an effective product development and maintenance process. The Capability Maturity Model Integration covers best-practices for planning, engineering and managing product development and maintenance. CMMI is the designated successor of the CMM. [CMMI] See also *Capability Maturity Model (CMM).*

capture/playback tool: A type of test execution tool where inputs are recorded during manual testing in order to generate automated test scripts that can be executed later (i.e. replayed). These tools are often used to support automated regression testing.

capture/replay tool: See *capture/playback tool.*

CASE: Acronym for Computer Aided Software Engineering.

CAST: Acronym for Computer Aided Software Testing. See also *test automation.*

causal analysis: The analysis of defects to determine their root cause. [CMMI]

cause-effect analysis: See *cause-effect graphing.*

cause-effect decision table: See *decision table.*

cause-effect diagram: A graphical representation used to organize and display the interrelationships of various possible root causes of a problem. Possible causes of a real or potential defect or failure are organized in categories and subcategories in a horizontal tree-structure, with the (potential) defect or failure as the root node. [After Juran]

cause-effect graph: A graphical representation of inputs and/or stimuli (causes) with their associated outputs (effects), which can be used to design test cases.

cause-effect graphing: A black box test design technique in which test cases are designed from cause-effect graphs. [BS 7925/2]

certification: The process of confirming that a component, system or person complies with its specified requirements, e.g. by passing an exam.

change control: See *configuration control.*

change control board: See *configuration control board.* **change management:** (1) A structured approach to transitioning individuals, teams, and organizations from a current state to a desired future state. (2) Controlled way to effect a change, or a proposed change, to a product or service. See also *configuration management.*

changeability: The capability of the software product to enable specified modifications to be implemented. [ISO 9126] See also *maintainability.*

charter: See *test charter.*

checker: See *reviewer.*

checklist-based testing: An experience-based test design technique whereby the experienced tester uses a high-level list of items to be noted, checked, or remembered, or a set of rules or criteria against which a product has to be verified.

Chow's coverage metrics: See *N-switch coverage*. [Chow]

classification tree: A tree showing equivalence partitions hierarchically ordered, which is used to design test cases in the classification tree method. See also *classification tree method*.

classification tree method: A black box test design technique in which test cases, described by means of a classification tree, are designed to execute combinations of representatives of input and/or output domains. [Grochtmann]

clear-box testing: See *white-box testing*.

code: Computer instructions and data definitions expressed in a programming language or in a form output by an assembler, compiler or other translator. [IEEE 610]

code analyzer: See *static code analyzer*.

code coverage: An analysis method that determines which parts of the software have been executed (covered) by the test suite and which parts have not been executed, e.g. statement coverage, decision coverage or condition coverage.

code-based testing: See *white box testing*.

codependent behavior: Excessive emotional or psychological dependence on another person, specifically in trying to change that person's current (undesirable) behavior while supporting them in continuing that behavior. For example, in software testing, complaining about late delivery to test and yet enjoying the necessary "heroism" working additional hours to make up time when delivery is running late, therefore reinforcing the lateness.

co-existence: The capability of the software product to co-exist with other independent software in a common environment sharing common resources. [ISO 9126] See also *portability*.

commercial off-the-shelf software: See *off-the-shelf software*.

comparator: See *test comparator*.

compatibility testing: See *interoperability testing*.

compiler: A software tool that translates programs expressed in a high order language into their machine language equivalents. [IEEE 610]

complete testing: See *exhaustive testing*.

completion criteria: See *exit criteria*.

complexity: The degree to which a component or system has a design and/or internal structure that is difficult to understand, maintain and verify. See also *cyclomatic complexity*.

compliance: The capability of the software product to adhere to standards, conventions or regulations in laws and similar prescriptions. [ISO 9126]

compliance testing: The process of testing to determine the compliance of the component or system.

component: A minimal software item that can be tested in isolation.

component integration testing: Testing performed to expose defects in the interfaces and interaction between integrated components.

component specification: A description of a component's function in terms of its output values for specified input values under specified conditions, and required non-functional behavior (e.g. resource-utilization).

component testing: The testing of individual software components. [After IEEE 610]

compound condition: Two or more single conditions joined by means of a logical operator (AND, OR or XOR), e.g. 'A>B AND C>1000'.

concrete test case: See *low level test case*.

concurrency testing: Testing to determine how the occurrence of two or more activities within the same interval of time, achieved either by interleaving the activities or by simultaneous execution, is handled by the component or system. [After IEEE 610]

condition: A logical expression that can be evaluated as True or False, e.g. A>B. See also *test condition*.

condition combination coverage: See *multiple condition coverage*.

condition combination testing: See *multiple condition testing*.

condition coverage: The percentage of condition outcomes that have been exercised by a test suite. 100% condition coverage requires each single condition in every decision statement to be tested as True and False.

condition determination coverage: The percentage of all single condition outcomes that independently affect a decision outcome that have been exercised by a test case suite. 100% condition determination coverage implies 100% decision condition coverage.

condition determination testing: A white box test design technique in which test cases are designed to execute single condition outcomes that independently affect a decision outcome.

condition outcome: The evaluation of a condition to True or False.

condition testing: A white box test design technique in which test cases are designed to execute condition outcomes.

confidence test: See *smoke test*.

configuration: The composition of a component or system as defined by the number, nature, and interconnections of its constituent parts.

configuration auditing: The function to check on the contents of libraries of configuration items, e.g. for standards compliance. [IEEE 610]

configuration control: An element of configuration management, consisting of the evaluation, co-ordination, approval or disapproval, and implementation of changes to configuration items after formal establishment of their configuration identification. [IEEE 610]

configuration control board (CCB): A group of people responsible for evaluating and approving or disapproving proposed changes to configuration items, and for ensuring implementation of approved changes. [IEEE 610]

configuration identification: An element of configuration management, consisting of selecting the configuration items for a system and recording their functional and physical characteristics in technical documentation. [IEEE 610]

configuration item: An aggregation of hardware, software or both, that is designated for configuration management and treated as a single entity in the configuration management process. [IEEE 610]

configuration management: A discipline applying technical and administrative direction and surveillance to: identify and document the functional and physical characteristics of a configuration item, control changes to those characteristics, record and report change processing and implementation status, and verify compliance with specified requirements. [IEEE 610]

configuration management tool: A tool that provides support for the identification and control of configuration items, their status over changes and versions, and the release of baselines consisting of configuration items.

configuration testing: See *portability testing*.

confirmation testing: See *re-testing*.

conformance testing: See *compliance testing*.

consistency: The degree of uniformity, standardization, and freedom from contradiction among the documents or parts of a component or system. [IEEE 610]

content-based model: A process model providing a detailed description of good engineering practices, e.g. test practices.

continuous representation: A capability maturity model structure wherein capability levels provide a recommended order for approaching process improvement within specified process areas. [CMMI]

control flow: A sequence of events (paths) in the execution through a component or system.

control flow analysis: A form of static analysis based on a representation of unique paths (sequences of events) in the execution through a component or system. Control flow analysis evaluates the integrity of control flow structures, looking for possible control flow anomalies such as closed loops or logically unreachable process steps.

control flow graph: An abstract representation of all possible sequences of events (paths) in the execution through a component or system.

control flow path: See *path*.

conversion testing: Testing of software used to convert data from existing systems for use in replacement systems.

corporate dashboard: A dashboard-style representation of the status of corporate performance data. See also *balanced scorecard, dashboard*.

cost of quality: The total costs incurred on quality activities and issues and often split into prevention costs, appraisal costs, internal failure costs and external failure costs.

COTS: Acronym for Commercial Off-The-Shelf software. See *off-the-shelf software*.

coverage: The degree, expressed as a percentage, to which a specified coverage item has been exercised by a test suite.

coverage analysis: Measurement of achieved coverage to a specified coverage item during test execution referring to predetermined criteria to determine whether additional testing is required and if so, which test cases are needed.

coverage item: An entity or property used as a basis for test coverage, e.g. equivalence partitions or code statements.

coverage measurement tool: See *coverage tool*.

coverage tool: A tool that provides objective measures of what structural elements, e.g. statements, branches have been exercised by a test suite.

critical success factor: An element which is necessary for an organization or project to achieve its mission. They are the critical factors or activities required for ensuring the success. See also *content-based model*.

Critical Testing Processes: A content-based model for test process improvement built around twelve critical processes. These include highly visible processes, by which peers and management judge competence and mission-critical processes in which performance affects the company's profits and reputation.

CTP: See *Critical Testing Processes*.

custom software: See *bespoke software*.

cyclomatic complexity: The number of independent paths through a program. Cyclomatic complexity is defined as: $L - N + 2P$, where
- L = the number of edges/links in a graph
- N = the number of nodes in a graph
- P = the number of disconnected parts of the graph (e. g. a called graph or subroutine).
- [After McCabe]

cyclomatic number: See *cyclomatic complexity*.

daily build: A development activity where a complete system is compiled and linked every day (usually overnight), so that a consistent system is available at any time including all latest changes.

dashboard: A representation of dynamic measurements of operational performance for some organization or activity, using metrics represented via metaphors such as visual "dials", "counters", and other devices resembling those on the dashboard of an automobile, so that the effects of events or activities can be easily understood and related to operational goals. See also *corporate dashboard, scorecard.*

data definition: An executable statement where a variable is assigned a value.

data driven testing: A scripting technique that stores test input and expected results in a table or spreadsheet, so that a single control script can execute all of the tests in the table. Data driven testing is often used to support the application of test execution tools such as capture/ playback tools. [Fewster and Graham] See also *keyword driven testing.*

data flow: An abstract representation of the sequence and possible changes of the state of data objects, where the state of an object is any of: creation, usage, or destruction. [Beizer]

data flow analysis: A form of static analysis based on the definition and usage of variables.

data flow coverage: The percentage of definition-use pairs that have been exercised by a test suite.

data flow testing: A white box test design technique in which test cases are designed to execute definition and use pairs of variables.

data integrity testing: See *database integrity testing.*

database integrity testing: Testing the methods and processes used to access and manage the data(base), to ensure access methods, processes and data rules function as expected and that during access to the database, data is not corrupted or unexpectedly deleted, updated or created.

dd-path: A path of execution (usually through a graph representing a program, such as a flow-chart) that does not include any conditional nodes such as the path of execution between two decisions.

dead code: See *unreachable code.*

debugger: See *debugging tool.*

debugging: The process of finding, analyzing and removing the causes of failures in software.

debugging tool: A tool used by programmers to reproduce failures, investigate the state of programs and find the corresponding defect. Debuggers enable programmers to execute programs step by step, to halt a program at any program statement and to set and examine program variables.

decision: A program point at which the control flow has two or more alternative routes. A node with two or more links to separate branches.

decision condition coverage: The percentage of all condition outcomes and decision outcomes that have been exercised by a test suite. 100% decision condition coverage implies both 100% condition coverage and 100% decision coverage.

decision condition testing: A white box test design technique in which test cases are designed to execute condition outcomes and decision outcomes.

decision coverage: The percentage of decision outcomes that have been exercised by a test suite. 100% decision coverage implies both 100% branch coverage and 100% statement coverage.

decision outcome: The result of a decision (which therefore determines the branches to be taken).

decision table: A table showing combinations of inputs and/or stimuli (causes) with their associated outputs and/ or actions (effects), which can be used to design test cases.

decision table testing: A black box test design technique in which test cases are designed to execute the combinations of inputs and/or stimuli (causes) shown in a decision table. [Veenendaal 04] See also *decision table.*

decision testing: A white box test design technique in which test cases are designed to execute decision outcomes.

defect: A flaw in a component or system that can cause the component or system to fail to perform its required function, e.g. an incorrect statement or data definition. A defect, if encountered during execution, may cause a failure of the component or system.

defect based technique: See defect based test design technique.

defect based test design technique: A procedure to derive and/or select test cases targeted at one or more defect categories, with tests being developed from what is known about the specific defect category. See also *defect taxonomy.*

defect density: The number of defects identified in a component or system divided by the size of the component or system (expressed in standard measurement terms, e.g. lines-of-code, number of classes or function points).

Defect Detection Percentage (DDP):   The number of defects found by a test phase, divided by the number found by that test phase and any other means afterwards.

defect management: The process of recognizing, investigating, taking action and disposing of defects. It involves recording defects, classifying them and identifying the impact. [After IEEE 1044]

defect management tool: A tool that facilitates the recording and status tracking of defects and changes. They often have workflow-oriented facilities to track and control the allocation, correction and re-testing of defects and provide reporting facilities. See also *incident management tool.*

defect masking: An occurrence in which one defect prevents the detection of another. [After IEEE 610]

defect report: A document reporting on any flaw in a component or system that can cause the component or system to fail to perform its required function. [After IEEE 829]

defect taxonomy: A system of (hierarchical) categories designed to be a useful aid for reproducibly classifying defects.

defect tracking tool: See *defect management tool.*

definition-use pair: The association of the definition of a variable with the use of that variable. Variable uses include computational (e.g. multiplication) or to direct the execution of a path ("predicate" use).

deliverable: Any (work) product that must be delivered to someone other than the (work) product's author.

Deming cycle: An iterative four-step problem-solving process, (plan-do-check-act), typically used in process improvement. [After Deming]

design-based testing: An approach to testing in which test cases are designed based on the architecture and/or detailed design of a component or system (e.g. tests of interfaces between components or systems).

desk checking: Testing of software or a specification by manual simulation of its execution. See also *static testing.*

development testing: Formal or informal testing conducted during the implementation of a component or system, usually in the development environment by developers. [After IEEE 610]

deviation: See *incident.*

deviation report: See *incident report.*

diagnosing (IDEAL): The phase within the IDEAL model where it is determined where one is, relative to where one wants to be. The diagnosing phase consists of the activities: characterize current and desired states and develop recommendations. See also *IDEAL.*

dirty testing: See *negative testing.*

documentation testing: Testing the quality of the documentation, e.g. user guide or installation guide.

domain: The set from which valid input and/or output values can be selected.

driver: A software component or test tool that replaces a component that takes care of the control and/or the calling of a component or system. [After TMap]

dynamic analysis: The process of evaluating behavior, e.g. memory performance, CPU usage, of a system or component during execution. [After IEEE 610]

dynamic analysis tool: A tool that provides run-time information on the state of the software code. These tools are most commonly used to identify unassigned pointers, check pointer arithmetic and to monitor the allocation, use and de-allocation of memory and to flag memory leaks.

dynamic comparison: Comparison of actual and expected results, performed while the software is being executed, for example by a test execution tool.

dynamic testing: Testing that involves the execution of the software of a component or system.

efficiency: The capability of the software product to provide appropriate performance, relative to the amount of resources used under stated conditions. [ISO 9126]

efficiency testing: The process of testing to determine the efficiency of a software product.

EFQM (European Foundation for Quality Management) excellence model: A non-prescriptive framework for an organisation's quality management system, defined and owned by the European Foundation for Quality Management, based on five 'Enabling' criteria (covering what an organisation does), and four 'Results' criteria (covering what an organisation achieves).

elementary comparison testing: A black box test design technique in which test cases are designed to execute combinations of inputs using the concept of condition determination coverage. [TMap]

emotional intelligence: The ability, capacity, and skill to identify, assess, and manage the emotions of one's self, of others, and of groups.

emulator: A device, computer program, or system that accepts the same inputs and produces the same outputs as a given system. [IEEE 610] See also *simulator.*

entry criteria: The set of generic and specific conditions for permitting a process to go forward with a defined task, e.g. test phase. The purpose of entry criteria is to prevent a task from starting which would entail more (wasted) effort compared to the effort needed to remove the failed entry criteria. [Gilb and Graham]

entry point: An executable statement or process step which defines a point at which a given process is intended to begin.

equivalence class: See *equivalence partition.*

equivalence partition: A portion of an input or output domain for which the behavior of a component or system is assumed to be the same, based on the specification.

equivalence partition coverage: The percentage of equivalence partitions that have been exercised by a test suite.

equivalence partitioning: A black box test design technique in which test cases are designed to execute representatives from equivalence partitions. In principle test cases are designed to cover each partition at least once.

error: A human action that produces an incorrect result. [After IEEE 610]

error guessing: A test design technique where the experience of the tester is used to anticipate what defects might be present in the component or system under test as a result of errors made, and to design tests specifically to expose them.

error seeding: See *fault seeding*.

error seeding tool: See *fault seeding tool*.

error tolerance: The ability of a system or component to continue normal operation despite the presence of erroneous inputs. [After IEEE 610].

establishing (IDEAL):   The phase within the IDEAL model where the specifics of how an organization will reach its destination are planned. The establishing phase consists of the activities: set priorities, develop approach and plan actions. See also *IDEAL*.

evaluation: See *testing*.

exception handling: Behavior of a component or system in response to erroneous input, from either a human user or from another component or system, or to an internal failure.

executable statement: A statement which, when compiled, is translated into object code, and which will be executed procedurally when the program is running and may perform an action on data.

exercised: A program element is said to be exercised by a test case when the input value causes the execution of that element, such as a statement, decision, or other structural element.

exhaustive testing: A test approach in which the test suite comprises all combinations of input values and preconditions.

exit criteria: The set of generic and specific conditions, agreed upon with the stakeholders, for permitting a process to be officially completed. The purpose of exit criteria is to prevent a task from being considered completed when there are still outstanding parts of the task which have not been finished. Exit criteria are used to report against and to plan when to stop testing. [After Gilb and Graham]

exit point: An executable statement or process step which defines a point at which a given process is intended to cease.

expected outcome: See *expected result*.

expected result: The behavior predicted by the specification, or another source, of the component or system under specified conditions.

experience-based technique: See *experience-based test design technique*.

experience-based test design technique: Procedure to derive and/or select test cases based on the tester's experience, knowledge and intuition.

exploratory testing: An informal test design technique where the tester actively controls the design of the tests as those tests are performed and uses information gained while testing to design new and better tests. [After Bach]

extreme programming: A software engineering methodology used within agile software development whereby core practices are programming in pairs, doing extensive code review, unit testing of all code, and simplicity and clarity in code. See also *agile software development*.

fail: A test is deemed to fail if its actual result does not match its expected result.

failure: Deviation of the component or system from its expected delivery, service or result. [After Fenton]

failure mode: The physical or functional manifestation of a failure. For example, a system in failure mode may be characterized by slow operation, incorrect outputs, or complete termination of execution. [IEEE 610]

Failure Mode and Effect Analysis (FMEA):   A systematic approach to risk identification and analysis of identifying possible modes of failure and attempting to prevent their occurrence. See also *Failure Mode, Effect and Criticality Analysis (FMECA)*.

Failure Mode, Effects, and Criticality Analysis (FMECA):   An extension of FMEA, as in addition to the basic FMEA, it includes a criticality analysis, which is used to chart the probability of failure modes against the severity of their consequences. The result highlights failure modes with relatively high probability and severity of consequences, allowing remedial effort to be directed where it will produce the greatest value. See also *Failure Mode and Effect Analysis (FMEA)*.

failure rate: The ratio of the number of failures of a given category to a given unit of measure, e.g. failures per unit of time, failures per number of transactions, failures per number of computer runs. [IEEE 610]

false-fail result: A test result in which a defect is reported although no such defect actually exists in the test object.

false-pass result: A test result which fails to identify the presence of a defect that is actually present in the test object.

false-positive result: See *false-fail result*.

false-negative result: See *false-pass result*.

fault: See *defect*.

fault attack: See *attack*.

fault density: See *defect density*.

Fault Detection Percentage (FDP):   See *Defect Detection Percentage (DDP)*.

fault masking: See *defect masking*.

fault seeding: The process of intentionally adding known defects to those already in the component or system for the purpose of monitoring the rate of detection and removal, and estimating the number of remaining defects. [IEEE 610]

fault seeding tool: A tool for seeding (i.e. intentionally inserting) faults in a component or system.

fault tolerance: The capability of the software product to maintain a specified level of performance in cases of software faults (defects) or of infringement of its specified interface. [ISO 9126] See also *reliability, robustness.*

Fault Tree Analysis (FTA): A technique used to analyze the causes of faults (defects). The technique visually models how logical relationships between failures, human errors, and external events can combine to cause specific faults to disclose.

feasible path: A path for which a set of input values and preconditions exists which causes it to be executed.

feature: An attribute of a component or system specified or implied by requirements documentation (for example reliability, usability or design constraints). [After IEEE 1008]

field testing: See *beta testing.*

finite state machine: A computational model consisting of a finite number of states and transitions between those states, possibly with accompanying actions. [IEEE 610]

finite state testing: See *state transition testing.*

formal review: A review characterized by documented procedures and requirements, e.g. inspection.

frozen test basis: A test basis document that can only be amended by a formal change control process. See also *baseline.*

Function Point Analysis (FPA): Method aiming to measure the size of the functionality of an information system. The measurement is independent of the technology. This measurement may be used as a basis for the measurement of productivity, the estimation of the needed resources, and project control.

functional integration: An integration approach that combines the components or systems for the purpose of getting a basic functionality working early. See also *integration testing.*

functional requirement: A requirement that specifies a function that a component or system must perform. [IEEE 610]

functional test design technique: Procedure to derive and/or select test cases based on an analysis of the specification of the functionality of a component or system without reference to its internal structure. See also *black box test design technique.*

functional testing: Testing based on an analysis of the specification of the functionality of a component or system. See also *black box testing.*

functionality: The capability of the software product to provide functions which meet stated and implied needs when the software is used under specified conditions. [ISO 9126]

functionality testing: The process of testing to determine the functionality of a software product.

glass box testing: See *white box testing.*

Goal Question Metric: An approach to software measurement using a three-level model: conceptual level (goal), operational level (question) and quantitative level (metric).

GQM: See *Goal Question Metric.*

hazard analysis: A technique used to characterize the elements of risk. The result of a hazard analysis will drive the methods used for development and testing of a system. See also *risk analysis.*

heuristic evaluation: A static usability test technique to determine the compliance of a user interface with recognized usability principles (the so-called "heuristics").

high level test case: A test case without concrete (implementation level) values for input data and expected results. Logical operators are used; instances of the actual values are not yet defined and/or available. See also *low level test case.*

horizontal traceability: The tracing of requirements for a test level through the layers of test documentation (e.g. test plan, test design specification, test case specification and test procedure specification or test script).

hyperlink: A pointer within a web page that leads to other web pages.

hyperlink test tool: A tool used to check that no broken hyperlinks are present on a web site.

IDEAL: An organizational improvement model that serves as a roadmap for initiating, planning, and implementing improvement actions. The IDEAL model is named for the five phases it describes: initiating, diagnosing, establishing, acting, and learning.

impact analysis: The assessment of change to the layers of development documentation, test documentation and components, in order to implement a given change to specified requirements.

incident: Any event occurring that requires investigation. [After IEEE 1008]

incident logging: Recording the details of any incident that occurred, e.g. during testing.

incident management: The process of recognizing, investigating, taking action and disposing of incidents. It involves logging incidents, classifying them and identifying the impact. [After IEEE 1044]

incident management tool: A tool that facilitates the recording and status tracking of incidents. They often have workflow-oriented facilities to track and control the allocation, correction and re-testing of incidents and provide reporting facilities. See also *defect management tool.*

incident report: A document reporting on any event that occurred, e.g. during the testing, which requires investigation. [After IEEE 829]

incremental development model: A development lifecycle where a project is broken into a series of increments, each of which delivers a portion of the functionality in the overall project requirements. The requirements are prioritized and delivered in priority order in the appropriate increment. In some (but not all) versions of this lifecycle model, each subproject follows a 'mini V-model' with its own design, coding and testing phases.

incremental testing: Testing where components or systems are integrated and tested one or some at a time, until all the components or systems are integrated and tested.

independence of testing: Separation of responsibilities, which encourages the accomplishment of objective testing. [After DO-178b]

indicator: A measure that can be used to estimate or predict another measure. [ISO 14598]

infeasible path: A path that cannot be exercised by any set of possible input values.

informal review: A review not based on a formal (documented) procedure.

initiating (IDEAL):   The phase within the IDEAL model where the groundwork is laid for a successful improvement effort. The initiating phase consists of the activities: set context, build sponsorship and charter infrastructure. See also *IDEAL.*

input: A variable (whether stored within a component or outside) that is read by a component.

input domain: The set from which valid input values can be selected. See also *domain.*

input value: An instance of an input. See also *input.*

inspection: A type of peer review that relies on visual examination of documents to detect defects, e.g. violations of development standards and non-conformance to higher level documentation. The most formal review technique and therefore always based on a documented procedure. [After IEEE 610, IEEE 1028] See also *peer review.*

inspection leader: See *moderator.*

inspector: See *reviewer.*

installability: The capability of the software product to be installed in a specified environment [ISO 9126]. See also *portability.*

installability testing: The process of testing the installability of a software product. See also *portability testing.*

installation guide: Supplied instructions on any suitable media, which guides the installer through the installation process. This may be a manual guide, step-by-step procedure, installation wizard, or any other similar process description.

installation wizard: Supplied software on any suitable media, which leads the installer through the installation process. It normally runs the installation process, provides feedback on installation results, and prompts for options.

instrumentation: The insertion of additional code into the program in order to collect information about program behavior during execution, e.g. for measuring code coverage.

instrumenter: A software tool used to carry out instrumentation.

intake test: A special instance of a smoke test to decide if the component or system is ready for detailed and further testing. An intake test is typically carried out at the start of the test execution phase. See also *smoke test.*

integration: The process of combining components or systems into larger assemblies.

integration testing: Testing performed to expose defects in the interfaces and in the interactions between integrated components or systems. See also *component integration testing, system integration testing.*

integration testing in the large: See *system integration testing.*

integration testing in the small: See *component integration testing.*

interface testing: An integration test type that is concerned with testing the interfaces between components or systems.

interoperability: The capability of the software product to interact with one or more specified components or systems. [After ISO 9126] See also *functionality.*

interoperability testing: The process of testing to determine the interoperability of a software product. See also *functionality testing.*

invalid testing: Testing using input values that should be rejected by the component or system. See also *error tolerance, negative testing.*

Ishikawa diagram: See *cause-effect diagram.*

isolation testing: Testing of individual components in isolation from surrounding components, with surrounding components being simulated by stubs and drivers, if needed.

item transmittal report: See *release note.*

iterative development model: A development lifecycle where a project is broken into a usually large number of iterations. An iteration is a complete development loop resulting in a release (internal or external) of an executable product, a subset of the final product under development, which grows from iteration to iteration to become the final product.

key performance indicator: See *performance indicator.*

keyword driven testing: A scripting technique that uses data files to contain not only test data and expected results, but also keywords related to the application being tested. The keywords are interpreted by special supporting scripts that are called by the control script for the test. See also *data driven testing.*

LCSAJ: A Linear Code Sequence And Jump, consists of the following three items (conventionally identified by line numbers in a source code listing): the start of the linear sequence of executable statements, the end of the linear sequence, and the target line to which control flow is transferred at the end of the linear sequence.

LCSAJ coverage: The percentage of LCSAJs of a component that have been exercised by a test suite. 100% LCSAJ coverage implies 100% decision coverage.

LCSAJ testing: A white box test design technique in which test cases are designed to execute LCSAJs.

lead assessor: The person who leads an assessment. In some cases, for instance CMMi and TMMi when formal assessments are conducted, the lead-assessor must be accredited and formally trained.

learnability: The capability of the software product to enable the user to learn its application. [ISO 9126] See also *usability.*

learning (IDEAL): The phase within the IDEAL model where one learns from experiences and improves one's ability to adopt new processes and technologies in the future. The learning phase consists of the activities: analyze and validate, and propose future actions. See also *IDEAL.*

level test plan: A test plan that typically addresses one test level. See also *test plan.*

lifecycle model: A partitioning of the life of a product or project into phases. [CMMI] See also *software lifecycle.*

link testing: See *component integration testing.*

load profile: A specification of the activity which a component or system being tested may experience in production. A load profile consists of a designated number of virtual users who process a defined set of transactions in a specified time period and according to a predefined operational profile. See also *operational profile.*

load testing: A type of performance testing conducted to evaluate the behavior of a component or system with increasing load, e.g. numbers of parallel users and/or numbers of transactions, to determine what load can be handled by the component or system. See also *performance testing, stress testing.*

load testing tool: See *performance testing tool.*

logic-coverage testing: See *white box testing.* [Myers]

logic-driven testing: See *white box testing.*

logical test case: See *high level test case.*

low level test case: A test case with concrete (implementation level) values for input data and expected results. Logical operators from high level test cases are replaced by actual values that correspond to the objectives of the logical operators. See also *high level test case.*

maintainability: The ease with which a software product can be modified to correct defects, modified to meet new requirements, modified to make future maintenance easier, or adapted to a changed environment. [ISO 9126]

maintainability testing: The process of testing to determine the maintainability of a software product.

maintenance: Modification of a software product after delivery to correct defects, to improve performance or other attributes, or to adapt the product to a modified environment. [IEEE 1219]

maintenance testing: Testing the changes to an operational system or the impact of a changed environment to an operational system.

management review: A systematic evaluation of software acquisition, supply, development, operation, or maintenance process, performed by or on behalf of management that monitors progress, determines the status of plans and schedules, confirms requirements and their system allocation, or evaluates the effectiveness of management approaches to achieve fitness for purpose. [After IEEE 610, IEEE 1028]

manufacturing-based quality: A view of quality, whereby quality is measured by the degree to which a product or service conforms to its intended design and requirements. Quality arises from the process(es) used. [After Garvin] See also *product-based quality, transcendent-based quality, user-based quality, value-based quality.*

master test plan: A test plan that typically addresses multiple test levels. See also *test plan.*

maturity: (1) The capability of an organization with respect to the effectiveness and efficiency of its processes and work practices. See also *Capability Maturity Model, Test Maturity Model.* (2) The capability of the software product to avoid failure as a result of defects in the software. [ISO 9126] See also *reliability.*

maturity level: Degree of process improvement across a predefined set of process areas in which all goals in the set are attained. [TMMi]

maturity model: A structured collection of elements that describe certain aspects of maturity in an organization, and aid in the definition and understanding of an organization's processes. A maturity model often provides a common language, shared vision and framework for prioritizing improvement actions.

Mean Time Between Failures: The arithmetic mean (average) time between failures of a system. The MTBF is typically part of a reliability growth model that assumes the failed system is immediately repaired, as a part of a defect fixing process. See also *reliability growth model.*

Mean Time To Repair: The arithmetic mean (average) time a system will take to recover from any failure. This typically includes testing to insure that the defect has been resolved.

measure: The number or category assigned to an attribute of an entity by making a measurement. [ISO 14598]

measurement: The process of assigning a number or category to an entity to describe an attribute of that entity. [ISO 14598]

measurement scale: A scale that constrains the type of data analysis that can be performed on it. [ISO 14598]

memory leak: A memory access failure due to a defect in a program's dynamic store allocation logic that causes it to fail to release memory after it has finished using it, eventually causing the program and/or other concurrent processes to fail due to lack of memory.

metric: A measurement scale and the method used for measurement. [ISO 14598]

migration testing: See *conversion testing*.

milestone: A point in time in a project at which defined (intermediate) deliverables and results should be ready.

mind-map: A diagram used to represent words, ideas, tasks, or other items linked to and arranged around a central key word or idea. Mind maps are used to generate, visualize, structure, and classify ideas, and as an aid in study, organization, problem solving, decision making, and writing.

mistake: See *error*.

modeling tool: A tool that supports the creation, amendment and verification of models of the software or system [Graham].

moderator: The leader and main person responsible for an inspection or other review process.

modified condition decision coverage: See *condition determination coverage*.

modified condition decision testing: See *condition determination testing*.

modified multiple condition coverage: See *condition determination coverage*.

modified multiple condition testing: See *condition determination testing*.

module: See *component*.

module testing: See *component testing*.

monitor: A software tool or hardware device that runs concurrently with the component or system under test and supervises, records and/or analyses the behavior of the component or system. [After IEEE 610]

monitoring tool: See *monitor*.

monkey testing: Testing by means of a random selection from a large range of inputs and by randomly pushing buttons, ignorant of how the product is being used.

MTBF: See *Mean Time Between Failures*.

MTTR: See *Mean Time To Repair*.

multiple condition: See *compound condition*.

multiple condition coverage: The percentage of combinations of all single condition outcomes within one statement that have been exercised by a test suite. 100% multiple condition coverage implies 100% condition determination coverage.

multiple condition testing: A white box test design technique in which test cases are designed to execute combinations of single condition outcomes (within one statement).

mutation analysis: A method to determine test suite thoroughness by measuring the extent to which a test suite can discriminate the program from slight variants (mutants) of the program.

mutation testing: See *back-to-back testing*.

N-switch coverage: The percentage of sequences of N+1 transitions that have been exercised by a test suite. [Chow]

N-switch testing: A form of state transition testing in which test cases are designed to execute all valid sequences of N+1 transitions. [Chow] See also *state transition testing*.

negative testing: Tests aimed at showing that a component or system does not work. Negative testing is related to the testers' attitude rather than a specific test approach or test design technique, e.g. testing with invalid input values or exceptions. [After Beizer]

non-conformity: Non fulfillment of a specified requirement. [ISO 9000]

non-functional requirement: A requirement that does not relate to functionality, but to attributes such as reliability, efficiency, usability, maintainability and portability.

non-functional test design technique: Procedure to derive and/or select test cases for non-functional testing based on an analysis of the specification of a component or system without reference to its internal structure. See also *black box test design technique*.

non-functional testing: Testing the attributes of a component or system that do not relate to functionality, e.g. reliability, efficiency, usability, maintainability and portability.

off-the-shelf software: A software product that is developed for the general market, i.e. for a large number of customers, and that is delivered to many customers in identical format.

operability: The capability of the software product to enable the user to operate and control it. [ISO 9126] See also *usability*.

operational acceptance testing: Operational testing in the acceptance test phase, typically performed in a (simulated) operational environment by operations and/or systems administration staff focusing on operational aspects, e.g. recoverability, resource-behavior, installability and technical compliance. See also *operational testing*.

operational environment: Hardware and software products installed at users' or customers' sites where the component or system under test will be used. The software may include operating systems, database management systems, and other applications.

operational profile: The representation of a distinct set of tasks performed by the component or system, possibly based on user behavior when interacting with the component or system, and their probabilities of occurence. A task is logical rather than physical and can be executed over several machines or be executed in non-contiguous time segments.

operational profile testing: Statistical testing using a model of system operations (short duration tasks) and their probability of typical use. [Musa]

operational testing: Testing conducted to evaluate a component or system in its operational environment. [IEEE 610]

oracle: See *test oracle*.

orthogonal array: A 2-dimensional array constructed with special mathematical properties, such that choosing any two columns in the array provides every pair combination of each number in the array.

orthogonal array testing: A systematic way of testing all-pair combinations of variables using orthogonal arrays. It significantly reduces the number of all combinations of variables to test all pair combinations. See also *pairwise testing*.

outcome: See *result*.

output: A variable (whether stored within a component or outside) that is written by a component.

output domain: The set from which valid output values can be selected. See also *domain*.

output value: An instance of an output. See also *output*.

pair programming: A software development approach whereby lines of code (production and/or test) of a component are written by two programmers sitting at a single computer. This implicitly means ongoing real-time code reviews are performed.

pair testing: Two persons, e.g. two testers, a developer and a tester, or an end-user and a tester, working together to find defects. Typically, they share one computer and trade control of it while testing.

pairwise testing: A black box test design technique in which test cases are designed to execute all possible discrete combinations of each pair of input parameters. See also *orthogonal array testing*.

Pareto analysis: A statistical technique in decision making that is used for selection of a limited number of factors that produce significant overall effect. In terms of quality improvement, a large majority of problems (80%) are produced by a few key causes (20%).

partition testing: See *equivalence partitioning*. [Beizer]

pass: A test is deemed to pass if its actual result matches its expected result.

pass/fail criteria: Decision rules used to determine whether a test item (function) or feature has passed or failed a test. [IEEE 829]

path: A sequence of events, e.g. executable statements, of a component or system from an entry point to an exit point.

path coverage: The percentage of paths that have been exercised by a test suite. 100% path coverage implies 100% LCSAJ coverage.

path sensitizing: Choosing a set of input values to force the execution of a given path.

path testing: A white box test design technique in which test cases are designed to execute paths.

peer review: A review of a software work product by colleagues of the producer of the product for the purpose of identifying defects and improvements. Examples are inspection, technical review and walkthrough.

performance: The degree to which a system or component accomplishes its designated functions within given constraints regarding processing time and throughput rate. [After IEEE 610] See also *efficiency*.

performance indicator: A high level metric of effectiveness and/or efficiency used to guide and control progressive development, e.g. lead-time slip for software development. [CMMI]

performance profiling: Definition of user profiles in performance, load and/or stress testing. Profiles should reflect anticipated or actual usage based on an operational profile of a component or system, and hence the expected workload. See also *load profile, operational profile*.

performance testing: The process of testing to determine the performance of a software product. See also *efficiency testing*.

performance testing tool: A tool to support performance testing that usually has two main facilities: load generation and test transaction measurement. Load generation can simulate either multiple users or high volumes of input data. During execution, response time measurements are taken from selected transactions and these are logged. Performance testing tools normally provide reports based on test logs and graphs of load against response times.

phase test plan: A test plan that typically addresses one test phase. See also *test plan*.

pointer: A data item that specifies the location of another data item; for example, a data item that specifies the address of the next employee record to be processed. [IEEE 610]

portability: The ease with which the software product can be transferred from one hardware or software environment to another. [ISO 9126]

portability testing: The process of testing to determine the portability of a software product.

postcondition: Environmental and state conditions that must be fulfilled after the execution of a test or test procedure.

post-execution comparison: Comparison of actual and expected results, performed after the software has finished running.

post-project meeting: See *retrospective meeting.*

precondition: Environmental and state conditions that must be fulfilled before the component or system can be executed with a particular test or test procedure.

predicted outcome: See *expected result.*

pretest: See *intake test.*

priority: The level of (business) importance assigned to an item, e.g. defect.

probe effect: The effect on the component or system by the measurement instrument when the component or system is being measured, e.g. by a performance testing tool or monitor. For example performance may be slightly worse when performance testing tools are being used.

problem: See *defect.*

problem management: See *defect management.*

problem report: See *defect report.*

procedure testing: Testing aimed at ensuring that the component or system can operate in conjunction with new or existing users' business procedures or operational procedures.

process: A set of interrelated activities, which transform inputs into outputs. [ISO 12207]

process assessment: A disciplined evaluation of an organization's software processes against a reference model. [After ISO 15504]

process cycle test: A black box test design technique in which test cases are designed to execute business procedures and processes. [TMap] See also *procedure testing.*

process improvement: A program of activities designed to improve the performance and maturity of the organization's processes, and the result of such a program. [CMMI]

process model: A framework wherein processes of the same nature are classified into a overall model, e.g. a test improvement model.

product-based quality: A view of quality, wherein quality is based on a well-defined set of quality attributes. These attributes must be measured in an objective and quantitative way. Differences in the quality of products of the same type can be traced back to the way the specific quality attributes have been implemented. [After Garvin] See also *manufacturing-based quality, quality attribute, transcendent-based quality, user-based quality, value-based quality.*

product risk: A risk directly related to the test object. See also *risk.*

production acceptance testing: See *operational acceptance testing.*

program instrumenter: See *instrumenter.*

program testing: See *component testing.*

project: A project is a unique set of coordinated and controlled activities with start and finish dates undertaken to achieve an objective conforming to specific requirements, including the constraints of time, cost and resources. [ISO 9000]

project retrospective: A structured way to capture lessons learned and to create specific action plans for improving on the next project or next project phase.

project risk: A risk related to management and control of the (test) project, e.g. lack of staffing, strict deadlines, changing requirements, etc. See also *risk.*

project test plan: See *master test plan.*

pseudo-random: A series which appears to be random but is in fact generated according to some prearranged sequence.

qualification: The process of demonstrating the ability to fulfill specified requirements. Note the term 'qualified' is used to designate the corresponding status. [ISO 9000]

quality: The degree to which a component, system or process meets specified requirements and/or user/customer needs and expectations. [After IEEE 610]

quality assurance: Part of quality management focused on providing confidence that quality requirements will be fulfilled. [ISO 9000]

quality attribute: A feature or characteristic that affects an item's quality. [IEEE 610]

quality characteristic: See *quality attribute.*

quality gate: A special milestone in a project. Quality gates are located between those phases of a project strongly depending on the outcome of a previous phase. A quality gate includes a formal check of the documents of the previous phase.

quality management: Coordinated activities to direct and control an organization with regard to quality. Direction and control with regard to quality generally includes the establishment of the quality policy and quality objectives, quality planning, quality control, quality assurance and quality improvement. [ISO 9000]

random testing: A black box test design technique where test cases are selected, possibly using a pseudo-random generation algorithm, to match an operational profile. This technique can be used for testing non-functional attributes such as reliability and performance.

Rational Unified Process: A proprietary adaptable iterative software development process framework consisting of four project lifecycle phases: inception, elaboration, construction and transition.

recorder: See *scribe.*

record/playback tool: See *capture/playback tool.*

recoverability: The capability of the software product to re-establish a specified level of performance and recover the data directly affected in case of failure. [ISO 9126] See also *reliability*.

recoverability testing: The process of testing to determine the recoverability of a software product. See also *reliability testing*.

recovery testing: See *recoverability testing*.

regression testing: Testing of a previously tested program following modification to ensure that defects have not been introduced or uncovered in unchanged areas of the software, as a result of the changes made. It is performed when the software or its environment is changed.

regulation testing: See *compliance testing*.

release note: A document identifying test items, their configuration, current status and other delivery information delivered by development to testing, and possibly other stakeholders, at the start of a test execution phase. [After IEEE 829]

reliability: The ability of the software product to perform its required functions under stated conditions for a specified period of time, or for a specified number of operations. [ISO 9126]

reliability growth model: A model that shows the growth in reliability over time during continuous testing of a component or system as a result of the removal of defects that result in reliability failures.

reliability testing: The process of testing to determine the reliability of a software product.

replaceability: The capability of the software product to be used in place of another specified software product for the same purpose in the same environment. [ISO 9126] See also *portability*.

requirement: A condition or capability needed by a user to solve a problem or achieve an objective that must be met or possessed by a system or system component to satisfy a contract, standard, specification, or other formally imposed document. [After IEEE 610]

requirements-based testing: An approach to testing in which test cases are designed based on test objectives and test conditions derived from requirements, e.g. tests that exercise specific functions or probe non-functional attributes such as reliability or usability.

requirements management tool: A tool that supports the recording of requirements, requirements attributes (e.g. priority, knowledge responsible) and annotation, and facilitates traceability through layers of requirements and requirements change management. Some requirements management tools also provide facilities for static analysis, such as consistency checking and violations to pre-defined requirements rules.

requirements phase: The period of time in the software lifecycle during which the requirements for a software product are defined and documented. [IEEE 610]

resource utilization: The capability of the software product to use appropriate amounts and types of resources, for example the amounts of main and secondary memory used by the program and the sizes of required temporary or overflow files, when the software performs its function under stated conditions. [After ISO 9126] See also *efficiency*.

resource utilization testing: The process of testing to determine the resource-utilization of a software product. See also *efficiency testing*.

result: The consequence/outcome of the execution of a test. It includes outputs to screens, changes to data, reports, and communication messages sent out. See also *actual result, expected result*.

resumption criteria: The testing activities that must be repeated when testing is re-started after a suspension. [After IEEE 829]

re-testing: Testing that runs test cases that failed the last time they were run, in order to verify the success of corrective actions.

retrospective meeting: A meeting at the end of a project during which the project team members evaluate the project and learn lessons that can be applied to the next project.

review: An evaluation of a product or project status to ascertain discrepancies from planned results and to recommend improvements. Examples include management review, informal review, technical review, inspection, and walkthrough. [After IEEE 1028]

review tool: A tool that provides support to the review process. Typical features include review planning and tracking support, communication support, collaborative reviews and a repository for collecting and reporting of metrics.

reviewer: The person involved in the review that identifies and describes anomalies in the product or project under review. Reviewers can be chosen to represent different viewpoints and roles in the review process.

risk: A factor that could result in future negative consequences; usually expressed as impact and likelihood.

risk analysis: The process of assessing identified risks to estimate their impact and probability of occurrence (likelihood).

risk-based testing: An approach to testing to reduce the level of product risks and inform stakeholders of their status, starting in the initial stages of a project. It involves the identification of product risks and the use of risk levels to guide the test process.

risk category: See risk type.

risk control: The process through which decisions are reached and protective measures are implemented for reducing risks to, or maintaining risks within, specified levels.

risk identification: The process of identifying risks using techniques such as brainstorming, checklists and failure history.

risk level: The importance of a risk as defined by its characteristics impact and likelihood. The level of risk can be used to determine the intensity of testing to be performed. A risk level can be expressed either qualitatively (e.g. high, medium, low) or quantitatively.

risk management: Systematic application of procedures and practices to the tasks of identifying, analyzing, prioritizing, and controlling risk.

risk mitigation: See *risk control.*

risk type: A set of risks grouped by one or more common factors such as a quality attribute, cause, location, or potential effect of risk. A specific set of product risk types is related to the type of testing that can mitigate (control) that risk type. For example the risk of user-interactions being misunderstood can be mitigated by usability testing.

robustness: The degree to which a component or system can function correctly in the presence of invalid inputs or stressful environmental conditions. [IEEE 610] See also *error-tolerance, fault-tolerance.*

robustness testing: Testing to determine the robustness of the software product.

root cause: A source of a defect such that if it is removed, the occurence of the defect type is decreased or removed. [CMMI]

root cause analysis: An analysis technique aimed at identifying the root causes of defects. By directing corrective measures at root causes, it is hoped that the likelihood of defect recurrence will be minimized.

RUP: See *Rational Unified Process.*

safety: The capability of the software product to achieve acceptable levels of risk of harm to people, business, software, property or the environment in a specified context of use. [ISO 9126]

safety critical system: A system whose failure or malfunction may result in death or serious injury to people, or loss or severe damage to equipment, or environmental harm.

safety testing: Testing to determine the safety of a software product.

sanity test: See *smoke test.*

scalability: The capability of the software product to be upgraded to accommodate increased loads. [After Gerrard]

scalability testing: Testing to determine the scalability of the software product.

scenario testing: See *use case testing.*

scorecard: A representation of summarized performance measurements representing progress towards the implementation of long-term goals. A scorecard provides static measurements of performance over or at the end of a defined interval. See also *balanced scorecard, dashboard.*

scribe: The person who records each defect mentioned and any suggestions for process improvement during a review meeting, on a logging form. The scribe should ensure that the logging form is readable and understandable.

scripted testing: Test execution carried out by following a previously documented sequence of tests.

scripting language: A programming language in which executable test scripts are written, used by a test execution tool (e.g. a capture/playback tool).

SCRUM: An iterative incremental framework for managing projects commonly used with agile software development. See also *agile software development.*

security: Attributes of software products that bear on its ability to prevent unauthorized access, whether accidental or deliberate, to programs and data. [ISO 9126] See also *functionality.*

security testing: Testing to determine the security of the software product. See also *functionality testing.*

security testing tool: A tool that provides support for testing security characteristics and vulnerabilities.

security tool: A tool that supports operational security.

serviceability testing: See *maintainability testing.*

session-based test management: A method for measuring and managing session-based testing, e.g. exploratory testing.

session-based testing: An approach to testing in which test activities are planned as uninterrupted sessions of test design and execution, often used in conjunction with exploratory testing.

severity: The degree of impact that a defect has on the development or operation of a component or system. [After IEEE 610]

simulation: The representation of selected behavioral characteristics of one physical or abstract system by another system. [ISO 2382/1]

simulator: A device, computer program or system used during testing, which behaves or operates like a given system when provided with a set of controlled inputs. [After IEEE 610, DO178b] See also *emulator.*

site acceptance testing: Acceptance testing by users/customers at their site, to determine whether or not a component or system satisfies the user/customer needs and fits within the business processes, normally including hardware as well as software.

smoke test: A subset of all defined/planned test cases that cover the main functionality of a component or system, to ascertaining that the most crucial functions of a program work, but not bothering with finer details. A daily build and smoke test is among industry best practices. See also *intake test*.

software: Computer programs, procedures, and possibly associated documentation and data pertaining to the operation of a computer system. [IEEE 610]

software attack: See *attack*.

Software Failure Mode and Effect Analysis (SFMEA): See *Failure Mode and Effect Analysis (FMEA)*.

Software Failure Mode, Effects, and Criticality Analysis (SFMECA): See *Failure Mode, Effects, and Criticality Analysis (FMECA)*.

Software Fault Tree Analysis (SFTA): See *Fault Tree Analysis (FTA)*.

software feature: See *feature*.

software lifecycle: The period of time that begins when a software product is conceived and ends when the software is no longer available for use. The software lifecycle typically includes a concept phase, requirements phase, design phase, implementation phase, test phase, installation and checkout phase, operation and maintenance phase, and sometimes, retirement phase. Note these phases may overlap or be performed iteratively.

Software Process Improvement: A program of activities designed to improve the performance and maturity of the organization's software processes and the results of such a program. [After CMMI]

software product characteristic: See *quality attribute*.

software quality: The totality of functionality and features of a software product that bear on its ability to satisfy stated or implied needs. [After ISO 9126]

software quality characteristic: See *quality attribute*.

software test incident: See *incident*.

software test incident report: See *incident report*.

Software Usability Measurement Inventory (SUMI): A questionnaire-based usability test technique for measuring software quality from the end user's point of view. [Veenendaal04]

source statement: See *statement*.

specification: A document that specifies, ideally in a complete, precise and verifiable manner, the requirements, design, behavior, or other characteristics of a component or system, and, often, the procedures for determining whether these provisions have been satisfied. [After IEEE 610]

specification-based testing: See *black box testing*.

specification-based technique: See *black box test design technique*.

specification-based test design technique: See *black box test design technique*.

specified input: An input for which the specification predicts a result.

SPI: See *Sofware Process Improvement*.

stability: The capability of the software product to avoid unexpected effects from modifications in the software. [ISO 9126] See also *maintainability*.

staged representation: A model structure wherein attaining the goals of a set of process areas establishes a maturity level; each level builds a foundation for subsequent levels. [CMMI]

standard: Formal, possibly mandatory, set of requirements developed and used to prescribe consistent approaches to the way of working or to provide guidelines (e.g. ISO/IEC standards, IEEE standards, and organizational standards). [After CMMI]

standard software: See *off-the-shelf software*.

standards testing: See *compliance testing*.

state diagram: A diagram that depicts the states that a component or system can assume, and shows the events or circumstances that cause and/or result from a change from one state to another. [IEEE 610]

state table: A grid showing the resulting transitions for each state combined with each possible event, showing both valid and invalid transitions.

state transition: A transition between two states of a component or system.

state transition testing: A black box test design technique in which test cases are designed to execute valid and invalid state transitions. See also *N-switch testing*.

statement: An entity in a programming language, which is typically the smallest indivisible unit of execution.

statement coverage: The percentage of executable statements that have been exercised by a test suite.

statement testing: A white box test design technique in which test cases are designed to execute statements.

static analysis: Analysis of software artifacts, e.g. requirements or code, carried out without execution of these software development artifacts. Static analysis is usually carried out by means of a supporting tool.

static analysis tool: See *static analyzer*.

static analyzer: A tool that carries out static analysis.

static code analysis: Analysis of source code carried out without execution of that software.

static code analyzer: A tool that carries out static code analysis. The tool checks source code, for certain properties such as conformance to coding standards, quality metrics or data flow anomalies.

static testing: Testing of a component or system at specification or implementation level without execution of that software, e.g. reviews or static analysis.

statistical testing: A test design technique in which a model of the statistical distribution of the input is used to construct representative test cases. See also *operational profile testing.*

status accounting: An element of configuration management, consisting of the recording and reporting of information needed to manage a configuration effectively. This information includes a listing of the approved configuration identification, the status of proposed changes to the configuration, and the implementation status of the approved changes. [IEEE 610]

STEP: See *Systematic Test and Evaluation Process.*

storage: See *resource utilization.*

storage testing: See *resource utilization testing.*

stress testing: A type of performance testing conducted to evaluate a system or component at or beyond the limits of its anticipated or specified work loads, or with reduced availability of resources such as access to memory or servers. [After IEEE 610] See also *performance testing, load testing.*

stress testing tool: A tool that supports stress testing.

structural coverage: Coverage measures based on the internal structure of a component or system.

structural test design technique: See *white box test design technique.*

structural testing: See *white box testing.*

structure-based test design technique: See *white box test design technique.*

structure-based testing: See *white-box testing.*

structured walkthrough: See *walkthrough.*

stub: A skeletal or special-purpose implementation of a software component, used to develop or test a component that calls or is otherwise dependent on it. It replaces a called component. [After IEEE 610]

subpath: A sequence of executable statements within a component.

suitability: The capability of the software product to provide an appropriate set of functions for specified tasks and user objectives. [ISO 9126] See also *functionality.*

suitability testing: The process of testing to determine the suitability of a software product.

suspension criteria: The criteria used to (temporarily) stop all or a portion of the testing activities on the test items. [After IEEE 829]

syntax testing: A black box test design technique in which test cases are designed based upon the definition of the input domain and/or output domain.

system: A collection of components organized to accomplish a specific function or set of functions. [IEEE 610]

system integration testing: Testing the integration of systems and packages; testing interfaces to external organizations (e.g. Electronic Data Interchange, Internet).

system of systems: Multiple heterogeneous, distributed systems that are embedded in networks at multiple levels and in multiple interconnected domains, addressing large-scale inter-disciplinary common problems and purposes, usually without a common management structure.

system testing: The process of testing an integrated system to verify that it meets specified requirements. [Hetzel]

Systematic Test and Evaluation Process: A structured testing methodology, also used as a content-based model for improving the testing process. Systematic Test and Evaluation Process (STEP) does not require that improvements occur in a specific order. See also *content-based model.*

technical review: A peer group discussion activity that focuses on achieving consensus on the technical approach to be taken. [Gilb and Graham, IEEE 1028] See also *peer review.*

test: A set of one or more test cases. [IEEE 829]

test approach: The implementation of the test strategy for a specific project. It typically includes the decisions made that follow based on the (test) project's goal and the risk assessment carried out, starting points regarding the test process, the test design techniques to be applied, exit criteria and test types to be performed.

test automation: The use of software to perform or support test activities, e.g. test management, test design, test execution and results checking.

test basis: All documents from which the requirements of a component or system can be inferred. The documentation on which the test cases are based. If a document can be amended only by way of formal amendment procedure, then the test basis is called a frozen test basis. [After TMap]

test bed: See *test environment.*

test case: A set of input values, execution preconditions, expected results and execution postconditions, developed for a particular objective or test condition, such as to exercise a particular program path or to verify compliance with a specific requirement. [After IEEE 610]

test case design technique: See *test design technique.*

test case specification: A document specifying a set of test cases (objective, inputs, test actions, expected results, and execution preconditions) for a test item. [After IEEE 829]

test case suite: See *test suite.*

test charter: A statement of test objectives, and possibly test ideas about how to test. Test charters are used in exploratory testing. See also *exploratory testing.*

test closure: During the test closure phase of a test process data is collected from completed activities to consolidate experience, testware, facts and numbers. The test closure phase consists of finalizing and archiving the testware and evaluating the test process, including preparation of a test evaluation report. See also *test process.*

test comparator: A test tool to perform automated test comparison of actual results with expected results.

test comparison: The process of identifying differences between the actual results produced by the component or system under test and the expected results for a test. Test comparison can be performed during test execution (dynamic comparison) or after test execution.

test completion criteria: See *exit criteria*.

test condition: An item or event of a component or system that could be verified by one or more test cases, e.g. a function, transaction, feature, quality attribute, or structural element.

test control: A test management task that deals with developing and applying a set of corrective actions to get a test project on track when monitoring shows a deviation from what was planned. See also *test management*.

test coverage: See *coverage*.

test cycle: Execution of the test process against a single identifiable release of the test object.

test data: Data that exists (for example, in a database) before a test is executed, and that affects or is affected by the component or system under test.

test data preparation tool: A type of test tool that enables data to be selected from existing databases or created, generated, manipulated and edited for use in testing.

test deliverable: Any test (work) product that must be delivered to someone other than the test (work) product's author. See also *deliverable*.

test design: (1) See *test design specification*. (2) The process of transforming general testing objectives into tangible test conditions and test cases.

test design specification: A document specifying the test conditions (coverage items) for a test item, the detailed test approach and identifying the associated high level test cases. [After IEEE 829]

test design technique: Procedure used to derive and/or select test cases.

test design tool: A tool that supports the test design activity by generating test inputs from a specification that may be held in a CASE tool repository, e.g. requirements management tool, from specified test conditions held in the tool itself, or from code.

test driven development: A way of developing software where the test cases are developed, and often automated, before the software is developed to run those test cases.

test driver: See *driver*.

test environment: An environment containing hardware, instrumentation, simulators, software tools, and other support elements needed to conduct a test. [After IEEE 610]

test estimation: The calculated approximation of a result related to various aspects of testing (e.g. effort spent, completion date, costs involved, number of test cases, etc.) which is usable even if input data may be incomplete, uncertain, or noisy.

test evaluation report: A document produced at the end of the test process summarizing all testing activities and results. It also contains an evaluation of the test process and lessons learned.

test execution: The process of running a test on the component or system under test, producing actual result(s).

test execution automation: The use of software, e.g. capture/playback tools, to control the execution of tests, the comparison of actual results to expected results, the setting up of test preconditions, and other test control and reporting functions.

test execution phase: The period of time in a software development lifecycle during which the components of a software product are executed, and the software product is evaluated to determine whether or not requirements have been satisfied. [IEEE 610]

test execution schedule: A scheme for the execution of test procedures. The test procedures are included in the test execution schedule in their context and in the order in which they are to be executed.

test execution technique: The method used to perform the actual test execution, either manual or automated.

test execution tool: A type of test tool that is able to execute other software using an automated test script, e.g. capture/playback. [Fewster and Graham]

test fail: See *fail*.

test generator: See *test data preparation tool*.

test harness: A test environment comprised of stubs and drivers needed to execute a test.

test implementation: The process of developing and prioritizing test procedures, creating test data and, optionally, preparing test harnesses and writing automated test scripts.

test improvement plan: A plan for achieving organizational test process improvement objectives based on a thorough understanding of the current strengths and weaknesses of the organization's test processes and test process assets. [After CMMI]

test incident: See *incident*.

test incident report: See *incident report*.

test infrastructure: The organizational artifacts needed to perform testing, consisting of test environments, test tools, office environment and procedures.

test input: The data received from an external source by the test object during test execution. The external source can be hardware, software or human.

test item: The individual element to be tested. There usually is one test object and many test items. See also *test object*.

test item transmittal report: See *release note*.

test leader: See *test manager*.

test level: A group of test activities that are organized and managed together. A test level is linked to the responsibilities in a project. Examples of test levels are component test, integration test, system test and acceptance test. [After TMap]

test log: A chronological record of relevant details about the execution of tests. [IEEE 829]

test logging: The process of recording information about tests executed into a test log.

test management: The planning, estimating, monitoring and control of test activities, typically carried out by a test manager.

test management tool: A tool that provides support to the test management and control part of a test process. It often has several capabilities, such as testware management, scheduling of tests, the logging of results, progress tracking, incident management and test reporting.

test manager: The person responsible for project management of testing activities and resources, and evaluation of a test object. The individual who directs, controls, administers, plans and regulates the evaluation of a test object.

Test Maturity Model (TMM): A five level staged framework for test process improvement, related to the Capability Maturity Model (CMM), that describes the key elements of an effective test process.

Test Maturity Model Integrated (TMMi): A five level staged framework for test process improvement, related to the Capability Maturity Model Integration (CMMI), that describes the key elements of an effective test process.

test monitoring: A test management task that deals with the activities related to periodically checking the status of a test project. Reports are prepared that compare the actuals to that which was planned. See also *test management.*

test object: The component or system to be tested. See also *test item.*

test objective: A reason or purpose for designing and executing a test.

test oracle: A source to determine expected results to compare with the actual result of the software under test. An oracle may be the existing system (for a benchmark), other software, a user manual, or an individual's specialized knowledge, but should not be the code. [After Adrion]

test outcome: See *result.*

test pass: See *pass.*

test performance indicator: A high level metric of effectiveness and/or efficiency used to guide and control progressive test development, e.g. Defect Detection Percentage (DDP).

test phase: A distinct set of test activities collected into a manageable phase of a project, e.g. the execution activities of a test level. [After Gerrard]

test plan: A document describing the scope, approach, resources and schedule of intended test activities. It identifies amongst others test items, the features to be tested, the testing tasks, who will do each task, degree of tester independence, the test environment, the test design techniques and entry and exit criteria to be used, and the rationale for their choice, and any risks requiring contingency planning. It is a record of the test planning process. [After IEEE 829]

test planning: The activity of establishing or updating a test plan.

Test Point Analysis (TPA): A formula based test estimation method based on function point analysis. [TMap]

test policy: A high level document describing the principles, approach and major objectives of the organization regarding testing.

test procedure: See *test procedure specification.*

test procedure specification: A document specifying a sequence of actions for the execution of a test. Also known as test script or manual test script. [After IEEE 829]

test process: The fundamental test process comprises test planning and control, test analysis and design, test implementation and execution, evaluating exit criteria and reporting, and test closure activities.

Test Process Group: A collection of (test) specialists who facilitate the definition, maintenance, and improvement of the test processes used by an organization. [After CMMI]

Test Process Improvement (TPI): A continuous framework for test process improvement that describes the key elements of an effective test process, especially targeted at system testing and acceptance testing.

test process improvement manifesto: A statement that echoes the agile manifesto, and defines values for improving the testing process. The values are:
 – flexibility over detailed processes
 – best practices over templates
 – deployment orientation over process orientation
 – peer reviews over quality assurance (departments)
 – business driven over model driven.
    [Veenendaal08]

test process improver: A person implementing improvements in the test process based on a test improvement plan.

test progress report: A document summarizing testing activities and results, produced at regular intervals, to report progress of testing activities against a baseline (such as the original test plan) and to communicate risks and alternatives requiring a decision to management.

test record: See *test log.*

test recording: See *test logging.*

test report: See *test summary report* and *test progress report*.

test reproducibility: An attribute of a test indicating whether the same results are produced each time the test is executed.

test requirement: See *test condition*.

test result: See *result*.

test rig: See *test environment*.

test run: Execution of a test on a specific version of the test object.

test run log: See *test log*.

test scenario: See *test procedure specification*.

test schedule: A list of activities, tasks or events of the test process, identifying their intended start and finish dates and/or times, and interdependencies.

test script: Commonly used to refer to a test procedure specification, especially an automated one.

test session: An uninterrupted period of time spent in executing tests. In exploratory testing, each test session is focused on a charter, but testers can also explore new opportunities or issues during a session. The tester creates and executes test cases on the fly and records their progress. See also *exploratory testing*.

test set: See *test suite*.

test situation: See *test condition*.

test specification: A document that consists of a test design specification, test case specification and/or test procedure specification.

test specification technique: See *test design technique*.

test stage: See *test level*.

test strategy: A high-level description of the test levels to be performed and the testing within those levels for an organization or programme (one or more projects).

test suite: A set of several test cases for a component or system under test, where the post condition of one test is often used as the precondition for the next one.

test summary report: A document summarizing testing activities and results. It also contains an evaluation of the corresponding test items against exit criteria. [After IEEE 829]

test target: A set of exit criteria.

test technique: See *test design technique*.

test tool: A software product that supports one or more test activities, such as planning and control, specification, building initial files and data, test execution and test analysis. [TMap] See also *CAST*.

test type: A group of test activities aimed at testing a component or system focused on a specific test objective, i.e. functional test, usability test, regression test etc. A test type may take place on one or more test levels or test phases. [After TMap]

testability: The capability of the software product to enable modified software to be tested. [ISO 9126] See also *maintainability*.

testability review: A detailed check of the test basis to determine whether the test basis is at an adequate quality level to act as an input document for the test process. [After TMap]

testable requirements: The degree to which a requirement is stated in terms that permit establishment of test designs (and subsequently test cases) and execution of tests to determine whether the requirements have been met. [After IEEE 610]

tester: A skilled professional who is involved in the testing of a component or system.

testing: The process consisting of all lifecycle activities, both static and dynamic, concerned with planning, preparation and evaluation of software products and related work products to determine that they satisfy specified requirements, to demonstrate that they are fit for purpose and to detect defects.

testware: Artifacts produced during the test process required to plan, design, and execute tests, such as documentation, scripts, inputs, expected results, set-up and clear-up procedures, files, databases, environment, and any additional software or utilities used in testing. [After Fewster and Graham]

thread testing: A version of component integration testing where the progressive integration of components follows the implementation of subsets of the requirements, as opposed to the integration of components by levels of a hierarchy.

time behavior: See *performance*.

top-down testing: An incremental approach to integration testing where the component at the top of the component hierarchy is tested first, with lower level components being simulated by stubs. Tested components are then used to test lower level components. The process is repeated until the lowest level components have been tested. See also *integration testing*.

Total Quality Management: An organization-wide management approach centered on quality, based on the participation of all its members and aiming at long-term success through customer satisfaction, and benefits to all members of the organization and to society. Total Quality Management consists of planning, organizing, directing, control, and assurance. [After ISO 8402]

TPG: See *Test Process Group*.

TQM: See *Total Quality Management*.

traceability: The ability to identify related items in documentation and software, such as requirements with associated tests. See also horizontal traceability, vertical traceability.

transactional analysis: The analysis of transactions between people and within people's minds; a transaction is defined as a stimulus plus a response. Transactions take place between people and between the ego states (personality segments) within one person's mind.

transcendent-based quality: A view of quality, wherein quality cannot be precisely defined, but we know it when we see it, or are aware of its absence when it is missing. Quality depends on the perception and affective feelings of an individual or group of individuals towards a product. [After Garvin] See also *manufacturing-based quality, product-based quality, user-based quality, value-based quality.*

understandability: The capability of the software product to enable the user to understand whether the software is suitable, and how it can be used for particular tasks and conditions of use. [ISO 9126] See also *usability.*

unit: See *component.*

unit test framework: A tool that provides an environment for unit or component testing in which a component can be tested in isolation or with suitable stubs and drivers. It also provides other support for the developer, such as debugging capabilities. [Graham]

unit testing: See *component testing.*

unreachable code: Code that cannot be reached and therefore is impossible to execute.

usability: The capability of the software to be understood, learned, used and attractive to the user when used under specified conditions. [ISO 9126]

usability testing: Testing to determine the extent to which the software product is understood, easy to learn, easy to operate and attractive to the users under specified conditions. [After ISO 9126]

use case: A sequence of transactions in a dialogue between an actor and a component or system with a tangible result, where an actor can be a user or anything that can exchange information with the system.

use case testing: A black box test design technique in which test cases are designed to execute scenarios of use cases.

user acceptance testing: See *acceptance testing.*

user-based quality: A view of quality, wherein quality is the capacity to satisfy needs, wants and desires of the user(s). A product or service that does not fulfill user needs is unlikely to find any users. This is a context dependent, contingent approach to quality since different business characteristics require different qualities of a product. [After Garvin] See also *manufacturing-based quality, product-based quality, transcendent-based quality, value-based quality.*

user scenario testing: See *use case testing.*

user test: A test whereby real-life users are involved to evaluate the usability of a component or system.

V-model: A framework to describe the software development lifecycle activities from requirements specification to maintenance. The V-model illustrates how testing activities can be integrated into each phase of the software development lifecycle.

validation: Confirmation by examination and through provision of objective evidence that the requirements for a specific intended use or application have been fulfilled. [ISO 9000]

value-based quality: A view of quality, wherein quality is defined by price. A quality product or service is one that provides desired performance at an acceptable cost. Quality is determined by means of a decision process with stakeholders on trade-offs between time, effort and cost aspects. [After Garvin] See also *manufacturing-based quality, product-based quality, transcendent-based quality, user-based quality.*

variable: An element of storage in a computer that is accessible by a software program by referring to it by a name.

verification: Confirmation by examination and through provision of objective evidence that specified requirements have been fulfilled. [ISO 9000]

version control: See *configuration control.*

vertical traceability: The tracing of requirements through the layers of development documentation to components.

volume testing: Testing where the system is subjected to large volumes of data. See also *resource-utilization testing.*

walkthrough: A step-by-step presentation by the author of a document in order to gather information and to establish a common understanding of its content. [Freedman and Weinberg, IEEE 1028] See also *peer review.*

WBS: See *Work Breakdown Structure.*

white-box technique: See *white-box test design technique.*

white-box test design technique: Procedure to derive and/or select test cases based on an analysis of the internal structure of a component or system.

white-box testing: Testing based on an analysis of the internal structure of the component or system.

Wide Band Delphi: An expert based test estimation technique that aims at making an accurate estimation using the collective wisdom of the team members.

wild pointer: A pointer that references a location that is out of scope for that pointer or that does not exist. See also *pointer.*

Work Breakdown Structure: An arrangement of work elements and their relationship to each other and to the end product. [CMMI]

ANSWERS TO SAMPLE EXAM QUESTIONS

This section contains the answers and the learning objectives for the sample questions in each chapter and for the full mock paper in Chapter 7.

If you get any of the questions wrong or if you weren't sure about the answer, then the learning objective tells you which part of the Syllabus to go back to in order to help you understand why the correct answer is the right one. The learning objectives are listed at the beginning of each section. For example, if you got Question 4 in Chapter 1 wrong, then go to Section 1.2 and read the first learning objective. Then re-read the part of the chapter that deals with that topic.

CHAPTER 1 FUNDAMENTALS OF TESTING

Question	Answer	Learning objective
1	A	1.1.3
2	B	1.1.5
3	C	1.1.5
4	A	1.2.1
5	A	1.2.3
6	C	1.4.1
7	B	1.5.1
8	D	1.2.3, 1.3.1 and 1.4.1

CHAPTER 2 TESTING THROUGHOUT THE SOFTWARE LIFE CYCLE

Question	Answer	Learning objective
1	D	2.1.3
2	D	2.1.3
3	B	2.3.1
4	B	2.3.3
5	C	2.3.1
6	D	2.4.3
7	C	2.3.5
8	B	2.3.1
9	A	2.2.1

CHAPTER 3 STATIC TECHNIQUES

Question	Answer	Learning objective
1	D	3.1.1
2	A	3.3.2
3	D	3.2.2
4	A	3.2.2
5	D	3.2.2
6	B	3.2.2
7	A	3.3.2
8	C	3.1.2
9	C	3.3.1

CHAPTER 4 TEST DESIGN TECHNIQUES

Question	Answer	Learning objective
1	D	4.1.1
2	A	4.1.4
3	C	4.1.4
4	A	4.2.1
5	B	4.2.2
6	C	4.3.1
7	D	4.3.1
8	B	4.3.1
9	B	4.3.2
10	C	4.4.2
11	A	4.3.3
12	C	4.4.2
13	C	4.4.4
14	A	4.5.1
15	D	4.5.2
16	B	4.6.1
17	A	4.3.1

CHAPTER 5 TEST MANAGEMENT

Question	Answer	Learning objective
1	B	5.1.1
2	D	5.1.4
3	B	Section 5.1
4	A	5.2.2
5	C	5.2.7
6	C	5.2.4
7	D	5.2.9
8	A	Section 5.2
9	C	5.3.1
10	B	5.3.2
11	A	5.3.3
12	C	5.4.1
13	D	5.5.1
14	B	5.5.2
15	A	5.5.3
16	A	5.5.5
17	B	Section 5.5
18	D	5.6.1
19	C	Section 5.6
20	A	Cross-section: 5.3, 5.5, 5.6

CHAPTER 6 TOOL SUPPORT FOR TESTING

Question	Answer	Learning objective
1	D	6.1.1
2	C	6.1.1
3	B	6.2.1
4	A	6.2.1
5	A	6.2.2
6	B	6.3.1
7	D	6.3.2

CHAPTER 7 MOCK EXAM

Question	Answer	Learning objective
1	B	4.2.2
2	A	Section 1.3
3	A	2.1.3
4	D	4.1.4 and 5.5.4
5	C	5.5.4
6	B	2.3.5
7	C	4.4.2
8	B	5.6.2
9	C	6.2.1
10	C	1.5.1
11	D	3.1.2
12	B	1.4.1
13	A	1.5.2
14	B	6.1.1
15	A	4.4.3
16	A	6.1.3
17	C	4.1.2
18	B	5.2.8
19	A	4.3.1
20	B	2.3.2
21	B	2.3.5
22	B	6.3.3
23	A	Section 2.2
24	B	1.1.5
25	C	1.1.2
26	C	4.3.1
27	C	4.3.1
28	D	4.5.1
29	B	4.4.1
30	C	5.2.1
31	B	4.1.3
32	C	3.3.1
33	D	Cross-section: 1.2, 1.4
34	D	5.4.1
35	C	4.3.1
36	C	Cross-section: 5.2, 5.5
37	B	3.2.3
38	A	2.4.3
39	D	4.3.1
40	D	5.1.2

REFERENCES

Key:
<u>In syllabus</u>
Extra to syllabus

PREFACE

ISTQB, www.istqb.org
ISTQB, *Certified Tester: Foundation Level Syllabus* (Version 2011)

CHAPTER 1 FUNDAMENTALS OF TESTING

<u>Beizer, B. (1990) *Software Testing Techniques* (2nd edition), Van Nostrand Reinhold: Boston</u>
<u>Black, R. (2009) *Managing the Testing Process* (3rd edition), John Wiley & Sons: New York</u>
Black, R. (2004) *Critical Testing Processes*, Addison Wesley: Reading MA
Gilb, T. (1993) *Software Inspection*, Addison Wesley: Reading, MA
<u>ISO/IEC 9126–1: 2001, Software Engineering – Software Product Quality</u>
Jones, C. (2008) *Estimating Software Costs, 3e*, McGraw Hill Education: New York

CHAPTER 2 TESTING THROUGHOUT THE SOFTWARE LIFE CYCLE

Agile Manifesto, www.agilemanifesto.org
<u>Chrissis, M.B., Konrad, M. and Shrum, S. (2004) *CMMI, Guidelines for Process Integration and Product Improvement*, Addison Wesley: Reading, MA</u>
DSDM, www.dsdm.org
<u>Hetzel, W. (1988) *Complete Guide to Software Testing*, QED: Wellesley, MA</u>
<u>ISO/IEC 12207 (1995) *Information Technology – Software Life Cycle Processes*</u>
Pol, M. and E. van Veenendaal, E. (1998) *Structured Testing of Information Systems,* Kluwer Bedrijfsinformatie: The Netherlands

CHAPTER 3 STATIC TECHNIQUES

<u>Gilb, T. and Graham, D. (1993) *Software Inspection*, Addison-Wesley: London</u>
Hatton, L. (1997) 'Reexamining the Fault Density-Component Size Connection' in *IEEE Software*, Vol. 14 Issue 2, March 1997: pp. 89–97
van Veenendaal, E. (1999) 'Practical Quality Assurance for Embedded Software' in *Software Quality Professional*, Vol. 1, no. 3, American Society for Quality, June 1999
van Veenendaal, E. and van der Zwan, M. (2000) 'GQM Based Inspections' in *Proceedings of the 11th European Software Control and Metrics Conference (ESCOM)*, Munich, May 2000
Weinberg, G.M. (1971) *The Psychology of Computer Programming*, Van Nostrand Reinhold: New York

CHAPTER 4 TEST DESIGN TECHNIQUES

Beizer, B. (1990) *Software Testing Techniques*, 2nd edition, Van Nostrand Reinhold: Boston

Black, R. (2007) *Pragmatic Software Testing*, John Wiley & Sons: New York.

Broekman, B. and Notenboom, E. (2003) *Testing Embedded Software*, Addison Wesley

BS7925-2, *Standard for Software Component Testing*

Copeland, L. (2003) *A Practitioner's Guide to Software Test Design*, Artech House: Norwood, MA

Craig, R. D. and Jaskiel, S. P. (2002) *Systematic Software Testing*, Artech House: Norwood, MA

Gilb, T. (1988) *Principles of Software Engineering Management*, Addison Wesley: Reading, MA

Hetzel, B. (1988) *The Complete Guide to Software Testing*, 2nd edition, QED Information Sciences

Hutcheson, M.L. (2003) *Software Testing Fundamentals*, Wiley: New York

IEEE (1998) *Standard for Software Test Documentation*, IEEE 829

Jacobson, I. (1992) *Object-Oriented Software Engineering: A Use Case Driven Approach*, Addison Wesley: Reading MA

Jorgensen, P. (1995) *Software Testing: A Craftsman's Approach*, CRC Press: New York

Kaner, C., Falk, J. and Nguyen, H.Q. (1993) *Testing Computer Software,* 2nd edition, John Wiley & Sons: New York

Kaner, C., Bach, J. and Petticord, B. (2002) *Lessons Learned in Software Testing*, John Wiley & Sons: New York

Marick, B. (1994) *The Craft of Software Testing*, Prentice Hall: New York

Myers, G. J. (1979) *The Art of Software Testing*, John Wiley & Sons: New York

Patton, R. (2001) *Software Testing*, SAMS, a division of MacMillan USA: Indianapolis

Pol, M., Teunissen, R. and van Veenendaal, E. (2001) *Software Testing: A Guide to the TMap Approach*, Addison Wesley

RTCA (1992) *Software Considerations in Airborne Systems and Equipment Certification,* D0178-B, RTCA: Washington

Testing Standards, www.testingstandards.co.uk

Whittaker, J. A. (2003) *How to Break Software: A Practical Guide to Testing*, Addison Wesley: Reading, MA

CHAPTER 5 TEST MANAGEMENT

Beizer, B. (1990) *Software Testing Techniques*, 2nd edition, van Nostrand Reinhold: Boston

Black, R. (2009) *Managing the Testing Process*, 3rd edition, John Wiley & Sons: New York

Black, R. (2004) *Critical Testing Processes*, Addison Wesley: Reading, MA

Brooks, F. (1995) *The Mythical Man Month and Other Essays on Software Engineering*, Addison Wesley: New York

Craig, R. D. and Jaskiel, S. P. (2002) *Systematic Software Testing*, Artech House: Norwood, MA

Drabick, R. (2004) *Best Practices for the Formal Software Testing Process: A Menu of Testing Tasks*, Dorset House: New York

Hetzel, W. (1988) *Complete Guide to Software Testing*, QED: Wellesley, MA

IEEE (1998) *Standard for Software Test Documentation*, IEEE 829

ISO (2001), *Software Engineering: Software Product Quality*, ISO/IEC 9126

Kaner, C., Bach, J. and Petticord, B. (2002) *Lessons Learned in Software Testing*, John Wiley & Sons: New York

Pol, M., Teunissen, R. and van Veenendaal, E. (2002), *Software Testing: A Guide to the TMap Approach*, Addison Wesley

Whittaker, J. (2002) *How to Break Software: A Practical Guide to Testing*, Addison Wesley

Whittaker, J. and Thompson, H.H. (2003) *How to Break Software Security*, Addison Wesley: Reading, MA

CHAPTER 6 TOOL SUPPORT FOR TESTING

Buwalda, H., Janssen, D. and Pinkster, I. (2001) *Integrated Test Design and Automation*, Addison Wesley: Reading, MA
Copeland, L. (2003) *A Practitioner's Guide to Software Test Design*, Artech House: New York
Fewster, M. and Graham, D. (1999) *Software Test Automation*, Addison Wesley: Reading MA
Hoffman, D. and Strooper, P. (1995) *Software Design, Automated Testing, and Maintenance*, International Thomson Computer Press
Mosley, D.J. and Posey, B.A. (2002) *Just Enough Software Test Automation*, Prentice Hall: New York
Siteur, M.M. (2005) *Automate Your Testing!*, Academic Service, Sdu Uitgevers bv

CHAPTER 7 ISTQB FOUNDATION EXAM

ISTQB, www.istqb.org
ISTQB, *Certified Tester: Foundation Level Syllabus* (Version 2011)
ISTQB, *Standard Glossary of Terms Used in Software Testing*, Version 2.1

GLOSSARY

BS 7925–2: 1998. *Software Component Testing*
DO-178B: 1992. *Software Considerations in Airborne Systems and Equipment Certification, Requirements and Technical Concepts for Aviation* (RTCA SC167)
IEEE 610.12: 1990. *Standard Glossary of Software Engineering Terminology*
IEEE 829: 1998. *Standard for Software Test Documentation*
IEEE 1008: 1993. *Standard for Software Unit Testing*
IEEE 1028: 1997. *Standard for Software Reviews and Audits*
IEEE 1044: 1993. *Standard Classification for Software Anomalies*
IEEE 1219: 1998. *Standard for Software Maintenance*
ISO 15504-9: 1998. *Information Technology – Software Process Assessment – Part 9: Vocabulary*
ISO/IEC 2382–1: 1993. *Data processing – Vocabulary – Part 1: Fundamental Terms*
ISO 9000: 2000. *Quality Management Systems – Fundamentals and Vocabulary*
ISO/IEC 9126–1: 2001. *Software Engineering – Software Product Quality – Part 1: Quality Characteristics and Sub-characteristics*
ISO/IEC 12207: 1995. *Information Technology – Software Life Cycle Processes*
ISO/IEC 14598–1: 1996. *Information Technology – Software Product Evaluation – Part 1: General Overview*
Abbott, J. (1986) *Software Testing Techniques*, NCC Publications
Adrion, W., Branstad, M. and Cherniabsky, J. (1982) 'Validation, Verification and Testing of Computer Software' in *Computing Surveys*, Vol. 14, No. 2, June 1982
Bach, J. (2004) 'Exploratory Testing' in E. van Veenendaal, *The Testing Practitioner*, 2nd edition, UTN Publishing
Beizer, B. (1990) *Software Testing Techniques*, van Nostrand Reinhold: New York
Chow, T. (1978) 'Testing Software Design Modeled by Finite-State Machines', in *IEEE Transactions on Software Engineering*, Vol. 4, No. 3, May 1978

Chrissis, M.B., Konrad, M. and Shrum, S. (2004) *CMMI, Guidelines for Process Integration and Product Improvement*, Addison Wesley: Reading, MA

Fenton, N. (1991) *Software Metrics: A Rigorous Approach*, Chapman & Hall: London

Fewster, M. and Graham, D. (1999) *Software Test Automation: Effective use of test execution tools*, Addison-Wesley: Reading, MA

Freedman, D. and Weinberg, G. (1990) *Walkthroughs, Inspections and Technical Reviews*, Dorset House Publishing: New York

Garvin, D.A. (1984), What does product quality really mean?, in: *Sloan Management Review*, Vol. 26, nr. 1 1984

Gerrard, P. and Thompson, N. (2002) *Risk-Based E-Business Testing*, Artech House Publishers: New York

Gilb, T. and Graham, D. (1993) *Software Inspection*, Addison-Wesley: Reading, MA

Grochtmann, M. (1994) 'Test Case Design Using Classification Trees' in *Conference Proceedings STAR* 1994

Hetzel, W. (1988) *The complete guide to software testing*, 2nd edition, QED Information Sciences

Juran, J.M. (1979), *Quality Control Handbook*, McGraw-Hill

McCabe, T. (1976) 'A complexity measure' *IEEE Transactions on Software Engineering*, Vol. 2, pp. 308–320

Musa, J. (1998) *Software Reliability Engineering*, McGraw-Hill Education: New York

Myers, G. (1979) *The Art of Software Testing*, Wiley: New York

Pol, M., Teunissen, R. and van Veenendaal, E. (2002) *Software Testing: A Guide to the TMap Approach*, Addison Wesley: Reading, MA

van Veenendaal, E. (2004) *The Testing Practitioner*, 2nd edition, UTN Publishing

van Veenendaal, E. (2008), Test Improvement Manifesto, in: *Testing Experience,* Issue 04/08, December 2008

AUTHORS

REX BLACK

With over a quarter century of software and systems engineering experience, Rex Black is President of RBCS (www.rbcs-us.com), a leader in software, hardware, and systems testing. For over 15 years, RBCS has delivered services in consulting, outsourcing and training for software and hardware testing. Employing the industry's most experienced and recognized consultants, RBCS conducts product testing, builds and improves testing groups and hires testing staff for hundreds of clients worldwide. Ranging from Fortune 20 companies to start-ups, RBCS clients save time and money through improved product development, decreased tech support calls, improved corporate reputation and more. As the leader of RBCS, Rex is the most prolific author practicing in the field of software testing today. His popular first book, *Managing the Testing Process*, has sold over 40,000 copies around the world, including Japanese, Chinese, and Indian releases, and is now in its third edition. In addition to *Managing the Testing Process* and *Foundations of Software Testing*, Rex has written five other books on testing, *Advanced Software Testing: Volume I, Advanced Software Testing: Volume II, Advanced Software Testing: Volume III, Critical Testing Processes* and *Pragmatic Software Testing*, which have also sold tens of thousands of copies, including Hebrew, Indian, Chinese, Japanese and Russian editions. He has written over 30 articles, presented hundreds of papers, workshops, and seminars, and given about 50 keynotes and other speeches at conferences and events around the world.

Rex is the immediate past President of the International Software Testing Qualifications Board and a Director of the American Software Testing Qualifications Board. He remains heavily involved in the ISTQB, serving on the Foundation Working Group, as the lead coordinator for test management materials in the Advanced Working Group, and as Chair of the Expert Test Manager subgroup within the Expert Working Group. He is also Governance Officer for the ISTQB.

Rex is married to his college girlfriend, Laurel Becker. They met in 1987 at the University of California, Los Angeles. They have two children, Emma and Charlotte, and two dogs, Hank and Cosmo. They currently live in the Hill Country of Texas, in the United States, but they travel extensively.

ERIK VAN VEENENDAAL

Dr Erik van Veenendaal, CISA, has been working as a practitioner and manager in the IT-industry since 1987. After a career in software development, he transferred to the area of software quality. As a test analyst, test manager and test consultant, Erik has over 20 years of practical testing experience. He has implemented structured testing, formal reviews and requirements processes, and has carried out test process improvement activities based on TMMi in a large number of organizations in different industries. Erik has also been a senior lecturer at the Eindhoven University of Technology, Faculty of Technology Management for almost ten years.

Erik founded Improve Quality Services BV (www.improveqs.nl) back in 1998 as an independent organization that focuses on advanced high quality services. He has been the company director for over 12 years. Under his direction Improve Quality Services became a leading testing company in http://www.improveqs.nl/TheNetherlands. Customers are especially to be found in the areas of embedded software (e.g. Philips, Océ en Assembléon) and in the finance domain (e.g. Rabobank, ING and Triodos Bank). Improve Quality Services offers international consultancy and training services with respect to testing (e.g. test process improvement using the TMMi framework), quality management and requirements engineering. Improve Quality Services BV was the second worldwide company to become accredited to perform TMMi assessments. They are a market leader for ISTQB Foundation and ISTQB Advanced training courses and a member of the International Requirements Engineering Board (IREB).

Erik is the (co-)author of numerous papers and a number of books on software quality and testing, including the best-sellers *The Testing Practitioner*, *Foundations of Software Testing* and *Testing according to TMap*. Erik was the first person to receive the ISEB Practitioner certificate with distinction and is also a Certified Information Systems Auditor (CISA). He is a regular speaker both at national and international testing conferences and a leading international trainer (ISTQB accredited) in the field of software testing. At EuroStar'99 (Usability testing), EuroStar'02 (Test Strategies and Planning) and EuroStar'05 (Inspection Leader), he received the best tutorial award.

He is a former vice president of the International Software Testing Qualification Board (ISTQB) (from 2005–2009). He is the editor of the ISTQB 'Standard Glossary of Terms Used in Software Testing' and vice-chair/chair of the ISTQB expert level working party since its inception in 2002. Erik is one of the founders of the TMMi Foundation and is currently the vice chair of the TMMi Foundation. He is the lead author of the TMMi model. Erik is actively involved in various working parties of the International Requirements Engineering Board (IREB). For his outstanding contribution to the field of testing Erik received the 'European Testing Excellence Award' in December 2007.

After having provided leadership to Improve Quality Services BV for over 12 years, Erik stepped down from that role in July 2010. Since that time he is living in Bonaire where Erik is involved in international test consultancy, training and international organizations (e.g. ISTQB, TMMi and IREB), publications and presentations. As a major shareholder, Erik will remain involved in Improve Quality Services.

Erik can be contacted via e-mail at eve@improveqs.nl and through his website www.erikvanveenendaal.nl.

DOROTHY GRAHAM

Dorothy Graham has been involved in software testing since the 1970s, where her first job (for Bell Labs in the US) was as a programmer in a testing group, and her task was to write two testing tools (test execution and comparison). After emigrating to the UK, she worked for Ferranti Computer Systems, developing software for UK Police forces. She then joined the National Computing Centre as a trainer and courseware developer, and then became an independent consultant (part-time while her children were young).

At that time, software testing was not a respected profession; in fact in the early 1990s, many thought of testing at best as a 'necessary evil' (if they thought of testing at all!). There were few people who specialized in testing, and it was seen as a 'second-class' activity, and not respected. There was a general perception that testing was easy, that anyone could do it, and that you were rather strange if you liked it. It was then that Dot decided to specialize in testing, seeing great scope for improvement in testing activities in industry, not only in imparting fundamental knowledge about testing (basic principles and techniques), but also in improving the view testers had of themselves, and the perceptions of testers in their companies. She developed training courses in testing, and began Grove Consultants, named after her house in Macclesfield. One of her most popular talks at the time was called 'Test is a four-letter word', reflecting the prevailing culture about testing.

It was into this context that the initiative to create a qualification for testers was born. Although not the initiator, Dot was involved from the first meetings and the earliest working groups that developed the first Foundation Syllabus, donating many hours of time to help progress this effort. This work was carried out with support from ISEB (Information Systems Examination Board) of the British Computer Society, and the testing qualification was modelled on ISEB's successful qualifications in Project Management and Information Systems Infrastructure. One of the aims at this time was to give people a common vocabulary to talk about testing, since at the time people seemed to be using many different terms for the same thing.

Grove Consultants (Dorothy Graham and Mark Fewster at the time) gave the first course based on the ISEB Foundation Syllabus in October 1998 and the first Foundation Certificates in Software Testing were awarded.

The success of the Foundation qualification took everyone by surprise – there seemed to be a hunger for a qualification that gave testers more respect: both for themselves and from their employers. It also gave testers a common vocabulary and more confidence in their work. The Foundation qualification had met its main objective of 'removing the bottom layer of ignorance' about software testing.

Work then began on extending the ISEB qualification to a more advanced level (which became the ISEB Practitioner qualification) and also to extending it to other countries, as news of the qualification spread in the international community. Dot was a facilitator at the meeting that formed ISTQB in 2001 in Sollentuna, Sweden. Now semi-retired, Dot has become much less involved in the ISTQB Advanced levels.

Dorothy's other activities over the years include being Programme Chair for the first European testing conference (EuroSTAR 1993); she was Programme Chair again in 2009. During the 1990s, she started and later co-authored *The CAST Report*, a summary of commercial testing tools (in the days before the internet!). In addition to this book, she co-authored *Software Inspection* (1993) with Tom Gilb, and *Software Test Automation* (1998) with Mark Fewster. Their new book *Experiences of Software Test Automation* is due to be published in 2011.

Dot continues do consultancy in test automation, and to be a popular speaker at testing conferences and events worldwide. She holds the European Excellence Award in Software Testing.

Her main non-testing activities include singing (choirs, madrigal groups and solos) and enjoyable holidays with her husband, Roger.

Visit Dorothy's website: www.DorothyGraham.co.uk.

COMPANIES

RBCS, INC.

Rex Black Consulting Services (RBCS) is a premier international testing consultancy specializing in consulting, outsourcing and training services. Led by one of the most recognized and published industry leaders, Rex Black, RBCS is an established company you can trust to show you results with the track record to prove it.

Since 1994, RBCS has been both a pioneer and leader in quality hardware and software testing. Through its training, consulting, and outsourcing services, RBCS has helped hundreds of companies improve their test practices and achieve quality results. RBCS has offices in the United States, New Zealand, Australia, and Sri Lanka with partners around the world.

RBCS utilizes deep industry experience to solve testing problems and improve testing processes. We help clients reduce risk and save money through higher-quality products and services. Our goal is to help clients avoid the costs associated with poor product quality – such as product recalls, tech support calls, lawsuits, reputation damage – by helping them understand and solve testing and performance issues and build better testing teams. Whether it's customizing a program to fit your company's needs, or providing the hands-on experience and resources that will allow your testing team to grow professionally, RBCS helps companies produce better products and increase ROI. RBCS pours its resources into ensuring our clients become successful.

Employing the industry's most experienced and recognized consultants, RBCS conducts product testing; builds and improves testing groups; and hires testing staff for hundreds of clients worldwide. Our principals include published, international experts in the area of hardware and software testing. Our skilled test managers and engineers all hold International Software Testing Qualifications Board (ISTQB) certifications and are highly trained.

RBCS believes in the value of real-life experience and leadership which is why the RBCS team is always striving to improve and perfect the testing process. Every trainer and consultant is ISTQB certified and encouraged to write articles and books, share leading ideas through presentations, and continuously research new ideas. In addition, as past President of the ISTQB and the ASTQB, Rex Black has more than a quarter-century of software and systems engineering experience and strongly leads the company with the most recent, proven testing methodologies and strategies.

Our client-centred approach helps companies deliver better quality products and reduce costs by improving their test practices. The difference? Our recognized industry experts started their careers in our customers' shoes; they have the real-world knowledge required to deliver the best services with proven practices.

From Fortune 100 to small and mid-size organizations, RBCS works with a variety of companies, in industries such as technology, finance, communications, retail, government and education.

RBCS offers customized consulting services that will not only help you solve your testing challenges, but provide you with the tools and framework for managing a successful testing organization. Our consulting methodology is based on successful, peer-reviewed publications with a customized approach that focuses on the individual needs of each client. Plus we have a long list of happy, reference-able customers around the globe that have benefited from RBCS expertise.

Rex Black Consulting Services, Inc.
31520 Beck Road
Bulverde, TX 78163
USA
www.rbcs-us.com
e-mail: info@rbcs-us.com

IMPROVE QUALITY SERVICES BV

Improve Quality Services BV was founded in 1998 by Erik van Veenendaal as an independent organization that focuses on advanced and high quality services in the area of testing and quality management. It offers (international) consultancy and training services with respect to testing, quality management, usability and inspections. Services include software process improvement, requirements engineering, IT-auditing, software quality assurance, inspection programs and, of course, test engineering, test management and consultancy and test process improvement.

Improve Quality Services is an accredited course provider for ISTQB Software Testing Foundation and all ISTQB Advanced modules (Test Manager, Test Analyst en Technical Test Analyst), Tmap Next foundation and Tmap Next Advanced and the 'IREB Certified Professional for Requirements Engineering' course and exam. In the area of test process improvement, they are accredited by the TMMi Foundation to perform formal TMMi assessments.

Quality is a key issue in all aspects of the company, whereby quality is translated into both customer and employee satisfaction. Customers vary from large multi-national companies to SME type companies and government bodies. Their most important customers are a number of major banks and a number of industrial engineering organizations.

Employees choose software quality and testing as their profession and career. They hold ISTQB testing certificates, PRINCE-2 project management certificates and are also accredited as Certified Information System Auditors (CISA). On a regular basis papers from employees are published in various international magazines. To provide leading edge services, Improve Quality Services has a close working relationship with the Eindhoven University of Technology and participates in (inter)national Research & Development projects.

Improve Quality Services BV
Laan van Diepenvoorde 1
5582 LA Waalre
The Netherlands
www.improveqs.nl
email: info@improveqs.nl

INDEX